The Defiant Muse

HEBREW FEMINIST POEMS

FROM ANTIQUITY TO THE PRESENT

THE HELEN ROSE SCHEUER JEWISH WOMEN'S SERIES

Streets: A Memoir of the Lower East Side
by Bella Spewack

The Maimie Papers: Letters of an Ex-Prostitute
by Maimie Pinzer
edited by Ruth Rosen and Sue Davidson

A Cross and a Star: Memoirs of a Jewish Girl in Chile
by Marjorie Agosín

Apples from the Desert: Selected Stories
by Savyon Liebrecht

Always from Somewhere Else: A Memoir of My Chilean Jewish Father
by Marjorie Agosín

The House of Memory: Stories by Jewish Women Writers of Latin America
edited by Marjorie Agosín

The Defiant Muse: Hebrew Feminist Poems from Antiquity to the Present, A Bilingual Anthology
edited by Shirley Kaufman, Galit Hasan-Rokem, and Tamar S. Hess

The Defiant Muse

HEBREW FEMINIST POEMS FROM ANTIQUITY TO THE PRESENT

A Bilingual Anthology

Edited by Shirley Kaufman, Galit Hasan-Rokem, and Tamar S. Hess

Foreword by Alicia Suskin Ostriker

The Helen Rose Scheuer Jewish Women's Series

THE FEMINIST PRESS
at the City University of New York

Published in 1999 by The Feminist Press at The City University of New York
365 Fifth Avenue
New York, NY 10016
www.feministpress.org

First edition

For copyright and credit information on poetry and translations, see pages 263–69, which constitute a continuation of this copyright page.

Steven H. Scheuer, in memory of his mother and in celebration of her life and the 100th anniversary of her birth (1995), has been pleased to endow the Helen Rose Scheuer Jewish Women's Series. *The Defiant Muse* is the seventh named book in the series.

This book was published with the financial support of the Steven and Alida Brill Scheuer Foundation. The Feminist Press thanks the Institute for the Translation of Hebrew Literature, Israel, for generously providing translation funding. The Feminist Press would also like to thank the Nathan Cummings Foundation, as well as Helene Goldfarb and Joanne Markell.

Library of Congress Cataloging-in-Publication Data
Hebrew feminist poems from antiquity to the present : a bilingual anthology / edited by Shirley Kaufman, Galit Hasan-Rokem, and Tamar S. Hess.
p. cm. — (The defiant muse) (The Helen Rose Scheuer Jewish women's series)
English and Hebrew.
Includes bibliographical references.
ISBN 1-55861-223-8 (hbk. : alk. paper). — ISBN 1-55861-224-6 (pbk. : alk. paper)
1. Hebrew poetry — Women authors. 2. Hebrew poetry — Women authors Translations into English. 3. Feminism poetry. I. Kaufman, Shirley II. Hasan-Rokem, Galit III. Hess, Tamar S. IV. Series V. Series: The Helen Rose Scheuer Jewish women's series.
PJ5040.H43 1999 99-35789
892.4'10809287—dc21 CIP

Text design by Dayna Navaro
Typeset by El Ot Ltd., Israel
Printed on acid-free paper by Transcontinental Printing
Printed in Canada

05 04 03 02 01 00 99 5 4 3 2 1

CONTENTS

FOREWORD

The poetry of women in the language of Hebrew. The poetry of women in the world's oldest and youngest language. It is like a small rootball, then an almost infinitely long stem, and at last an immense blossom. A long fuse, then the explosion. The wildfire. And a book of fiery language, collected and laid out before us.

Who wrote the Bible? We cannot know. We know only that the aggregation of texts called by that name was composed over a period of three thousand years and edited over a period of more than a thousand years, and that some of its sources are even older. Might some of the Bible's poetry have been created by women? We cannot know. Yet women, in many traditional societies, are singers as well as storytellers. And some of the most powerful and beautiful verses in the Bible are placed in the mouths of women. Miriam, the sister of Moses and Aaron, leads the Israelite women in a song and dance of triumph, praising God, after the crossing of the Red Sea. Deborah, who is judge, prophetess, military commander-in-chief and "mother in Israel" rolled into one, sings the defeat of an enemy general—"The stars fought from heaven / Fought from their courses against Sisera"—and of his death at the hand of Yael, another woman. In the Song of Songs, a woman's voice celebrates the beauty of her lover, invites his caresses, and rejoices in his love, in language that has become a major source of erotic poetry throughout Western and Middle Eastern literature. Ruth's famous declaration of loyalty to Naomi in the Book of Ruth—"whither thou goest, I will go"—and Naomi's bitter complaint of her widowhood and the death of her sons, touch a universal chord of human feeling. In the biblical book of Lamentations, the desolate city of Jerusalem is personified as a grieving woman. As the editors of this volume remind us, the role of bewailing the dead is in many cultures the task of women.

However speculatively, the editors enable us to hear the voices of women poets in the ancient world, creating poetry of love, pain, relationship, triumph, defeat. Culling from rabbinic texts of late antiquity, they have found anonymous folk verses, some of which are attributed to women; and from the medieval period and the period of the early modern world, the archives of Hebrew literature have yielded a few women poets whose names we can confidently know.

Why only a few? As the introduction to this volume explains, the silence of women was, for better or worse, built into the culture of Hebrew as a sacred language. Talmudic study was not for women, nor was the language of liturgy; women's worship was separated from men's; *tkhines,* special prayers for women, were usually written in Yiddish, the "mother tongue." Thus the sacred linguistic soil from which Hebrew poetry—sacred and secular—sprang for nearly two millennia, was off-limits for most women. Cynthia Ozick, in her landmark feminist essay "Notes Toward Finding the Right Question," has strikingly—if shockingly—lamented the exclusion of women from the tradition of Jewish learning and creativity as "one of the cruelest events in Jewish history."

But when we reach the modern era, the marginality of women to Hebrew culture becomes, interestingly, an advantage. Unburdened by the massive authoritative weight of religious study laid on men, when Hebrew began to reinvent itself as a secular language in the land that would become Israel, women were more free than men to create a fresh and vital idiom. "The woman writes with the pen of a bird, the man with a pen of iron and lead," remarked the poet and literary critic Yehuda Leib Gordon. Especially from the 1920s onward, women's poetry in Israel has become increasingly a force to be reckoned with.

In the poetry of nineteenth- and twentieth-century women translated for this volume, we see many themes familiar to modern women's writing in other languages. There is the trope of ambiguously ironic modesty and humility in a poet like Rachel Morpurgo, which so recalls Emily Dickinson, or the sensual assertiveness of Esther Raab, whose first book, *Kimshonim* (Thistles), wonderfully recalls Edna St. Vincent Millay's *A Few Figs from Thistles,* and who, like Millay, had a long and increasingly politically engaged career, or the acerbic passion of Dahlia Ravikovitch, which has caused her to be compared with Sylvia Plath. A focus on the body, the insistence on a self not to be defined by others, outrage at oppression, revisionist use of traditional texts—especially of biblical and Zionist texts—mark many of these poems. We might draw a straight line, for example, from Shulamit Kalugai's amazingly sympathetic "Jezebel" (1941) to Shulamith Hareven's version of Job's wife asking "where are the black-coated boys / to whom she gave birth when she still feared God / and avoided evil" (1962) to Nurit Zarchi's gender-bending "She Is Joseph" (1983). The yearning for peace is a recurring theme, as is resistance to the uncompromising stances of Zionism, and (more recently) poetry dealing with issues of ethnicity within Israel, along with Holocaust poetry. The overtly feminist poetry beginning in the late 1970s interrogates sexuality—most scandalously in the writing of Yona Wallach, whose poems "Tefillin" (1983) and "Hebrew" (1985) brilliantly reveal the links between gender war and the core religious and linguistic realities of Hebrew and Jewish culture.

To read through this newest volume in the Defiant Muse series is to be thrilled with the work of the editors and translators, and even more thrilled with the poets. In this collection of more than one hundred poems by over fifty poets, I have encountered numerous women writers whose names I never heard of before now, who have never before been translated into English, and whom I will treasure. Individually and collectively, these poets bring into play their love and anger, their experience of sex, motherhood, war, and religion, their critiques of society, myth, and language. Thanks to the work of feminist critics writing in Hebrew, the value of these poets is increasingly acknowledged in Israel. Now, thanks to The Feminist Press, speakers and readers of English have the opportunity to be awestruck by the fiery vision of these relentlessly forceful female poets.

Alicia Suskin Ostriker
Rutgers University
May 1999

ACKNOWLEDGMENTS

This project has offered the possibility, for the first time, of a systematic effort to redeem hidden voices in Hebrew and to gather outstanding women's poetry over a span of nearly three thousand years. After three years of sifting through biblical and rabbinic texts and thousands of Hebrew poems by women; after three years of selecting poems, finding or assigning translations, and collaborating with many capable translators in Israel and the United States; after consulting with generous scholars, both women and men, engaged in research and teaching in every area of Hebrew literature; and after studying and considering everything that has gone into this first comprehensive anthology of feminist Hebrew poetry; we are pleased to express, above all, our gratitude to each other and to our husbands.

To each other we give thanks for a powerful and enriching mutual learning experience and for the growth of a new friendship.

And, for their steady interest and encouragement, we give thanks to our husbands, Ronnen Segman, Freddie Rokem, and especially Bill Daleski—for his good humor and availability, his always insightful advice, his sensitivity to style and to the poetic texts, and his editorial wisdom.

We thank those who worked closely with us on this project's development.

We are deeply indebted to Hamutal Bar-Yosef for the skill and dedication she brought to this project in its early stages—initiating, supervising, and participating in the search for lost and forgotten poets in archives and journals—and for making numerous helpful suggestions about which poets and poems to include.

Mia Barzilai prepared the typescript in both Hebrew and English, with exceptional devotion, equanimity, and an alertness to errors.

Invaluable advice was given to us by the following scholars and friends in various areas of Hebrew literature: on biblical literature, Sarah Japhet, Ilana Pardes, Yair Zakovitch, and especially Moshe Greenberg; on rabbinic literature, Charlotte Fonrobert and Dina Stein, Shaul Shaked, David Stern, and especially Daniel Boyarin; on medieval poetry, Ezra Fleischer, Tova Rosen, Yehoshua Granat, and especially Matti Huss; on early modern poetry, Ephraim Hazan, Chava Weissler, and especially Chava Turniansky; on modern and contemporary poetry: Ruth and Ariel Ginzburg, Hanan Hever and Ezra Mendelsohn, Ariel Hirschfeld and Iris Parush, Malka and Gershon Shaked, and Rotem Wagner, Anat Weissman, and especially Hamutal Tsamir.

Special thanks to others whose time, suggestions, and support were generously given: Lois Bar-Yaacov, Peter Cole, Alice and Moshe Shalvi, and Ilana Zuckerman.

Following up on some of the texts suggested to us was often like detective work, and one little drama deserves mention. Judith Olszowy, an Israeli scholar engaged in research on women's letters among the Genizah documents stored at Oxford, did not find any poems for us among the letters but told us about her work with David Money, a senior research fellow at Wolfson College, Cambridge University, who, in the course of writing about Robert Boyle, had discovered a seventeenth-century letter to Boyle by Bathsheva Maikin in which a poetic passage from the Bible is quoted in Hebrew. Money wrote to us that a Bathsheva Rainolds, who lived at the same time and wrote poetry, might be the same person as Maikin, and that Rainolds might be of interest to us since she wrote in Greek, Latin, and French, and "some in Hebrew." He knew of a book she had published in 1616, referred to in *Intellectual Culture in Elizabethan and Jacobean England* by J. W. Binns (1990). We immediately turned to Binns, where we found a paragraph about this remarkable young woman, the daughter of a schoolmaster. We knew that there were hardly any Jews in England at the time (Jews having been expelled in 1290 and again in 1608), but we were excited by the idea of publishing an unknown non-Jewish poet writing in Hebrew. A letter to the keeper of rare books at Cambridge University library inquiring about the 1616 book was never answered. A year later, however, an Israeli historian, Shulamith Shahar, was working at Cambridge, and offered to look for the book. Imagine our triumph when she telephoned from England that she had found it and was bringing a copy back with her to Jerusalem. And with what delight we received this precious document, *Musa Virginiea: Graeco-Latino-Gallica* by Bathseva R. (*filia* Henrici Reginaldi), London, 1616. The book did indeed contain poems in Greek, Latin, and French, written by a talented sixteen-year-old schoolgirl, who also showed off her beginner's Hebrew with a three-line epigraph in Hebrew (full of mistakes) to one of her Greek poems, and on another page, two mysterious lines of indecipherable kabbalistic numerology. Bathsheva's ambition was commendable but, unfortunately, not appropriate for our anthology. The process of uncovering her work, however, suggests that other voices, too, are buried. We hope that the publication of this anthology will inspire others to unearth these voices.

We are grateful for the financial and administrative assistance of the Institute for the Translation of Hebrew Literature and the staff of the Association of Composers, Authors, and Publishers of Music in Israel (ACUM), and for making their resources available to us, the Jewish National and University Library, and Genazim (the Archive of the Association of Hebrew Writers).

The Feminist Press at The City University of New York, notably its director, Florence Howe, who initiated this project, and our editor, Sara Cahill, have been generous beyond words, with enthusiasm and practical advice. We also extend our thanks to David Sulomm Stein for his careful proofreading, Dayna Navaro, the design and production manager at The Feminist Press, for the beautiful design of the book, and El Ot typesetting for their exceptional work.

We are grateful for the financial support provided by the Steven and Alida Brill Scheuer Foundation through the Helen Rose Scheuer Jewish Women's Series. We also thank the Institute for the Translation of Hebrew Literature, Israel, for their assistance with translation funding.

We cannot end these acknowledgments without praise for the gifted and hardworking translators, most of whom are accomplished poets in their own right; they have brought the richness of the original Hebrew into English with great care. The translations, most of which were specially commissioned for this volume, have been carefully read and modified by the editors, always in consultation with the translators. Over many years, up to the last days before his death, Robert Friend was assisted by Shimon Sandbank. And Shirley Kaufman is especially indebted for help with the Hebrew to her co-editors, and also to Shimon Sandbank.

INTRODUCTION

"Ten portions of speech came down to the world—nine of them were women's," the rabbis of late antiquity assert in one of their texts.[1] The opposite, however, seems to be true of writing. Although the Hebrew language takes pride in an uninterrupted written tradition of close to three thousand years, there are few texts prior to the nineteenth century that are unequivocally attributed to women.

Amalia Kahana-Carmon, a major contemporary Israeli novelist, has compared the marginality of women in Hebrew literature to their seating in an orthodox synagogue: the significant action seems to take place only in the main—that is, men's—hall, where the holy scrolls are kept and read. Upstairs, in the women's gallery, one is expected to stay invisible and unheard. The prayer is led by the (male) cantor, who speaks for the whole congregation. The writer in Hebrew, like the cantor, according to Kahana-Carmon, speaks for the community. The writer is the eye, the consciousness, and the alter ego of the community. As in the Orthodox synagogue, women have been hindered from making their voice heard in Hebrew literature.[2]

This anthology, with more than one hundred poems by over fifty poets, recovers such hidden voices and includes poetry from Israel and the diaspora, from the tenth century B.C.E. to the present. Compiling this anthology has reshaped our perception of feminist poetry. The poems collected here represent a broad feminist perspective. As in the other volumes in the Defiant Muse series, the selected poems are characterized by a feminist inclination to rebel openly against patriarchal oppression of women, or to assert a woman's subjectivity, or even to appropriate an area of experience usually confined to men, such as writing, supporting a family economically, expressing an outspoken and active sexuality, or—alas—fighting in wars.

In addition to considering thematic diversity, we made our selections with an appreciation for the circumstances surrounding the work: that a verse in the Bible or a text in the Talmud or Midrash could be ascribed to a woman seemed too historically significant to ignore. Similarly, through the succeeding centuries, that a woman in Andalusia, Tunisia, Morocco, Kurdistan, Italy, Russia, or Palestine (before the state of Israel) dared to study and master the Hebrew language well enough to write verse in Hebrew made these writers early feminists—women who could stand on their own and express ideas and feelings in a language hitherto owned by men.

Choosing among the modern and contemporary work—poems written after women had learned, grown up in, and were at ease with the Hebrew language, and had begun to use it as creatively as men—was more difficult. Working together, we shared our personal tastes. We sought poems with arresting voices, poems not afraid to press beyond the boundaries of the expected, well-wrought poems with a clarity of vision, accessible and translatable. Diverse in genre and theme, this collection seeks to reshape the traditional Hebrew canon, while illuminating the continuity and breadth of women's poetic tradition in Hebrew.

The Hebrew language and its literature are geographically connected with the area in the eastern Mediterranean in which the state of Israel exists today. The most ancient known texts in Hebrew were authored when the political entities Israel and Judah existed in this region.[3] Not unlike other languages—for example, French and English—Hebrew was transported with its users into the Jewish diaspora, partially functioning in the textual and expressive tradition of the Jews. Hebrew was mainly associated with religion: the ongoing interpretation of biblical texts, including their application to everyday life, prayer, and liturgical literature. Parallel to this, however, in various locations and at different times, Hebrew literature encompassed wider fields of experience. Babylonia in late antiquity (from approximately the second to the sixth century C.E.) was, in addition to Palestine, a place where Hebrew literature was written, often in intense diglossia with Aramaic. Aramaic, a north Semitic language written in the same characters as Hebrew, was then the lingua franca of the Near East, extant in the later books of the Hebrew Bible and coexisting with Hebrew in most texts of late antiquity and the early Middle Ages. The most notable works of the period are the Palestinian and Babylonian Talmud and the Midrash—postbiblical Hebrew and Aramaic texts containing biblical interpretation and legal deliberations, as well as stories. These texts together comprise what is known as classical rabbinic literature, and developed in the wake of the destruction of Jerusalem and its temple in 70 C.E. From the mid-first century to the end of the fifth century, rabbis in Palestine and Babylonia established centers of learning in which these texts were orally created and transmitted and then later put into writing.

Hebrew literature was written from time to time in other places, but almost exclusively by men. During the eleventh to fifteenth centuries in Spain, especially in Andalusia's flourishing Arab culture, the cultural and political interaction of Jews with Moslems produced some of the greatest Hebrew poetry of all times. Centuries later, the rise of nationalism, which often involved pervasive forms of anti-Semitism, gave Jews serious social reasons to consolidate their national identity. Jewish national identity in Europe encompassed two different, almost contradictory linguistic identities: Yiddish and Hebrew. Alignment with Yiddish stressed a vision of cultural and national autonomy in the diaspora of Europe, whereas those who chose Hebrew as their language for the most part envisioned the future of Jewish national life in Palestine, the ancient homeland of Hebrew literature. The practical obliteration of European Yiddish culture during the Holocaust settled the choice between the two languages. Toward the end of the twentieth century, Hebrew has again become the language in which the Jewish experience is culturally expressed, particularly in Israel, the place where its earliest utterances are still being unearthed.

This introduction, as well as the arrangement of poems in the volume, follows the standard periodization of Hebrew literature: the ancient period, identified with the texts of the Hebrew Bible; late antiquity, whose Hebrew literature was mainly transmitted to us through rabbinic literature; and the medieval, early modern, modern, and contemporary periods. Following the usage of the *Encyclopaedia Judaica*,[4] we have called the birth ground of Hebrew literature *Israel* in the ancient era, *Roman and Byzantine Palestine* in late antiquity, *Ottoman Palestine* under Turkish rule (1516–1917), *Mandatory Palestine* under British rule (1917–48), and *Israel* from the establishment of the modern state in 1948.

Our concern is with women in all these periods and places.

Ancient Hebrew Texts: The Bible

Feminist interpretation is an indispensable prism for viewing the masses of Hebrew texts written before the modern era. This interpretative perspective may, in the study of ancient and medieval texts especially, be applied in a twofold manner: the exposure of the oppressive mechanisms of male-authored texts or the revelation of what has been considered by some unlikely: the presence of women's voices in these texts. It is mainly a search for these voices that has yielded some of the texts that we have presented here as women's poetry in Hebrew in antiquity, late antiquity, and the Middle Ages.[5]

That future research might discover female-authored texts in the biblical texts or their cognates does have a critical precedence.[6] Recognition that women have shaped—or even authored—these texts is already part of a venerable tradition. Modern readings of passages of the biblical Song of Songs have emphasized the distinctive presence of the woman's voice and its strength, highlighting that the verses sung by the female figure outnumber those sung by the male and that the woman's lines are more openly and assertively erotic than the man's.[7] Other scholars have made claims for female authorship, questioning conventional notions of the composition of the Bible. Other claims for women's authorship are readily supported by the ancient texts themselves, such as the mention of Miriam and Deborah in the introductory passages of the poems that carry their names.[8] Shlomo D. Goitein has even ventured that Miriam's line, "Sing ye to the LORD, / for he hath triumphed gloriously; / the horse and his rider / hath he thrown into the sea" (Exodus 15.21), inspired the Song at the Sea sung by her brother Moses (Exodus 15.1–18).[9] The Song of Deborah, said to be the oldest long poem of the Hebrew Bible, seems to open with a double attribution—"Deborah and Barak, son of Abinoam." The feminine singular form of the Hebrew verb for *sang*, however, clearly indicates Deborah's primacy. Biblical Hebrew verb form often conforms, in case and gender, to the "more important" of two actors.[10] The primacy of Deborah is doubly revealed in the linguistic form. In the translation of the song, we have stressed Deborah's authorship by placing Barak's name after the verb *sang*.

The Song of Deborah, in particular, has a feminist point of view, actually a double one: Yael's heroism[11] and the mourning "other," mother of Sisera, whose pain includes sorrow for the women raped by the enemy. A feminist reading enables empathy for women's suffering and opens new meaning for lines that have conventionally been interpreted as gloating at the mortification of the enemy women.[12] In any case, without diminishing the level of aggression, the effect of war is rendered through its impact on women, as a woman's victory and a woman's ruin.

Some scholars have asserted that a specifically female voice informs the Books of Ruth and Esther, especially the former. The agency of strong women in the plots of these two narratives, as well as the intimate bonding and loyalty between Ruth and Naomi, motivate such approaches.[13] Although predominantly prose, the first-person passages spoken by the heroines themselves lend themselves to interpretation as women's poetry.[14] Some recent authorities have claimed that the distinction between prose and poetry is not clearly upheld in biblical texts. Two passages in the Book of Ruth, however, namely the protagonist's loving words to her mother-in-law (1.16–17) and the words of Naomi to the women of Bethlehem (1.20–21), deserve to be regarded as poetry by women.[15]

Laments are a genre of folk poetry practiced by women in most cultures, and have been well documented for ages on the eastern coasts of the Mediterranean. Most of the biblical Book of Lamentations is composed of poems lamenting the destruction of Jerusalem and the Temple of Solomon by the Babylonians in the sixth century B.C.E. It should be mentioned that the word *city* is a feminine noun in Hebrew, and Jerusalem is personified as a woman in many verses of the book. A number of passages retain the flavor and rhetoric of the womanly poetry of wailing over the dead mentioned by the prophet Jeremiah, "and teach your daughters wailing and every one her neighbor lamentation" (Jeremiah 9.19). Most of the poetry in Lamentations is articulated in a male voice, although according to biblical texts, women had a central role in collectively lamenting defeat, as well as in singing victory songs.[16]

The most well-known texts in Hebrew in the period when the biblical text was in the process of canonization, from approximately the first century B.C.E. to the first century C.E., are the Dead Sea Scrolls. Work on these texts has so far not revealed female authorship or recognizable female voices.[17]

Late Antiquity: Rabbinic Texts

The main postbiblical Hebrew text, the Talmud—both the Babylonian and the Palestinian—is a collectively compiled text. It is juridical and ethnographic in its character, dialogical and anthological in its composition, and encyclopedic in its scope. The two editions emerged around the middle of the first millennium C.E. in Mesopotamia and Byzantine Palestine. The texts themselves reflect the creative process of the scholarly debates from which they emerged. The major parts concern legal and ritual matters and principles rooted in biblical law. The dialectic thinking and the collective negotiations construct a system of adjustments of the ancient law to new conditions. The discourse is richly interwoven with various prose narratives: legends, myths, fantastic tales, and biographies. It was compiled by men, but its polyphony includes women's voices. The same is largely true of the contemporaneous texts of the aggadic[18] Midrash, structured mainly as a running commentary on and elaboration of the books of the Torah (Genesis, Exodus, Leviticus, Numbers, and Deuteronomy) and the Five Scrolls (Esther, Song of Songs, Ruth, Lamentations, and Ecclesiastes). These were composed mainly in Palestine, and we have quoted from Leviticus Rabbah and Lamentations Rabbah. The Palestinian sources are, in general, more tolerant regarding the expression of women in the study of Torah, "the Learning."[19]

Women's authorship in postbiblical Hebrew literature may be inferred from introductory formulae such as "the women of Shkanziv[20] say," which precedes the lamentations from the Babylonian Talmud's tractate Moed Katan, or "mother told me," which introduces the poetry of healing, nurturing, sex, and magical traditions in a number of tractates of the Babylonian Talmud. In these texts there is not only a heightened awareness of women's firsthand knowledge of the origin of human life and the body but also testament to the passing on of this knowledge through oral tradition.

Like the earlier biblical texts, women's dominant role in lamenting the dead is revealed in the sources of this period: "What is *wailing*—when all the women wail in unison; and *lamenting*—when one speaks out and the others answer after her" (Mishna, Moed Katan 3:9). In other cases, where the woman's voice is not as explicitly marked, we have conjectured about the social creation of the text. The rabbinic literature of late antiquity, unlike quite a few books of the Hebrew Bible (e.g., those of the prophets) and most modern poetry, was composed collectively, both in its overall structure and in its discrete components such as specific tractates, narratives, or legal discussions. Whereas this collective oeuvre often credits the male participants in its rich multivocal chorus, it only rarely spells out the explicit participation of women. On the other hand, being collective and largely anonymous, this literary corpus is marked by a profound interaction between written and oral modes of creativity. The poetic characteristics of the verse in its use of stress and parallelism are not different from biblical poetics in any notable degree. Women have been acknowledged for their central role in crafting oral poetry not only in Hebrew tradition but in other traditions as well. We have therefore posited female authorship of poetic passages that relate to the folk traditions on pregnancy and birth from Midrash Leviticus Rabbah, and of the balladlike short narrative of Rachel's redemptive power from Midrash Lamentations Rabbah. Both of these belong to the Palestinian aggadic Midrash, previously mentioned for its relatively more open approach to women's cultural participation.[21]

Medieval Hebrew Poetry: Lonely Voices

Great gaps of time as well as considerable geographical leaps characterize the movement of women's voices in Hebrew poetry. It is hundreds of years later, far from Palestine and Mesopotamia, that the next identifiable woman's voice appears. It appears within a literary context where, for the most part, the names and identities of individual authors are acknowledged; yet this woman's name remains unknown, her work subsumed into the work of her husband. Dunash ben Labrat was the first great poet of the classical "golden age" of Hebrew poetry in Andalusia, Moslem southern Spain. The poem of his anonymous wife, scolding him for having wandered to foreign lands and leaving her with the children, is the first Hebrew poem of a woman who gives lyrical expression to her own intimate cares. It may well be the very first poem of the classical era, and has been recognized for its superb poetic qualities, rare specificity, and strength of emotion. This poem has survived thanks to the practice of Genizah, the careful preservation of all Hebrew texts lest they, and especially the holy names of God inscribed in them, be defiled. The poem existed in the most famous Genizah, the attic of the ancient synagogue of Cairo, together with an enormous number of diverse texts, ranging from the greatest poetry of such masters as Shmuel Ha-Nagid, Yehuda Halevi, Solomon ibn-Gabirol, Moses ibn-Ezra, and others who were active mostly in Moslem Spain, Andalusia, to quotidian documents such as invoices, contracts, and private letters. This treasure, discovered at the end of the nineteenth century, has revolutionized research into the lives of Jews around the Mediterranean in the Middle Ages.

The poem of Dunash ben Labrat's wife has always aroused interest and discussion, even by those contesting the view, now accepted by specialists in the field, that the poem was indeed written by the wife and not by the much better known husband. So great has been the impression made by this one poem that its discovery has caused one of the foremost experts of the poetry of the era to ponder a radically innovative view of the development of Hebrew poetry in Spain: positing a sudden birth of perfectly mature poetry rather than a slow evolution.[22] Given the pervasive silencing of female voices in standard poetic practice at the time, the hatching of this poem at the earliest stage of Spanish classical Hebrew poetry is all the more impressive.[23]

Perhaps more Hebrew poems by women in Spain are waiting to be discovered, but we have found only one other, written more than four centuries later by an unknown woman. Religious in nature, it begins with the line "Blessed, majestic, and terrible."[24] Her name is revealed by means of the poem's acrostic: the first letter of each line, read vertically, spells Merecina. In a note preceding the poem, the manuscript also gives the name Merecina, as well as the place where she lived—Gerona, in northern Christian Spain. Interpretations of her name vary, but the sense of "meritorious" has been favored.[25] Her use of language suggests that she was a refined woman, well-educated in the Hebrew Bible.

Dunash ben Labrat's wife and Merecina are the only women whose voices have been found so far in all the Spanish Hebrew poetry of the Middle Ages. Both transcend the limitations of their culture in Spain which was unfavorable to public female creativity.[26]

Early Modern Women's Poetry: Scattered Voices

Two major cataclysms dramatically affected Jewish culture during this period: the first, a physical calamity, was the expulsion of the Jews of Spain in 1492 by the Catholic monarchs Ferdinand and Isabella. As a result of the expulsion, many Jews perished, while others sought asylum elsewhere in Europe, North

Africa, and the Ottoman Empire. Forced conversions to Christianity took place mainly in Spain and its colonies. The second cataclysm, a spiritual upheaval, more than a hundred and fifty years later and probably related to the first, was the movement known as Shabbatean Messianism, named after its founder Shabbetai Zevi. In the Ottoman Empire, where many Jews had found refuge after the expulsion, some of the descendants of those expelled from Spain, together with local Jews, converted to Islam, following Shabbetai Zevi. In both cases, whether Catholicism or Islam, the new religious identity was assimilated with Judaism, often serving as a cover for the continuation of the secret practice of Judaism.

Writing in Hebrew by Jewish women virtually disappeared during this period for other reasons as well. Monastic institutions in Christian Europe, and the cloistering of thousands of women as nuns, enabled women's creativity, which reached one of its peaks in the twelfth century. Jewish women of the Middle Ages, however, had no sanctioned institutional way out of matrimonial obligations. Furthermore, they were not initiated into the secrets of kabbalah, which had a profound effect on the creative expression of men. Although the theology of kabbalah had room for a female as well as male component in the godhead, and the female component, the Shekhina, was considered beneficial,[27] women were, for the most part, excluded. Some scholars have understood the marginalization of women in kabbalistic study to be the result of the demonization of the female Lilith.[28] Women's creative expression was affected by their exclusion from kabbalistic learning and experience.

At the same time, Jewish cultural expression resurfaced in vernacular forms. Hebrew has always coexisted in Jewish culture in close dialogue with other languages, those spoken exclusively by Jews as well as those dominant in the countries of the Jewish diaspora. The emergence of Jewish vernacular literatures such as Judeo-Arabic, Judeo-Spanish, Yiddish, and so on, in various countries opened up creative possibilities in those languages for women, further minimizing women's reading and writing in Hebrew. Legend ascribes Hebrew lines and stanzas to daughters and wives of famous poets such as Spanish Hebrew masters Shmuel Ha-Nagid, Yehuda Halevi, and Abraham ibn-Ezra, but these accounts have not yet been corroborated. The accomplished Arabic poetry of Qasmuna, Ha-Nagid's daughter, has been discovered, however, as well as studied.[29]

A woman in Kurdistan in the sixteenth century, Asenath, daughter of Rabbi Samuel Adoni Barzani, wrote a long poem of lament and petition in the form of a rhymed letter. Newly widowed by her husband Rabbi Jacob of Mosul, Asenath addressed the leaders of the city of Amadiya, another Jewish community in the same area of Kurdistan as Mosul. Both Mosul and Amadiya were established centers of Jewish learning, continuing in the Babylonian Jewish tradition but also reshaping literary conventions in response to the influence of Arabic and Spanish Hebrew poetry. Asenath wrote her poem in the traditional monorhymed metrical form, in the Arabic tradition, with considerable skill and an excellent command of the Hebrew language. It is written as a letter of supplication, a convention often used by the Hebrew poets of Spain. A rhymed prose section of her letter, which follows the poem we have translated for our anthology, reveals deep erudition in rabbinic literature. It is clear from her plea to the leaders of Amadiya that she was actively involved in her husband's scholarly institution even before his death. After Rabbi Jacob's death, Asenath's economic and spiritual survival was endangered: her son was still a child and could not continue his father's enterprise. She therefore courageously presents herself as a worthy follower of her husband, a very unusual stance for a woman in Jewish tradition. From another letter, written by her son as an adult, we are informed that her appeal met with little response.[30]

Among women who wrote in Yiddish, one, Glikl bas Leyb (better known as Glückel of Hameln), who lived in the second half of the seventeenth century and the beginning of the eighteenth, has become especially famous for her informative, moving, and entertaining memoirs.[31] Women also wrote poetry in Yiddish at least a century before Glikl.[32] In the early modern era, Jewish women in central and eastern Europe created specific women's supplications, *tkhines,* a genre which has been extensively studied by the scholar Chava Weissler. Most of these supplications are in Yiddish and therefore do not appear in this anthology. One such text, however, was written by its author both in Yiddish and Hebrew, actually mostly in Aramaic. The poet—daughter of the well-known central European rabbi Jacob Yokl Horowitz, who lived in the mid-eighteenth century—bore the impressive name Sarah Rebecca Rachel Leah Horowitz, the names of all the four matriarchs, usually invoked in the genre of the supplications. Leah, apparently the name by which she was usually called, was one of seven children. Three of her brothers were rabbis in various communities in central and eastern Europe. Her sister Pessil was known to be of such spiritual stature that her grandnephew, a famous Hassidic rabbi, reportedly declared that she had the soul of the matriarchs. Both Leah and Pessil disproved the old saying that the only educated women were the daughters of learned rabbis who had no sons.[33]

Leah Horowitz's poetry weaves together collective concerns with private matters, combining the rhetoric of communal prayer with the intimacy of the lyrical poem. The power ascribed to the matriarchs gives the poem a feminist thrust, since the matriarchs are thought to influence God and forward the supplication to Him as messengers. The mention of all four matriarchs in the poem serves as a variation of the acrostic technique, forming the poet's name in initial letters of the lines, a literary device often employed by Hebrew poets of the classical medieval period in Spain and, thereafter, by their followers. Although her final prayer for male sons reflects the conventions of the time, in composing her poem Leah assumed an unusual stance for a woman of her time.

Some years later, at the end of the eighteenth century or at the beginning of the nineteenth century, another woman poet—in North Africa—wrote in Hebrew the first "Zionist" manifesto by a woman. The poem is composed of four couplets abiding by the strict poetics of liturgical form and following classical Hebrew Andalusian models. The poet—whose Arabic name, Freyha, is inscribed in the opening letters of each couplet in both of her poems that have been discovered—was, apparently, of Moroccan descent. Freyha Bat Avraham Bar-Adiba's assertive stance and her adoption of the rhetorical position of a leader of her people earn the poems their place in the anthology. Her two poems are the only Hebrew poems written by a woman found, so far, among thousands of poems belonging to the genre of sacred poetry written by Jews in North Africa in late medieval and early modern to modern times. Women's creativity is well known in oral poetry in the Judeo-Arabic dialects of North Africa. The scholar Joseph Chetrit, who uncovered Freyha's poems in a library in Strasbourg, has also published extensively on the oral poetry of Moroccan women—in Judeo-Arabic—basing his scholarship largely on his recordings. According to Chetrit, Freyha must have had an education not much different from men's, and the quality of her poetry ranks with that of male poets in the same area, period, and genre.[34]

Whereas the hidden treasures of medieval Hebrew poetry have yielded only two clear women's voices, the early modern Hebrew texts—from Asenath Barzani to Sarah Rebecca Rachel Leah Horowitz to Freyha Bat Avraham Bar-Adiba—although still few in number, testify to women's creative production before the modern era. The breadth and diversity of work by women stemming from the periods that follow disclose a great, but not easily achieved, change.

Enlightenment and the Beginning of Modernity

The birth of modern Hebrew literature in Europe is related to historical processes that shaped Jewish life from the French revolution to the first half of the twentieth century: the slow struggle for and attainment of Jewish civil emancipation, Jewish assimilation in the surrounding cultures, secularization, the emergence, at the turn of the eighteenth century, of the Enlightenment in Jewish culture—the Haskalah[35]—ongoing persecution, mass emigration, and the rise of nationalism. The political and social developments that shaped the Western world at the threshold of modernity had a significant impact on the structure of Jewish society. Although these social and cultural changes took different directions in different parts of Europe, their ultimate outcome was similar. The Jewish community opened itself to outside influences. These influences were willingly absorbed in central Europe, where emancipation was achieved in the second half of the nineteenth century; and accepted with more resignation in eastern Europe, where they were imposed on Jews by regimes advocating for complete assimilation, yet not offering civil emancipation until the early twentieth century. Nevertheless, the values of the Haskalah were ardently supported by some factions within Jewish society. The *maskilim*—those who embraced the Haskalah—introduced secular studies into traditional Jewish education. They encouraged the acquisition of local national languages (German, Russian, or Polish) and a change in traditional Jewish dress and manners.

The limitations and restrictions under which Jews lived in eastern Europe naturally influenced their cultural expression. In czarist Russia the Jewish settlement was restricted, until World War I, to the area of the Pale of Settlement, twenty-five provinces in Poland, Lithuania, Belorussia, Bessarabia, the Crimea, and the Ukraine. Although this confinement permitted Russian and Polish Jews to develop their own culture, it also cut them off from the surrounding society.

Traditional Jewish society encouraged Jewish men to devote themselves to religious study. Women were expected to apply themselves as breadwinners, in addition to running their homes. As a result, women came in daily contact with non-Jewish society and some were provided with a rudimentary secular education. Oddly enough, as Iris Parush has pointed out, women, who had been largely excluded from traditional Jewish religious schooling, enjoyed an advantage in secular studies. They were allowed relatively free access to world literature, and became instrumental in advancing Haskalah values.[36]

Although women became readers of literature in European languages and influenced male reading habits, and although they were the largest number of readers of modern Yiddish fiction, which was also taking its first steps in the second half of the nineteenth century, their education did not give them access to Hebrew texts. Yiddish may have been an option open both to men and to women who aspired to write secular literature, but the men had an alternative: their religious training and Torah studies enabled them to write in Hebrew as well. Most women lacked even a basic knowledge of Hebrew, and could not follow a prayer in the synagogue, let alone compose a prayer or an expression of their own.[37] It is thus no wonder that Yiddish is known as the *"Mame Loshen"* (the mother tongue) as opposed to Hebrew, which has been called *"Leshon Avot"* (the fathers' language).[38]

Although many *maskilim* did not oppose Jewish religious belief or ritual, their actions were seen as a severe threat to traditional Jewish society. The threat of assimilation and the fear of losing Jewish national distinction were instrumental in the birth of modern Hebrew literature. *Maskilim* who wished to promote the promise of the Enlightenment, while preserving a national identity, chose to promote their new principles in Hebrew.

Writing in Hebrew, therefore, was an ideological choice, which required considerable effort, especially for women. Rachel Morpurgo (1790–1871), Elisheva (1888–1949), Rahel (1890–1931), Yokheved Bat-Miriam (1901–1980), Anda Pinkerfeld-Amir (1902–1981), and Lea Goldberg (1911–1970) all had to learn the language they used in their poetry. They were often accused of not knowing Hebrew well enough or were condescendingly complimented for mastering it. Though her mother tongue was Yiddish, Esther Raab (1894–1981) is the first poet in this anthology to have spoken Hebrew as a child, in the Hebrew-speaking environment of Petah Tikvah in Ottoman Palestine. Bat-Hamah (1898–1979) and Haya Ginzburg (1900–1985) grew up in Hebrew-speaking households in Lipniki, a Ukrainian town where Yiddish and Russian were spoken. Miri (1911–1945) is the first to have been brought up in a Hebrew-speaking household in Mandatory Palestine.[39]

For generations, Hebrew was hardly used as a secular tongue. When it was more widely spoken again, Hebrew needed to be adjusted, "revived," and expanded for modern use. A secular aesthetic, which could grow out of and relate to the sacred Hebrew canon, had to be developed. As Yehuda Leib Gordon, the foremost male poet of the late Haskalah period in Russia saw it, women were to play a vital part in this process: that women had been prevented from reading and writing in Hebrew turned out to be a blessing in disguise.[40] In traditional Jewish society, most women were barely acquainted with the already existing body of Hebrew literature. Unburdened by the traditions of generations of schooling, the female pen could liberate Hebrew idiom from the clutches of tradition and create a freer, truer poetry. Gordon said, "The woman writes with the pen of a bird, and the man with a pen of iron and lead."[41] Hebrew poetry was perceived as stagnant, stifled by centuries of written rather than spoken usage, and women were expected, by Gordon at least, to give it a vitalizing shake. The transformation, however, evolved slowly. Fifty years after Gordon's remark, Rahel was still boasting of her rare, "pure," and unburdened language, "innocent as a baby" ("A Way of Speaking").[42] Lea Goldberg, whose first poems were published a decade later, had written her Ph.D. thesis on the Samaritan translation of the Bible and specialized in Semitic languages. Although traditional sources were easily accessible to her, Goldberg's poetry is not weighed down by them; rather, she forges her own language.

Historians of Hebrew literature generally agree that women's poetry fulfilled Gordon's predictions. They are divided on the causes and effects of this transformation. Dan Miron, the first to attempt an inclusive scholarly description of women's Hebrew poetry of the 1920s, has written that until the 1920s, the representative voice of Hebrew poetry was strictly male and that there was no space for women's poetry. According to Miron, once the obligation to speak for the nation diminished, nonrepresentative voices—or voices that had shed the prophets' robes—could be heard, and when they spoke they could express themselves in a new idiom.[43]

The absence of women poets before the 1920s is mirrored to some extent in this anthology; there seem to be, however, many reasons for this absence. Ziva Shamir stresses the educational barrier women faced in Hebrew. The rare appearances of women writers, such as the gifted feminist prose writer Devorah Baron (1887–1956) and the poet Sarah Shapira (c. 1870–c. 1930), only emphasize the existence of the barrier. Both women, despite convention, learned Hebrew. Moreover, even women who knew Hebrew were more inclined to write prose or memoir, since Hebrew poetry exposed its author in a way that stood in opposition to the code of modesty women were reared to obey.[44]

Michael Gluzman, an innovative feminist voice, sees the women poets of the 1920s (Elisheva, Rahel, Raab, and Bat-Miriam) as the pioneers of one of the greatest revolutions Hebrew poetry has known: the release from the traditional idiom. Gluzman thus revises the history of Hebrew poetry, re-evaluating and positioning formerly marginal poetry at the center of the canon.[45]

The conventional canon of modern Hebrew poetry allows for *one* woman poet, at most, in each poetic generation before the 1960s. This canon, which resembles other national literary canons prior to their expansion by feminist historians and critics, is being revised since the discovery and the new appraisal of formerly discarded voices, such as those presented in this anthology. The few select women who were historically admitted into the canon are Rachel Morpurgo, Sarah Shapira, Rahel, Lea Goldberg, Dahlia Ravikovitch (1936–), and Yona Wallach (1944–1985). Each was admitted into the canon for different reasons, most of which had little to do with the value of her poetry. The reception of Morpurgo's poetry was, for example, facilitated by her family connections. Her famous cousin, the poet and scholar Samuel David Luzzatto [ShaDaL] acted as a mediator between Morpurgo and Mendel Stern, editor of the periodical *Kokhavey Yizhak*, where her poems were published. When ShaDaL died in 1865, Morpurgo ceased to publish, although she continued to write.[46] Shapira was accepted on similar grounds: her father's connections. Shapira is better known for the encouraging letters that the poet Yehuda Leib Gordon wrote her, than by her own work. She never published a book, and only two of her poems are known. The first, an untitled poem that begins "let there be no dew and let there be no rain," is a short, zealous, Zionist hymn, which has been widely anthologized. The feminist poem we offer here, "Remember the Horn," has been largely ignored.

Shapira and Morpurgo were both, in their own times, celebrated as singular novelties, occupying the space allotted by the literary system for a token woman poet but perhaps not opening the way for others. The reception of Rahel's poetry was probably aided by an obtuse misreading: her work was interpreted as light, simple, pleasant, and unsophisticated. Rahel's wide popularity during her lifetime might account for the scorn and condescension held for her by major figures on the literary scene at the time. Her early death of tuberculosis contributed to the construction of her fragile and overprotected literary persona, in contrast to that of Raab, whose very strength probably kept her out of the canon.[47] Supportive critics of the time hailed Goldberg's early work for what they saw as its total devotion to the quest for love. Her poetry, like Rahel's, was read as "pure," "clean," and "simple,"—that is, mood poetry that had little to do with the world outside its speaker's perception.[48] It was seen as confessional, and although it demonstrated a clear intimacy with world literature and an exquisite command of prosody, because the themes addressed did not range beyond the poet's personal sphere, critics tended to perpetuate an image of the poet as a vulnerable woman.

Goldberg attained an eminent position in the literary establishment of her generation, which was dominated, from the 1930s until the 1950s, by her contemporaries Avraham Shlonsky[49] and Nathan Alterman.[50] Often Goldberg was the single woman in a group of male writers and artists—a queen bee, denying the sexist slant of the criteria for canonization and declaring poetry sexless. Like Wallach after her, Goldberg stated more than once that she wanted to be evaluated simply as a poet, not as a female poet. When her poetry was judged as a woman's, she felt it was being reduced.[51]

Ravikovitch was not part of a literary group. Although her early poems were printed in 1955 along with those of the esteemed male writers Yehuda Amichai, David Avidan, and Nathan Zach, she did not collaborate in the writing of their literary manifestos or their editing activities. Her early interest in traditional lyric forms and rhyme and her fascination with biblical language won over a major voice in the critical establishment of Israel in the mid-1950s—that of Baruch Kurzweil. Kurzweil placed Ravikovitch apart from her contemporaries; disregarding her intrinsic connections to these poets, he mistook her for a "nonthreatening" voice and thus opened a way for her into the canon. Another major critic, Mordechai Shalev, described Ravikovitch as a "lamenting poetess" in the ancient biblical tradition.[52]

The 1960s mark a divide in the history of Israeli poetry. The centralized structure of literary cliques, which characterized Hebrew poetry from Haim Nahman Bialik[53] at the turn of the nineteenth century onward, was weakened. Several poets of Yona Wallach's generation formed a close social circle in Tel-Aviv but did not present a united front in formulated literary manifestos. The reasons for Wallach's acceptance into the canon are complex. As soon as her first poems were published in 1964, critical consensus seems to have been established that her poetry—whether praised or rejected—was beyond most readers' comprehension. A typical headline from the late 1960s exclaims "Who Understands the Poet Yona Wallach?"[54] The obscureness of her poetry contributed to the mystification of her figure. Early criticism of Wallach's poetry often refers to her in the masculine, citing her as "perhaps the most innovative author in young Hebrew poetry," noting that her poetry cannot be judged in the category of "women's poetry," and aligning her within the male tradition as "a poet who has no fathers."[55] Although Wallach pronounced herself a feminist, feminist readings of her poetry are relatively new[56] and did not influence her entry into the canon.

Reconsidering Literary History

A review of the recent contribution of feminist critics, along with a thorough bibliographic search of periodicals and archives, leads us to a revised map of women's Hebrew poetry in the modern era. This new map reveals that women's Hebrew poetry developed gradually rather than erupting, as the conventional view suggests, in the early 1920s.[57] In order to outline this gradual development, one needs to reconsider its early stages.

In the first half of the nineteenth century, Italian Jewish scholars and poets were among the leading figures of the Haskalah movement. It is thus perhaps not surprising that Morpurgo, the first modern woman poet who wrote in Hebrew, was a member of the Jewish community in Italy. The Italian Jewish community had consciously maintained a continuity with poetic tradition from the Middle Ages onward. Italian Jews did not see Haskalah as being in sharp conflict with the traditional way of Jewish life, which in Italy was relatively moderate in many of its rulings, especially with regard to women's social and cultural roles.[58] Morpurgo was descended from a line of great Italian poets and scholars. This talented woman was fortunate enough to be taught and to master the Hebrew language, from biblical to rabbinic sources. Her deeply religious poetry was written in elaborate patterns, artfully exploiting the art of allusion and adhering to intricate classic poetic forms, such as the sonnet. Although her poetry was conventional in form, thematically it was innovative and revolutionary. Morpurgo signed her poems "*R*achel *M*orpurgo *H*a-ketana" (Little Rachel Morpurgo) or just with the initials RMH (רמה), which in Hebrew constitute the word *rima* (literally *worm*) to which she sometimes added the idiomatic *tola'a* (maggot), creating the idiomatic phrase *rima ve-tola'a,* meaning utter worthlessness. Critic Yaffa Berlowitz has argued that Morpurgo was not devaluing herself or her work by using these signatures. Berlowitz regards the signatures as a metaphoric extension of the poems and a protest against the status of women in Jewish religious culture as nonpersons, as good as dead. The poet provocatively confronted her readers with the marginality of women in Jewish culture and insisted that they read her poems as those of a woman—and not of an aberration.[59] Morpurgo also signed some of her poems *"nefel eshet Ya'akov Morpurgo"* (stillborn, the wife of Yaakov Morpurgo), an expression of her bitter-ironic view of herself as a wife and poet. The phrase *nefel eshet* (a woman's stillbirth) appears only once in the Bible (Psalms 58.9),[60] exhibiting Morpurgo's erudition beneath feigned modesty.

Women's poetry in eastern Europe internalized and conformed to the period's poetics, just like Morpurgo's oeuvre in Italy, but seemingly without any knowledge of her work. Their writing, in general, more often appeared in prose—essays and letters—than in poetry. Only Shapira, twenty years later, was well-known as a poet, though occasionally other women poets would be published in eastern European Hebrew journals.[61]

Later, under the Soviet regime, Hebrew literature was stifled, and many Russian poets were exiled to Siberia, imprisoned, and murdered. Many poets, including Bat-Miriam[62] and Haya Ginzburg, left the Soviet Union, while others like Bat-Hamah were cut off from the lifeline of Hebrew literature and resigned themselves to literary isolation and oblivion. Bat-Hamah's poetry, along with that of Raab and later on Miri,[63] spoke out against sexual oppression in Jewish society. Bat-Hamah's themes—arranged marriages ("The Vigil") and divorce—are early evidence of a woman poet celebrating her own sexuality. In a striking narrative poem of 1922, "The Harlot," Bat-Hamah created a Jewish heroine who loses her fiancé in a pogrom. Determined on revenge, she seduces his murderers, arouses their jealousy, and sets them against one another. A bloodbath ensues, and the avenger proudly returns home, where she is rejected and punished for having associated with non-Jewish men. Bat-Hamah's early poetic attempt to link gender and national issues was never published.[64]

Revisionist Mythmaking

The early writing of Bat-Miriam may be read as a painful struggle for the right to speak. The verse included from a poem of this period, "Hidden Treasures," is pivotal in this respect. In these early poems she seeks ratification in traditional women's prayers: the *tkhines.*[65] Later on, as she drew nearer to symbolist poetics, Bat-Miriam reached out to her chosen biblical namesake as a source of strength in affirming her poetic license. Embracing the rejected Miriam, Bat-Miriam rehabilitates the castigated leprous "matriarch."[66] In "Hagar," Bat-Miriam rehabilitates another biblical outcast, giving the narrative voice to Hagar and omitting God from the story.

Biblical mothers nurture the muse of many modern poets. Similarly, Rahel finds her poetic voice and connects herself to the Palestinian landscape by reviving her biblical matriarchal namesake—"it is her blood that flows in my blood, / her voice that sings in me"—("Rachel"), and Raab adopts the prophet Deborah as a congenial role model ("[Holy grandmothers in Jerusalem]"). Neglected or ostracized biblical women are redeemed by a feminist retelling, as in Shulamit Kalugai's (1891–1972) "Jezebel."

Biblical and postbiblical traditional Jewish texts remain the bedrock of Hebrew poetry. Women poets derive their own vocabulary from this foundation, though no longer from a disadvantaged position. Ravikovitch appropriates biblical idiom to create a powerful, culturally significant, and distinct poetic language. Shulamith Hareven (1932–), Hedva Harechavi (1941–), Nurit Zarchi (1941–), Bracha Serri (1942–), Galit Hasan-Rokem (1945–), and Rivka Miriam (1952–) all cultivate a complex and fruitful relationship with traditional Hebrew texts,[67] akin to the developments Alicia Suskin Ostriker has described as "revisionist mythmaking" in her influential study of women's poetry in America.[68]

Whereas most Hebrew poets today secularize sacred texts, Zelda (1914–1984) stands out in her religious devotion and pious mysticism. Her poetry is prayer; more than this it is a mystical union with divinity, which subverts traditional Jewish gender roles of religious discourse. Zelda, an observant Orthodox poet, over fifty when her first book was published, was admiringly embraced by a literary canon that extolled secularism and youth. Her successful reception by diverse audiences has been critically marveled at by her major interpreter, Hamutal Bar-Yosef.[69] Zelda may be seen as a forerunner of spiritual poetry that has gained greater prominence since the 1980s. Women's contribution to this development is clearly manifest in the literary periodical *Dimui* (Image), edited by the poet Hava Pinchas-Cohen (1955–).

The Emergence of Zionism and Israel

From the end of the nineteenth century, Hebrew literature and Zionism have been involved in a close symbiotic relationship. As writers immigrated to Palestine, initially under the Ottoman Empire and then later under the British Mandate, Hebrew literature once again took root there. The emerging pioneer society expected literature to promote its values and to valorize its achievements. Most poets found these demands burdensome and, on occasion, even contrary to the nature of poetry. This situation was particularly complicated for women poets. National accomplishments were represented as male; male-authored literature cast women in supportive, submissive, sometimes destructive, but never in leading roles. Hebrew poetry was also intensely engaged with the unfamiliar Palestinian landscape, and as in many colonialist literatures, the landscape was assumed to be feminine. Since all nouns in Hebrew are gendered, it should be noted that the Hebrew word for land, *adama,* is feminine (making the assumption easier). Such gender-marking established an exploitive and sexual relationship between the masculine settler and the land awaiting to be colonized. In literary depiction, land and the national settlement project took the place of women.[70]

Rahel, who first came to Palestine in 1909, and native Raab both contributed to reversing such imbalances.[71] Rahel discards "the great deeds of a hero / or the spoils a battle yields" ("To My Country") in favor of the mother-daughter ties she forms with her adopted land.[72] Raab also revises dominant male-centered poetic iconography. She communicates an autoerotic intimacy with the landscape and a familiarity with native Palestinian flora and fauna. Both poets, in different ways, subvert and expand the conventional poetic norms. Whereas Hebrew modernism of the time was heavily inclined toward Russian futurism and French symbolism, Rahel and Raab preferred a more direct and allegedly "simple" poetics.[73] Rahel's poetics were mistakenly interpreted as naïve and submissive to national ideals, as Alterman sarcastically put it, aiming a direct affront at Rahel's Zionist poem "My Country," "Blessed is the poetry which writes 'my country' / without feeling it has stepped on a snake."[74]

Israel's history and especially its wars and war poetry have marginalized women,[75] and their personal experience has not been acknowledged as a representative part of the collective ethos. Pinkerfeld-Amir's long epic poem of Israel's War of Independence, "Ahat" (The one), too long to be included here, is groundbreaking in this respect. Based on a true story, "Ahat" treats the Holocaust, national revival, and rehabilitation through the story of a mother, and her daughter Rachel Zeltser (1927–1948) who died in the battle for the Jewish Quarter in the Old City of Jerusalem.

The conflict between personal and collective demands characterizes all national literatures.[76] Freeing a personal voice from the grip of the collective is an ongoing project in Hebrew literature. Women's writing has contributed to the loosening of these individual voices. Although political and social issues are often part of this configuration, as in Serri's "Aliza Says," Ravikovitch's "Hovering at a Low Altitude" and Maya Bejerano's (1949–) "War Situations," women's writing has persistently sought an individual identity. Goldberg asserted that Hebrew poetry need not serve as the nation's "court jester." During World War II she launched a direct attack on demands to represent the community. She refused to harness her poetry to the service of war and national travail. The living—their joy and their pain—were more important than the dead, even if they had died a hero's death: "A wheat field will eternally be more precious and more beautiful than a wasteland which the tanks have trampled, even if the cause of those tanks is highly worthy."[77]

Although Goldberg participated in the debate over the politicization of poetry, she did not overtly address such themes in her own poetry, which was largely devoted to the expression of beauty and emotion. Goldberg's skillful practice of metrical and rhymed forms she derived from European and world literature[78] are probably the most accomplished in modern Hebrew poetry; included in this anthology are a section from "The Flowering" in terza rima form, and two sonnets from "The Love of Teresa de Meun." Her heightened awareness of the mystifying power of the poetic craft is suggested in the gendered context of "A Look at a Bee."

Unlike Goldberg, other women writers did openly confront public issues in their poetry. A singular case in point is that of Haya Vered (1922–1998). Vered's "The Zero Hour" is an exceptional expression of the bitter disillusion that took hold of Israeli society once the Zionist dream had been realized, and a Jewish state had been established in 1948.[79] Vered, whose speaker addresses her country as a "wounded five-year-old child," bluntly parodies Alterman's canonized poem "The Silver Platter."[80] Written in 1947, "The Silver Platter" had, by the early 1950s, become a national emblem. Frequently recited at official memorial services, it is a poem in which the nation expresses its gratitude to its young war dead, laid out as a silver platter on which the state has established its independence. As the critic Hannan Hever has shown, Vered is one of the few writers, mainly women, who, during this period, vehemently denies any justification for the loss of life, using extreme images of amputated bodies and materialistic corruption to demonstrate the high costs of war. Vered expands the sacrifice beyond the combat soldiers of "The Silver Platter" to encompass the Israeli people as a whole, including Holocaust survivors and refugees from all over the world. Pinkerfeld-Amir, Ayin Tur-Malka (1926–), Bat-Miriam, and later on Rahel Chalfi (c. 1945–) also reject the metaphoric "cleansing" of death in battle, legitimating the position of mourning mothers. Most male war poetry of the 1950s did not allow for the intimacy of personal grief and loss.[81]

It should be noted that Vered's parody, although iconoclastic, was written from the safe seat of early Israeli hegemony. Vered mourned the decline of idealized pioneer Palestine and the rise of materialism. She also associated the vast changes in the state with the arrival of Jewish immigrants from Arab and North African countries, together with European Holocaust survivors. While she did refer to these immigrants as "brothers," the ethnic stereotypes figured in "The Zero Hour" tend to persist in Hebrew poetry. The complexity of Israeli society as a community of immigrants is reflected with more diversity in contemporary women's poetry. Jews of Middle Eastern or North African origin comprise half the Israeli population today, but their poets are still in a minority. Those who explore their ethnic identity within a feminist context are fewer still. Simcha Zarmati-Atzta (1927–1992), Serri, Amira Hess (1943–), and Miri Ben-Simhon (1954–1996) deal with ethnicity as a personal and political issue in Israeli society, exposing and opposing the double oppression that women from Arab and African countries suffer, both as women and as eastern (Mizrahi) Jews.

Toward the Twenty-First Century

In the last quarter of this century, European Jewish identity has become a subject for poetry.[82] Although the Holocaust profoundly affected Israeli society, especially through the direct impact of the thousands of families who fled Europe for Palestine before the war and the hundreds of thousands of survivors who arrived immediately after the war, we found fewer Holocaust poems than we expected.[83] Few survivors adopted Hebrew as their literary language, although the male survivors Abba Kovner and Dan Pagis are outstanding Hebrew poets. Even memoirs written by women about the Holocaust are often written in their mother tongue and translated into Hebrew. There are some Israeli women, however, who have written poems relating to the Holocaust; these range from a commemoration of the dead to laments and bitter accusations. In one of Zelda's early poems, published in 1942, "The Girl's Poem" (not included here), the poet exclaims, "God, how can You command me to bloom? / You have planted my life in the river of death— / Shall I blossom in my brothers' blood? // Answer: Shall I clothe myself in happiness, bear fruit, / in front of amputated bodies, / in front of faceless corpses? / Answer—."[84]

Raab wrote a poem cursing Adolph Eichmann; Bat-Miriam published a cycle weighing the possibility and value of poetry after the Holocaust entitled "Ghetto Poems." A more contemplative and elegiac mode distinguishes Goldberg's cycle, "From My Old Home," which resurrects the charm of Kovno, her lost hometown of childhood. Ruth Alpern Ben-David (1936–), an Israeli-born poet, was entrapped on a prewar visit to Poland yet survived the Holocaust. She has written a poem about coming to terms with Germany and German tourists visiting in Israel today, "Setting Out for Convalescence." Poets of the second and third generation following the Holocaust are beginning to write about the experience and feelings of survival and its significance in Israeli society; consider the poetry of Hareven, Devorah Amir (1948–), and Leah Aini (1962–).

The genocide of the Jewish people during World War II, followed by the military struggles of the state of Israel, which continue to take a high number of lives, are perhaps, as Lesley Hazleton has suggested, responsible for the importance Israeli society attaches to childbirth. In Hazleton's words, "fertility is a national priority in Israel."[85] As feminism has become a growing influence, motherhood is experienced less in the national context (as in Pinkerfeld-Amir's long poem "Ahat" and Tur-Malka's poem "Memorial Service") and more in a personal light (as in Harechavi's "A Very Cheerful Girl," Zarchi's "Baby Blues," and Leah Ayalon's [c. 1951–] "Golden Girl"). Motherhood nevertheless continues to be viewed from a national perspective (as in Serri's "Aliza Says," Ravikovitch's "A Mother Walks Around," and Chalfi's "Tel-Aviv Beach, Winter '74"). Israeli women's poetry now also considers the politics of mothering (as in Zarchi's "She Is Joseph").

Forging a Feminist Consciousness

The feminist movement's history in Israel is as old as the history of the Zionist movement.[86] From the outset, however, feminist issues have been subordinated to the national interest and, thus, marginalized. Many poets who made their debuts, beginning in the late 1950s, wrote their openly feminist poetry only from the late 1970s onward. Our choice of poems reflects this tendency. Second wave feminism and the Civil Rights movement, which shook women's lives in the United States and Europe in the 1960s, left barely any mark on Israeli women. It took twenty more years for women's issues to gain ground in Israel, especially in matters of peace and civil rights, but now feminist organizations have a lively and productive presence—although still a marginal one. The influence of Anglo-American and French feminist theory and literary criticism in the universities has also contributed to this progress. Departments of Hebrew literature have expanded curricula to include a variety of approaches to women's literature.

Poetry possibly preceded women activists in raising a feminist agenda. The greatest and most consistent contribution to the construction of a feminist consciousness in Israeli poetry is surely that of Dahlia Ravikovitch. Self-reflection led Ravikovitch to expose stereotypical feminine images, carrying them to their utmost extreme and creating an ostensibly passive and submissive persona who finally rages against them (as in "Clockwork Doll"). Ravikovitch highlights and unmasks the conventional association of women with vulnerability, dependence, seduction, violence, hysteria, witchcraft, and charms. Her early tendency toward traditional forms and language facilitated her warm reception by male critics and the general reading public from the very start, and probably blinded them to her overt feminist stand. The pattern noted at the beginning of modern Hebrew women's poetry, in the writing of Rachel Morpurgo one hundred years earlier, is thereby repeated.

The young Ravikovitch exhibits a close affinity to Goldberg. But unlike her mentor, Ravikovitch takes a personally involved political stand and confronts, in feminist terms, the oppression of Palestinians in Lebanon and in the occupied West Bank (as in "Hovering at a Low Altitude" and "A Mother Walks Around").

That Ravikovitch was not identified with feminism served Wallach in constructing her own poetic persona as a feminist forerunner. Wallach maintained Ravikovitch was "not feminist."[87] In retrospect Wallach, whose first poems were published only five years after Ravikovitch's first volume of poetry appeared, was clearly following in Ravikovitch's footsteps. She herself led Hebrew poetry into a new phase. Ever since, Hebrew poets of both sexes have explored the possibilities that she opened up, in widening varieties. Poets as diverse as Bejerano, Hess, Zarchi, and Ayalon have assimilated Wallach's influence in genuine and innovative ways.

With Wallach the unconscious entered the foreground of Israeli poetry. As she gave voice to explicit, detailed, sometimes humorous, often violent sexual fantasies and practice, and reached deep into the human psyche, Wallach committed herself to the construction and deconstruction of fundamental emotional, ideological, and social attitudes. Her poetic experiments with gender crossings often have a dazzling effect (as in "[A grizzly she-bear reared me]" and "Absalom"). Sex in Ravikovitch's poetry is highly symbolic, and far from physiological; she might mention a nail or a tongue but never sexual organs. Wallach's blatant exposure of the female (as well as the male) body in her poetry is daring and provocative (as in "Tefillin").

The voyage inward initiated by Wallach[88] is still pursued, in various ways, by Harechavi, Hess, Ayalon, and others. The influence of the Hebrew canon is still potent as Hebrew women poets begin to find the canon increasingly accessible. Along with the mainstream of Israeli poetry, women's poetry has turned from the earlier influence of Russian and European models to poets writing in English. Israeli women poets have especially been drawn to American women's poetry (Emily Dickinson, Muriel Rukeyser, and Sylvia Plath). Zarchi acknowledges these and other feminist influences in her essays, as well as in her poetry. Ayalon shows a great fondness for popular American culture; anything from fast food restaurants to scenes from recent American films may be found in her poetry. "I'll Speak with You in September" brings together and then disarms two powerful representatives of American literature, William Faulkner and Ernest Hemingway. The speaker adopts the persona of Emily, the heroine of Faulkner's short story "A Rose for Emily," ascribing a "macho" voice to the silenced and oppressed character. The poem is set in the diner of Hemingway's story "The Killers." Instead of silently revering the two masters of prose, Ayalon mixes their two stories together, diffusing their sharp characteristic lines. If there is a murder in this poem, it is the murder of the authors, a liberating act, that frees writer and reader to create their own new text.

Women's poetry has often been described in male Hebrew criticism, as previously noted, as "simple," "transparent," and linguistically flat.[89] Perhaps in reaction to this criticism, many contemporary women poets compose allusive, somewhat elite work, layered with fantastic imagery and intertextual references. Contemporary Israeli women's writing challenges the Hebrew language, tearing it at its seams, invading areas formerly restricted to masculine discourse (as Bejerano does in her "Data Processing" poems) and eroding the phallocentric system.

Chalfi first explored a powerful feminist persona in aquatic imagery: in the poem "The Water Queen of Jerusalem," the city is overwhelmed by its cultural baggage, while the protagonist herself is almost drowned. She triumphs, mutating into a fishlike being in a process of evolution that also defines her subjectivity. Thereafter, Chalfi adopted medieval witch trials as a poetic framework, acting in defense of the falsely accused. Her poetry is exploratory, forever aware of the futile effort to grasp or to define a given moment, yet cherishing the attempt itself.

Bejerano has chosen, especially in her early poetry, a technical, seemingly "unpoetic" language. Against the commonplace, she introduces astronomy, computer technology, and science fiction to signal that the future belongs to women. The poetic voice in these poems unabashedly positions itself at the center of the universe's orbit. Her later poetry, especially in the cycle "The Hymns of Job," draws on mythical imagination, confronting existential and political questions. Her 1997 volume, *Trying to Touch My Belly-Button,* takes an autobiographical direction.

Agi Mishol (1947–) pokes fun at the Zionist sanctification of agricultural labor and establishes a relationship with the land on her own terms ("Estate"). Introducing herself as "the supermarket bard" ("In the Supermarket") with a nod to

Allen Ginsberg, she demystifies the poetic muse. Like Bejerano in "Poetry," Mishol develops poetics that are grounded in a woman's experience—for example, as she faces herself in the morning in the mirror ("Estate").

Younger poets such as Ben-Simhon, Efrat Mishori (1964–), and Sharon Hass (1966–) actively forge a Hebrew (M)other tongue, and pursue the possibilities that present themselves when a woman's body meets her language. Mishori performs her poetry, accentuating the corporeal dimension of language. As womanhood comfortably settles into Hebrew, "compulsory heterosexuality" is also being dissolved. Hebrew poetry is discovering a lesbian voice in some recent poems by Harechavi and Hass.

Male poets such as Gordon, Bialik, Shlonsky, and Alterman were the leading figures in modern Hebrew literature from the turn of the nineteenth century until the late 1950s, when the dominance of poetry receded in favor of prose. Literary periodicals continuously reflected and contributed to this development. As narrative fiction has come to the fore in Israeli literature, and volumes of poetry are more difficult to publish (even major poets must often finance the publication of their books), the role of periodicals has become crucial. Publications such as *Achshav* and *Keshet* (from the late 1950s), *Siman Kri'a, Prosa, Iton 77* (from the 1970s) and *Hadarim* (from the 1980s) have provided a continuous platform for women's—and men's—poetry. The theme-centered anthologies issued by Helicon (begun in the early 1990s) have become a notably supportive environment for fledgling as well as established poets. Poetry workshops also have proliferated in the last two decades, allowing new poetic voices to surface. The Helicon workshop has shown constant involvement in issues of gender and poetry. Enterprises such as the young poets' group *Ev* have displayed an equal presence of women and men poets.

The last quarter of the twentieth century has witnessed an enormous surge of women's literary creativity, in poetry as well as in prose. Women have now taken their place in Israeli literature.[90] Women poets need no longer be subversive; and they are continuing to develop an open and self-assured feminist outlook. Taken together, the poets collected in this volume have a powerful impact. Their integration into Hebrew literature, within a securely rooted feminist tradition, constitutes the fruition of a long and laborious process. But even as the fruition is recognized, the convulsive history of Israel's young statehood has foregrounded and empowered male-dominated institutions, primarily the Orthodox rabbinate and the army. These institutions have little tolerance for women's rights and women's presence in the public arena. As in the moving prose poem from the Midrash about Rachel and Leah, women's sisterhood and their brave, outspoken voices are needed.

Shirley Kaufman, Galit Hasan-Rokem, and Tamar S. Hess
Jerusalem, Israel
Nisan 5759 / April 1999

Notes

A note on transliteration of Hebrew proper names and titles of works. Our chief concern in transliteration has been to create a readable text. Since there are a great number of different conventions, some of which present typographic difficulties and some of which seem to us awkward or unpronounceable in English, we referred most often to the *Encyclopaedia Judaica* (Jerusalem: Keter, 1971), usually accepting the most common usage. With regard to living poets, we followed their own requests.

1. Babylonian Talmud, Tractate Kiddushin 49b.

2. Amalia Kahana-Carmon, "Brenner's Wife Rides Again," (in Hebrew) *Moznaim* (October 1985).

3. The Gezer Calendar, attributed to the tenth century B.C.E., is the oldest poetic text written in the ancient Hebrew alphabet yet discovered. Discovered in 1908 at a site of an ancient city in central Israel between Ramla and Latrun, the tablet is inscribed with the calendar of the ancient Israelites—according to some views, the text of a folk song about the seasons and the agricultural tasks associated with each.

4. *Encyclopaedia Judaica* (Jerusalem: Keter, 1971).

5. Dating biblical texts is a precarious task. There is no scholarly consensus regarding the dating of the songs of Miriam and Deborah. We have therefore decided to avoid specific dating by generally dating all our biblical texts from the tenth century to the third century B.C.E. Our decision concerning dates was arrived at after many discussions with scholars, notably Professors Moshe Greenberg, Sarah Japhet, and Yair Zakovitch, all at the Hebrew University of Jerusalem.

6. For a review of this tradition, see Shlomo D. Goitein, "Women's Poetry in the Bible," (in Hebrew) *Molad* 14 (December 1956): 533.

7. Yair Zakovich, introduction and commentary to the Hebrew original, (in Hebrew) *Song of Songs,* Mikra leyisra'el: "A Bible Commentary for Israel," eds. Moshe Greenberg and Shmuel Ahituv (Tel-Aviv: Am Oved; Jerusalem: The Magnes Press, 1992), especially 11–14. For a comprehensive scholarly discussion in English of the composition of the Song of Songs, see the new translation by Ariel Bloch and Chana Bloch (New York: Random House, 1995), their introduction, 3–41, especially 33–34, comparing the song to wedding songs sung by women. See also Marcia Falk's translation and commentary (New York: Harcourt Brace Jovanovich, 1977; Sheffield: The Almond Press, 1982; San Francisco: Harper San Francisco, 1990). For feminist readings of the Bible, see Phyllis Trible, *God and the Rhetoric of Sexuality* (Philadelphia: Fortress Press, 1978), and Ilana Pardes, *Countertraditions in the Bible: A Feminist Approach* (Cambridge, Mass.: Harvard University Press, 1992), on the Song of Songs, 118–43.

8. See also, the attribution of the songs of David's victory to women (1 Samuel 18.7), as well as the explicit mention of women as lamenters (Jeremiah 9.16–19).

9. For a review of literature concerning this, see Goitein, "Women's Poetry," 532.

10. Other examples of such alterations in verb agreement include Numbers 12.1, in which although the verb form is singular and feminine, two speakers follow, Miriam *and* Aaron, and also Genesis 3.8, in which the masculine singular verb form is followed by the two actors Adam and Eve.

11. Tikva Frymer-Kensky characterizes Yael's heroism as part of a larger phenomenon in biblical narratives about women, what she calls "stories of deception," which impart an acceptance of female strategies in patriarchal society. See Frymer-Kensky, *In the Wake of the Goddesses: Women, Culture, and the Biblical Transformation of Pagan Myth* (New York: The Free Press, 1992), 137.

12. This reinterpretation is sustained by the contemporary male poet Haim Gouri in his poem "His Mother," written in the late fifties, which describes Sisera's mother in an empathetic way. Gouri, *Compass Rose* (Shoshanat haruhot) (Tel-Aviv: Hakibbutz Hameuchad, 1990); *In My Lovesick Blood,* tr. Stanley Chyet (Detroit: Wayne State University Press, 1996), 44–45.

13. Other explicit attributions of poetic expressions to women appear in the stories of the matriarchs Leah and Rachel, who name their sons in succinct words of poetry (Genesis 29:32–35 and 30:6, 8, 11, 13). The naming of sons by women has been considered a rare instance of authoritative female behavior in this patriarchal text. See Pardes, *Countertraditions,* "Beyond Genesis 3: The Politics of Maternal Naming," chap. 3, 39–59. We thank Tirzah Meacham of the University of Toronto for suggesting this idea. Scholarly readings of Proverbs clearly show that the book is composed from varied sources. Chapter 31 of the book records explicitly the source of the text, King Lemuel, who quotes his mother's admonitions, thus giving voice to another ancient woman whose poem we did not include because of its insistent patriarchal bias: "'*No, my son! No, O son of my womb! No O son of my vows! Do not give your strength to women, Your vigor to those who destroy kings*'" (Proverbs 31.2–3).

14. Pardes, *Countertraditions,* chap. 6. Also see, Yair Zakovich, introduction and commentary to the Hebrew original, (in Hebrew) *Book of Ruth,* Mikra leyisra'el: "A Bible Commentary for Israel," eds. Moshe Greenberg and Shmuel Ahituv (Tel-Aviv: Am Oved; Jerusalem: The Magnes Press, 1990).

15. For comprehensive treatments of the question of biblical poetry versus prose, see James L. Kugel, *The Idea of Biblical Poetry: Parallelism and Its History* (New Haven: Yale University Press, 1981); Robert Alter, *The Art of Biblical Poetry* (New York: Basic Books, 1985). See also T. Carmi, *The Penguin Book of Hebrew Verse* (Harmondsworth: Penguin Books, 1981), introduction, 13–55; Benjamin Hrushovski (Harshav), "Prosody," *Encyclopaedia Judaica,* vol. 13 (Jerusalem: Keter, 1971), 1195–1240. Some of the newest English Bible translations have reinforced the identification of these lines as poetry, and we have used the lineation from *The New Oxford Annotated Bible: New Revised Standard Version* (New York: Oxford University Press, 1991) although the translation itself is taken from *The Holy Bible, Authorized King James Version* (1611; reprint, New York: Oxford University Press, 1967).

16. For an example of a victory song, see 1 Samuel 18.7, and for lamenting collective disasters, see Jeremiah 49.3 and Ezekiel 32.16.

17. Female participation in ritual performance of texts has been discussed in recent research. Joseph Baumgarten, "4Q502, Marriage or Golden Age Ritual," *Journal of Jewish Studies* 37 (1983): 124–35. We thank Esther Chazon of the Hebrew University for this reference.

18. The belletristic, nonlegal parts of rabbinic literature.

19. Daniel Boyarin, *Carnal Israel: Reading Sex in Talmudic Culture* (Berkeley, Los Angeles, Oxford: University of California Press, 1993), 169–70.

20. Shkanziv, a township in Babylonia mentioned three other times in the Talmud, all three related to women: once there is a warning against marrying women from Shkanziv (Pesahim 112b), as it is the seat of jesters, and in the other two (more or less identical) passages (Yoma 18b; Yevamot 38b) it is mentioned as a distant place where rabbis might have been engaged in temporary wedlock with local women. Also see Aharon Oppenheimer, *Babylonia Judaica in the Talmudic Period* (Wiesbaden: L. Reichert, 1983, 397–401). We thank Shaul Shaked of the Hebrew University.

21. For the theoretical argument on women's voices in rabbinic literature of late antiquity, see Galit Hasan-Rokem, *The Web of Life—Folklore in Rabbinic Literature* (in Hebrew) (Tel-Aviv: Am Oved, 1996), especially chap. 6.

22. Ezra Fleischer, "On Dunash ben Labrat, His Wife and His Son; New Light on the Beginnings of the Hebrew-Spanish School," (in Hebrew) *Jerusalem Studies in Hebrew Literature* 5 (Joseph Ewen In Memoriam) (1984): 189–202.

23. Tova Rosen, "On Tongues Being Bound and Let Loose: Women in Medieval Hebrew Literature," *Prooftexts* 8, no. 1 (1988): 67–87.

24. Avraham M. Haberman, *Studies in Sacred and Secular Poetry of the Middle Ages* (in Hebrew) (Jerusalem: Reuben Mass, 1972), 265–67. According to Haberman, the manuscript was sent to him in Jerusalem by a Viennese Jewish bookseller, Rabbi David Fraenkel, in the late thirties. We thank Yehoshua Granat for this information.

25. Haberman, *Studies,* quotes Haim Beinart, famous historian of the Jews in medieval Spain, to this effect.

26. A permitted expression of female creativity was the incorporation of lines in Spanish, composed by women, into the Hebrew poems of men: "girdle poems." Emilio Garcia-Gomez, "La poesie lyrique hispano-arabe et l'apparition de la lyrique romane" (Hispanic-Arabic poetry and the appearance of Romance lyric poetry) *Arabica* 5 (1958): 113–44. Samuel M. Stern, *Hispano-Arabic Strophic Poetry: Studies,* ed. L. P. Harvey, (Oxford: Oxford University Press, 1974), 56–62. Tova Rosen-Moked, *The Hebrew Girdle Poem (Muwashshah) in the Middle Ages* (in Hebrew) (Haifa: Haifa University Press, 1985), 95–97.

27. Raphael Patai, "The Shekhina," *Journal of Religion,* 44 (1964): 275–88; Gershom Scholem, "Ha-shekhina," (in Hebrew) *Elements of the Kabbalah and Its Symbolism* (Jerusalem: The Bialik Institute, 1980), 259–307. Gerda Lerner, *The Creation of Feminist Consciousness from the Middle Ages to Eighteen-Seventy* (New York and Oxford: Oxford University Press, 1993), 112–13, citing Gershom G. Scholem, *Major Trends in Jewish Mysticism* (New York: Schocken Books, 1941), 37–38. The same holds true for the later Hassidism, see Ada Rapoport-Albert, "On Women in Hassidism: S. A. Horodecky and the Maid of Ludomir Tradition," in *Jewish History: Essays in Honour of Chimen Abramsky,* eds. Ada Rapoport-Albert and Steven J. Zipperstein (London: Peter Halban, 1988), 518.

28. Gershom Scholem, "Lilith," *Encyclopaedia Judaica,* vol. 14 (Jerusalem: Keter, 1971), 1349–54 (especially 1353–54); reprinted in *Kabbala* (Jerusalem: Keter, 1974), 356–61.

29. James Mansfield Nichols, "The Arabic Verses of Qasmuna Bint Isma'il Ibn Naghalah," *International Journal of Middle East Studies* 13 (1981): 155–58, quotes the poems; James Belamy, "Qasmuna the Poetess: Who Was She?" *American Oriental Society* 103 (1983): 423–24, identifies her without doubt as Ha-Nagid's daughter.

30. Jacob Mann, *Texts and Studies in Jewish History and Literature,* vol. 1 (Cincinnati: Hebrew Union College Press, 1931), 483; and for "The text of the Hebrew poem of the Kurdish woman, Asenath the daughter of Rabbi Samuel Adoni Barzani," see section IV, 507–15. See also Yona Sabar, ed. and trans., *The Folk Literature of the Kurdistani Jews: An Anthology,* Yale Judaica Series 23 (New Haven and London: Yale University Press, 1982), xxxvi. On p. xx, Sabar actually refers to her as "the famous female Rabbi Asenath." On Asenath's legendary biography, see Sabar, *Folk Literature,* 123–24. On legendary and historical attributions of poems—Hebrew and other—to Jewish women, see Avraham M. Habermann, "Jewish Poetesses of Ancient Times," (in Hebrew) *Mi-pri Ha-et Ve-ha-'et* (Jerusalem: Reuven Mass, 1981), 93–99.

31. Natalie Zemon Davis, *Women on the Margins: Three Seventeenth-Century Lives* (Cambridge, Mass., and London: Harvard University Press, 1995), especially "Arguing with God: Glikl bas Judah Leib," 5–62; see also, Chava Turniansky, "'A Jewish Woman's Life': The Memoirs of Glikl (Hamel)," (in Hebrew) *Sexuality and the Family in History,* eds. Israel Bartal and Isaiah Gafni (Jerusalem: The Zalman Shazar Center for Jewish History, 1998), 177–91.

32. Ezra Korman, ed., *Yidishe dikhterins: antologye* (Yiddish women poets: Anthology) (Chicago: L. M. Stein, 1928).

33. Weissler supplied us with the information about the poem and about the poet's life and family. See her *The Voices of the Matriarchs: Listening to the Prayers of Early Modern Jewish Women* (Boston: Beacon Press, 1998) 104–25.

34. Joseph Chetrit, "Freyha Bat Yosef: A Hebrew Poetess in Eighteenth-Century Morocco," (in Hebrew) *Peamim: Studies in the Cultural Heritage of Oriental Jewry* 4 (1980): 84–93; "Freha bat Rabbi Avraham: More on a Hebrew Poetess in Morocco in the Eighteenth Century," (in Hebrew) *Peamim: Studies in the Cultural Heritage of Oriental Jewry* 55 (1993): 124–30. It has not been clarified until now why she uses a different patronym, Bat Yosef, in the acrostic of her first poem.

35. "Etymologically *Haskalah* is derived from the root *skl* (שכל) denoting understanding, reason or intelligence. *Haskalah* meant a commitment to reason rather than to revelation as the source of truth, or perhaps more correctly, the identification of revelation with reason," *Encyclopaedia Judaica,* vol. 8, (Jerusalem, Keter, 1971), 179.

36. Iris Parush, "Women Readers As Agents of Social Change Among Eastern European Jews in the Late Nineteenth Century," *Gender and History* 9, no. 1 (April 1997): 60–82.

37. During the same period, in Italy, Jewish women were certainly the performers, if less certainly the authors, of situational poems in Hebrew recited at rituals, such as the donation of a candelabra to a synagogue after a happy birth. Oral communications with Tirza Meacham of the University of Toronto, who is currently working on such texts with Harry Fox, also of the University of Toronto.

38. It might further be noted that the two languages had a definite hierarchical relationship: Hebrew being the holy tongue "*Leshon Kodesh*") and Yiddish marking the daily mundane. For a lucid and illuminating discussion of the gendered significance of the relation between Yiddish and Hebrew, see Naomi Seidman, *A Marriage Made in Heaven: The Sexual Politics of Hebrew and Yiddish* (Berkeley, Los Angeles, and London: University of California Press, 1997).

39. Many of these poet-immigrants made a vital contribution to Hebrew literature through translations. Lea Goldberg translated Petrarch into Hebrew. Ella Amitan, Shulamit Kalugai, and Anda Pinkerfeld-Amir also translated poetry and prose from different European languages. The Israeli-born Shin Shifra has lately completed a monumental project of translating the *Gilgamesh Epic*.

40. Gordon as cited in Iris Parush, "The Hebrew Tongue: A Man's Tool or a Woman's Garment?" (in Hebrew) in *Literature and Society: Papers Written in Honor of Gershon Shaked,* eds. Judith Bar-El and Yigal Schwartz (Tel-Aviv: Hakibbutz Hameuchad, forthcoming); see also her "Readers in Cameo: Woman Readers in Jewish Society of Nineteenth-Century Eastern Europe," *Prooftexts* 14 (1994): 1–23.

41. From a Hebrew letter to Sheine Wolf, 8 November 1881, from *Iggerot Yehuda Leib Gordon* (Collected letters of Y. L. Gordon) vol. 2 (Warsaw: n. p., 1794), 5 (letter no. 203). Quoted by Parush, "Readers in Cameo," 18.

42. Michael Gluzman, "The Exclusion of Women from Hebrew Literary History," *Prooftexts* 11 (1991): 259–78. Major critics, however, still view Rahel's poetic manifestos as deriving from her elementary proficiency in Hebrew. See Ziva Shamir, *The Origins of Originality: The Poetry of Jonathan Ratosh, Father of the Hebrew Youth "Canaanites")* (in Hebrew) (Tel-Aviv: Hakibbutz Hameuchad, 1993), 192–200.

43. Dan Miron, *Founding Mothers, Stepsisters: The Emergence of the First Hebrew Poetesses and Other Essays* (in Hebrew) (Tel-Aviv: Hakibbutz Hameuchad, 1991); also excerpted in English as "Why Was There No Women's Poetry in Hebrew Before 1920?" in *Gender and Text in Modern Hebrew and Yiddish Literature,* eds. Naomi B. Sokoloff, Anne Lapidus Lerner, and Anita Norich (New York and Jerusalem: The Jewish Theological Seminary of America, 1992), 65–91.

44. Shamir, *The Origins,* 196.

45. Gluzman, "The Exclusion of Women."

46. Yaffa Berlowitz, "Rachel Morpurgo: The Death Wish, The Poem's Wish—On the First Hebrew Poet in Modern Times," (in Hebrew) in *Sadan: Studies in Hebrew Literature,* vol. 2, eds. Ziva Shamir and Hanna David (Tel-Aviv: Tel-Aviv University, 1996), 11–40.

47. For more on the reception of Raab's work, see Hamutal Tsamir, "Love of the Homeland and a Deaf Dialogue: A Poem by Esther Raab and Its Masculine Critical Reception," (in Hebrew) *Theory and Criticism* 7 (1995): 125–45; and for the reception of Rahel, see Miron, *Founding Mothers,* 114–50.

48. Yaakov Fichmann, "A New Poet," (in Hebrew) in *Lea Goldberg, A Selection of Critical Essays on Her Writings,* ed. Avraham B. Yoffe (Am Oved: Tel Aviv, 1980), 38–40; Haya Shaham, "A Woman Poet in a Crowd of Men Poets: The Reception of Lea Goldberg's and Dahlia Ravikovitch's Poetry in the Criticism of Their Time," (in Hebrew) in *Sadan: Studies in Hebrew Literature,* vol. 2, eds. Ziva Shamir and Hanna David (Tel-Aviv: Tel-Aviv University, 1996), 203–40.

49. The poet Avraham Shlonsky (1900–1973) had a vast influence on Israeli literature from the mid-1920s until the 1950s, not only as bearer of the symbolist and expressionist torch but also as a prolific and innovative translator into Hebrew and as an editor of the leading modernist periodicals of the time.

50. Nathan Alterman (1910–1970) was the foremost Hebrew poet from the late 1930s until the mid-1950s. He was a prolific writer, and produced drama as well as lyrical and polemical political poetry. His work had an immense influence on the development of Israeli poetry.

51. Drora Idelman, "Woman in Literature: A Conversation with Lea Goldberg," (in Hebrew) *Hapoel Hatsair* 35, no. 11, 15 December 1959, 19.

52. Mordechai Shalev, "Dahlia Ravikovitch: A Lamenting Poet," (in Hebrew) *Ha'aretz* (daily newspaper) 2 April 1969. For a psychological feminist discussion of the conflicts in Goldberg's life as a woman poet and professor, see Amia Lieblich, *El Lea* (Towards Lea) (Tel-Aviv: Hakibbutz Hameuchad, 1995).

53. Haim Nahman Bialik (1873–1934), the leading Hebrew poet at the turn of the century, often crowned as Hebrew's "national poet," is considered the greatest poet modern Hebrew literature has known.

54. Eli Mohar, "Who Understands the Poet Yona Wallach?" (in Hebrew) *Be-mahne Nahal,* Tel-Aviv, 1 October 1969, no. 1 (215), p. 17.

55. Gabriel Moked, "Poetry as a Renewal of Significance," (in Hebrew) *Prosa* 10 (October 1976): 3, 20. The noun *author* is in the masculine form, to signify the neutral "universal" rather than gendered character of the nomination; Moshe Ben Shaul, "Romanticism and Myth in Yonah Wallach's Poetry," *Moznaim* 43, no. 4 (1977): 303–06; David Carmi, *Ba-mahane,* Tel-Aviv, 20 October 1966.

56. Hamutal Tsamir, "Femininity and Utopia in Yonah Wallach's Early Poetry" in "The Porter Institute Pre-Publication Collection," vol. 2, ed. Hannan Hever (Tel-Aviv: Tel-Aviv University, 1996), 119–43.

57. Berlowitz, "Rachel Morpurgo," 40.

58. There is evidence of women studying the Talmud and appreciating, as well as financially supporting, Hebrew literature in Italy from the sixteenth century. Dan Pagis, "The Poetic Debate on the Nature of Women: A Mirror of Changes in Hebrew Poetry in Italy" (in Hebrew) in *Poetry Aptly Explained: Studies and Essays on Medieval Hebrew Poetry,* ed. Ezra Fleischer (Jerusalem: The Magnes Press, 1993), 161; Robert Bonfil, *Jewish Life in Renaissance Italy,* tr. Anthony Oldcorn (Berkeley, Los Angeles, London: University of California Press, 1994). Howard Adelman, "Finding Women's Voices in Italian Jewish Literature," in *Women of the Word: Jewish Women and Jewish Writing,* ed. Judith R. Baskin (Detroit: Wayne State University Press, 1994), 50–69.

59. Berlowitz, "Rachel Morpurgo," 23–26.

60. For this translation, see *The Writings: A New Translation of The Holy Scriptures According to The Traditional Hebrew Text* (Philadelphia: The Jewish Publication Society, 1982).

61. An example of conformity to male poetics is a long poem by the poet Hanna Blume Solz, published in 1883, in which only two out of eighteen stanzas are written in the female first person. The persona has a prophetic Zionist vision.

62. The names Bat-Hamah and Bat-Miriam are matrilineal pseudonyms, see Ilana Pardes, "Yocheved Bat Miriam: The Poetic Strength of a Matronym," in *Gender and Text in Modern Hebrew and Yiddish Literature,* eds. Naomi B. Sokoloff, Anne Lapidus Lerner, and Anita Norich (New York and Jerusalem: The Jewish Theological Seminary of America, 1992), 39–63. In reviewing the history of women's Hebrew poetry during this period, one cannot fail to appreciate the active feminist strategies of women poets in their choice of names. Some dropped their father's or husband's name, and some chose new matronyms such as Bat-Hamah and Bat-Miriam. Others decided to use only their first name, as it was given or newly adopted.

63. Ziva Shamir, "A Distant Sister: Miri Dor—The First Modernist Poet," (in Hebrew) in *Sadan: Studies in Hebrew Literature,* vol. 2, eds. Ziva Shamir and Hanna David (Tel-Aviv: Tel-Aviv University, 1996), 241–63.

64. For the text of the poem, see the Archive of the Association of Hebrew Writers (Genazim), file 525, document c-34088.

65. Ruth Kartun-Blum, *Receding Horizons: Studies in the Poetry of Bat-Miriam* (in Hebrew) (Ramat-Gan: Masada Press, 1977), 13.

66. Pardes, "Yocheved Bat Miriam."

67. So do some poets not included here such as Ella Bat-Zion (Gavriela Elisha), Nitsa Kann, Haviva Pedaya, and others.

68. Alicia Suskin Ostriker, *Stealing the Language: The Emergence of Women's Poetry in America* (Boston: Beacon Press, 1986), chap. 6, 210–38. For an example of the fertile influence that American feminist criticism has had on Israeli literary criticism, see Tova Cohen, "Within Culture and Without: On the Appropriation of the 'Father's Tongue' As an Intellectual Shaping of the Feminine 'I'," (in Hebrew) in *Sadan: Studies in Hebrew Literature,* vol. 2, eds. Ziva Shamir and Hanna David (Tel-Aviv: Tel-Aviv University, 1996), 69–110, and Lily Rattok, "Like Water She Carves: Motifs in Women's Hebrew Poetry," (in Hebrew) in *Sadan: Studies in Hebrew Literature,* vol. 2, eds. Ziva Shamir and Hanna David (Tel-Aviv: Tel-Aviv University, 1996), 165–202.

69. Hamutal Bar-Yosef, *On Zelda's Poetry* (in Hebrew) (Tel-Aviv: Hakibbutz Hameuchad, 1988), 39.

70. Annette Kolodny, *The Lay of The Land: Metaphor as Experience and History in American Life and Letters* (Chapel Hill: The University of North Carolina Press, 1975).

71. For an in-depth close reading of "[I'm under the bramble]" and other Raab poems, see Chana Kronfeld, *On the Margins of Modernism: Decentering Literary Dynamics* (Berkeley: University of California Press, 1996), especially 76–77; Tsamir, "Love of the Homeland"; Hamutal Bar-Yosef, "In the Trap of Equations: 'Woman=Nature, Man=Culture' and Esther Raab's poem 'Holy Grandmothers of Jerusalem,'" in *A View into the Lives of Women in Jewish Societies: Collected Essays,* ed. Yael Azmon (Jerusalem: The Zalman Shazar Center for Jewish History, 1995), 337–47; Anne Lapidus Lerner, "The Naked Land: Nature in the Poetry of Esther Raab," in *Women of the Word: Jewish Women and Jewish Writing,* ed. Judith R. Baskin (Detroit: Wayne State University Press, 1994), 236–57.

72. Tali Asher, "'I have known how to tell of myself': Re-reading Rahel" (paper presented at the Hebrew University of Jerusalem, Israel, Winter 1996).

73. For further discussion of these poets' poetics, see our biographical notes and our discussion of "simple" poetics, see page 12 of this introduction.

74. Quoted by Ziva Shamir, "The Author's Apology on the Status of the Artist in Time of War" (in Hebrew) in *Literature and Society: Papers Written in Honor of Gershon Shaked,* eds. Judith Bar-El and Yigal Schwartz (Tel-Aviv: Hakibbutz Hameuchad, forthcoming).

75. The Israeli military has preserved an image of egalitarianism that may be traced back to the War of Independence, and might have been enhanced by photographs of women soldiers carrying arms. This myth, however, has long been shattered. Today, although women are required to do almost two years of compulsory military service at the age of eighteen (men serve three years), their military contribution remains mostly within prescribed roles (that is, noncombat units, usually secretarial work). In 1995 Alice Miller, then a twenty-three-year-old aeronautics engineer, won a precedent-setting high court ruling enabling women to enroll as pilot trainees in the Israeli Air Force. Other restrictions are slowly being challenged in the navy and in other corps.

76. Eavan Boland has written about this in a notably poignant memoir, with reference to Irish poetry, in her *Object Lessons: The Life of the Woman and the Poet in Our Time* (New York and London, W. W. Norton and Company, 1995), especially 185, "given the force of the national tradition and the claim it had made on Irish Literature, the political poem stood in urgent need of a subversive private experience to lend it true perspective and authority. An authority which in my view, could be guaranteed only by an identity—and this included a sexual identity—which the poetic tradition, and the structure of the Irish poem had almost stifled."

77. Quoted by Tuvia Ruebner, *Lea Goldberg: A Monograph* (in Hebrew) (Tel-Aviv: Sifriat Poalim, 1980), 70. Also see, Virginia Woolf, *Three Guineas* (London: The Hogarth Press, 1938).

78. Ruebner, *Lea Goldberg,* 58–60, describes Goldberg's poetics as inspired by German neoromantic poetry, including Rainer Maria Rilke, Stefan George, and Hugo von Hofmannsthal, among other influences.

79. For more on the nature of this disillusion, see Gershon Shaked, ed., *Hebrew Narrative Fiction 1880–1980,* vol. 4 (in Hebrew) (Tel-Aviv and Jerusalem: Hakibbutz Hameuchad and Keter Publishing Houses, 1995), 87–92.

80. Hannan Hever, "The Poetry of the National Body: Women Poets in the War of Independence," (in Hebrew) *Theory and Criticism,* 7 (1995): 99–123.

81. Hever, "Poetry of the National Body," 99–123.

82. See, for example, Ravikovitch's "We Had an Understanding" and Agi Mishol's (1947–) "[The transistor muezzin]."

83. Research has not yet provided answers into the reasons why women survivors did not write poetry in Hebrew. Until the 1980s Israelis addressed the Holocaust almost exclusively in the public sphere, such as the trial of Adolph Eichmann for crimes against humanity, construction of monuments, and the annual memorial day. Collective practice may have prevented private expression in literary form. Early personal poems by women about the Holocaust are rare. In 1946 an unknown poet, going only by the first name Nurit, published a poem entitled "No Address." In the poem the speaker addresses her infant son, telling him "To whom will I write a letter? / All the addresses are lost. / Smoke rose on the horizon / And above our heads the cloud / And eternal silence. // .... // My child, my child do you know / We have no addresses / There is no mother, no father / And in their ruined home / only eternal silence." Other survivors who have written poetry are Bat-Sheva Dagan and Halina Birenbaum. Second generation poets not in this anthology include Nitsa Kann and Tania Hadar.

84. *Dvar Ha-poelet* (in Hebrew) 9, no. 9, 27 September 1943, p. 129.

85. Lesley Hazleton, *Israeli Women: The Reality Behind the Myths* (New York: Simon and Schuster, 1977), 65. For an Israeli and more recent survey, see Dafna N. Israeli, Ariella Friedman, Ruth Schrift, Francis Raday, and Judith Buber-Agassi, eds., *The Double Bind: Women in Israel* (in Hebrew) (Tel-Aviv: Hakibbutz Hameuchad, 1982).

86. Deborah Bernstein, ed., *Pioneers and Homemakers: Jewish Women in Pre-State Israel* (Albany: State University of New York Press, 1992).

87. Helit Yeshurun, "Yona Wallach, April 1984, an Interview," (in Hebrew) *Hadarim* 4 (1984): 108.

88. Before Wallach, the poet Dahlia Hertz took up these themes. Due to the poet's explicit wish, Hertz's poetry does not appear here.

89. Shaham, "A Woman Poet," 203–40.

90. One indication of the change in the position of Israeli women in poetry is their relation to children's literature. Women have played a key role in the creation of literature for children in Hebrew. Women's contributions to children's Hebrew literature were recognized much earlier than their contributions to adult literature. Many women poets, such as Kalugai and Ella Amitan (1900–1995) (and Miriam Yelan-Shtekelis and Fanya Bergstein, not included here) wrote few poems for adults but found children's literature more accessible. When Pinkerfeld-Amir received the distinguished Israel Prize, it was for her poetry for children, not for adults. When Lea Goldberg, whose children's books still rank high among Israeli classics, became an editor in a publishing house (Sifriat Poalim), she edited children's literature. Women poets still write for children, but this no longer marks their marginalization in Hebrew literature. When Zarchi implements motifs from her children's poetry in her adult poetry, she demonstrates an intentional disregard for generic and hierarchical classification.

A NOTE ON TRANSLATION

Hebrew is a woman bathing
Hebrew is Batsheva clean
Hebrew is an unsculpted sculpture
with tiny beauty marks and stretch marks from giving birth
the older she gets the more beautiful she is
her judgment is sometimes prehistoric
"Hebrew" by Yona Wallach, translation by Lisa Katz

This anthology begins with the Bible, which has probably been translated more than any other text. In choosing among the various English translations of the biblical passages included here, we had to make our way through a confusing assortment, from the King James Version, with its familiar and often majestic poetry, to the more accurate but prosaic revisions published by the Jewish Publication Society. There have been many competent versions published in the three hundred years between these two major translations, and some especially fine ones in recent years. We were looking for fidelity to the original Hebrew text combined with the magic of poetry, for music and words that would reflect the beauty and power of the source language.

Consider the interpretative ingenuity and poetic sensibility (and probably, too, a confident personal taste) required in order to find English equivalents of half of one verse from the Song of Songs 2.5:[1]

Stay me with flagons, comfort me with apples (King James Version, 1611)
Sustain me with raisins, / Refresh me with apples (Revised Standard Version, 1952)
He refreshed me with raisins, he / revived me with apricots (New English Bible, 1971)
Sustain me with raisin cakes, / Brace me with apples (translation by Marvin Pope, 1977)
Sustain me with raisin cakes, / Refresh me with apples (Jewish Publication Society, 1982)
Put me to bed among fruit clusters, / spread me my bed among apricots (translation by Michael Fox, 1985)
Feed me raisincakes and quinces! (translation by Marcia Falk, 1977, reprint 1990)
Let me lie among vine blossoms, / in a bed of apricots! (translation by Ariel Bloch and Chana Bloch, 1995)

The meanings of Hebrew words have shifted over the more than three thousand years of the history of Hebrew literature. For example, whereas the word *tappuhim* (which appears at the end of the lines quoted above) is unequivocally *apples* in modern Hebrew, historical linguistics and botanical research raise other possibilities, including apricots and quinces.

That Hebrew was a "holy language," used mainly for prayer and study until the end of the nineteenth century, contributed significantly to the need to reshape and expand its vocabulary. Not only did many new words have to be invented in modern Hebrew, but colloquial speech, part of the fabric of contemporary poetry, has had to absorb the ancient vocabulary, to make it live in a modern context. Because of the dominance of biblical words in modern Hebrew, one cannot translate poetry, whose very energy is connotative, without being alert to possible biblical contexts. A biblical concordance is an indispensable tool in translation. A simple word such as *hair* may, in specific contexts, recall both the physical power of Samson and the narcissism of Absalom. When the Hebrew word for *reeds* appears in Dahlia Ravikovitch's poem "Little Child's Head on the Pillow," it conjures the infant Moses, as does the "basket in the river" in Nurit Zarchi's poem "Baby Blues." Numerous idioms connote ethnographic, ideological, and religious frameworks of different ages and places. In some cases we have added short footnotes in order to provide the necessary context, but sometimes the allusions and idiomatic richness are lost in translation.

Semitic languages are based on roots, generally of three consonants, transformed in certain paradigms in which the vowels are inflected with diacritical marks, to define the specific temporality, mode, number, and gender of verbs, nouns, and adjectives. The verb is central and may encompass personal pronouns as well. The language tends, therefore, to be more condensed than Indo-European languages in general, and English in particular. For instance, in Zelda's poem "Each Rose," we read, "Inside the petals / of each rose dwells / a sapphire bird called / 'And They Shall Beat Their Swords.'" In Hebrew the fourth line of the stanza is one compact word of five letters—*ve'khitetu* (וְכִתְּתוּ)—which requires four words in English translation— *and they shall beat*. Since this did not fully connote the specific biblical allusion to swords being beaten into ploughshares (Isaiah 2.4), Barbara Goldberg wisely decided to include the swords. Although the biblical allusion is sustained in the English translation, the onomatopoeic value of the Hebrew, which sounds like a bird chirping, is lost.[2]

Sometimes we are lucky enough to capture an onomatopoeic sound in the translation, such as Zvi Jagendorf's happy choice of *rustle* for the Hebrew *terashresh* in Yokheved Bat-Miriam's "Hagar." At other times, to compensate for lost music elsewhere, translators use alliteration and assonance in English in places that do not appear in Hebrew. In Rahel Chalfi's poem "'I Went to Work As an Ostrich' Blues," the last three lines repeat the syllable *na* five times, even in a nonsense word *hushana,* which rhymes with the preceding word and connotes sensuality, without really meaning anything. Here is Shirley Kaufman's compensatory translation of these three lines: "it's so sensual   it's so dimensual / Na! It's not a matter of feathers, they yell at me, it's a matter of savvy. / Of sand and savvy!"

The inflection, by gender, of Hebrew verbs, as well as nouns and adjectives, poses difficulties for translators who have to cope with transgendering as in Nurit Zarchi's "She Is Joseph," or with even more intricate problems, such as the subversive exposure of gendered words in many of Yona Wallach's poems.

Wallach addresses this in her widely quoted poem "Hebrew":

About pronouns and sex English leaves its options open
in practice each *I*
has all the options
she is *he* when it's *you*
I doesn't have a sex
there's no difference between she-*you* and he-*you*
and all *things* are *it*—not man not woman
no need to think before relating to sex
Hebrew is a sex maniac.

When Leah Ayalon switches to the masculine first-person verb form in "Dark Thoughts and I'm Even the Opposite of What You Think"—"I want to undress and remove the clothes from all those women"—the translator, Rachel Tzvia Back, has to specify, "As a man I want to undress..." We have had to leave out a number of poems we wanted to include because the translations were impossible without gender marking in English.

An imperative of women's feminist poetry in Israel has been to claim the "sacred language," traditionally the exclusive domain of men. For example, Esther Ettinger's poem "The Sadness Cage" establishes a distinct feminist context by challenging verses traditionally recited by men addressing women at the Friday night ritual Sabbath dinner (Kabbalat Shabbat). By calling up these sacred words, Ettinger constructs her sadness cage against the ceremonial dinner that symbolically epitomizes blissful Jewish family life. The phrase, "*the meat of her household,*" which ends the second stanza, is a quotation from Proverbs 31.15, a passage which ostensibly praises the virtuous housewife as "a woman of valor" (*eshet hayil*) but, in effect, endorses patriarchal values. Furthermore, the people who encourage the lioness to "rise up go forth" speak the words of "*Lekha Dodi,*" a traditional song in which the Sabbath is metaphorically greeted as a bride going to meet her groom. The bars of the cage are thus fortified by generations of social and cultural indoctrination. The voices which call "rise up" suggest that a form of salvation may come through the revision of such oppressive ancient texts, through confronting and reframing them, which is precisely what "The Sadness Cage" does. Many Hebrew readers, whether religious or not, are sufficiently steeped in Jewish tradition to grasp these allusions, which deepen their reading of the poem. The challenge for the translator, in this case, is to render the poem in a way that is powerful and affecting, even without the layers accessible only to those with the linguistic and cultural context.

Reading in Hebrew, one can perceive how words with different meanings are derived from the same root consonants. This is one of the delights of the language. In Maya Bejerano's "Data Processing 60," the speaker's face serves as a metonymy for her spiritual and emotional identity; in the words of the poem, it may expose her "internal structure." The word *internal* in Hebrew has the same three consonants *pnm* (פנם) as the word *face*. The same phonological elements express the internal and "face" value, encapsulating—through semantics—the connection between the two. Another aspect of the linguistic density and layered content of this poem that defies translation is the allusion to the ritual "showbread," which in Hebrew is literally called "face-bread" (*lehem ha-pannim*). Here the poet revives a dead metaphor by reconnecting the idiom to its linguistic root—the face (*pannim*). Bejerano plays an additional deconstructive game: her poem masquerades as an exegesis of biblical decrees:

> Perhaps the face is an abstraction too,
> as it is said in Scripture
> from the moment it's offered—first
> one sacrifices the showbread,
> which means:
> the forehead, the mouth and the nose, cheeks, eyes.
> Take the showbread and break it into pieces—
> then the face will disappear, will be sacrificed,
> and what will remain in its place is only the abstract riddle.

An innocent reading accepts the lines "first one sacrifices the showbread" and "Take the showbread and break it into pieces" as quotations from the Bible since they are introduced with the words "as it is said in Scripture." But Bejerano has created her own synthetic biblical verses; although similar sayings do appear in the Bible, there are no verses identical to the ones she "quotes" here. What appears at first to be a secularizing use of a hallowed text is actually a subversive act of appropriation. The text, which rejects women from its sacrificial rulings as "impure," is rewritten in a way that hallows the feminine persona, as well as the act of listening to and understanding of her. Bejerano further glorifies her persona by modeling her stance after the prophet Ezekiel's vision. When she writes the word "electric"—which appears in two verses of Ezekiel 1.4 and 1.27 (no one knows what it really means), and with a slight difference in Ezekiel 8.2—and then adds, "Surrounding objects dance resembling / vast glowing vessels," she gives a prophetic dimension to her self-discovery.

The process of translation has to accept a loss of ambiguity. The translation of Wallach's poem "Absalom" ends with the questions: "what will you fight / and on what will the wind / rest / where will it carry you / the wind my son." The Hebrew word for *wind* (*ruah*) denotes both wind and spirit. Translator Linda Zisquit wrestled with this poem, which is included in her collection of Wallach translations, and we joined her in lengthy debates on which noun would be best in translation. The double meaning was inevitably lost. Translation forces one to interpret, whereas the condensed Hebrew allows a double meaning.

Chana Bloch, whose translations of the Song of Songs and of Dahlia Ravikovitch appear in this anthology, has written about the consequences of "uprooting a poem from its homeland" and sending it "into exile," quoting from Psalms 137.4: "How shall we sing the Lord's Song in a strange land?"[3] How can any song in its mother tongue be sung in another language? The translators in this volume, almost all of them poets themselves, have tried their best.

Notes

1. Chana Bloch, "Translating the *Song of Songs*" (paper presented at the International Conference for Translators of Hebrew Literature, Jerusalem, 2–8 January 1994).

2. We thank Hamutal Bar-Yosef for this observation.

3. Chana Bloch, "The Politics of Translation: Amichai and Ravikovitch in English," *Tikkun* 4, no. 4 (1989): 72.

שירת מרים

שמות טו 21–20

וַתִּקַּח מִרְיָם הַנְּבִיאָה אֲחוֹת אַהֲרֹן
אֶת־הַתֹּף בְּיָדָהּ
וַתֵּצֶאןָ כָל־הַנָּשִׁים אַחֲרֶיהָ;
בְּתֻפִּים וּבִמְחֹלֹת.

וַתַּעַן לָהֶם מִרְיָם:
שִׁירוּ לַיהוָה
כִּי־גָאֹה גָּאָה;
סוּס וְרֹכְבוֹ
רָמָה בַיָּם.

שירת דבורה

שופטים ה 31–1

וַתָּשַׁר דְּבוֹרָה וּבָרָק בֶּן־אֲבִינֹעַם בַּיּוֹם הַהוּא לֵאמֹר:

בִּפְרֹעַ פְּרָעוֹת בְּיִשְׂרָאֵל,
בְּהִתְנַדֵּב עָם—
בָּרְכוּ יְהוָה

שִׁמְעוּ, מְלָכִים, הַאֲזִינוּ, רֹזְנִים
אָנֹכִי לַיהוָה, אָנֹכִי אָשִׁירָה
אֲזַמֵּר לַיהוָה אֱלֹהֵי יִשְׂרָאֵל.

יְהוָה, בְּצֵאתְךָ מִשֵּׂעִיר,
בְּצַעְדְּךָ מִשְּׂדֵה אֱדוֹם—
אֶרֶץ רָעָשָׁה,
גַּם־שָׁמַיִם נָטָפוּ,

גַּם־עָבִים נָטְפוּ מָיִם.
הָרִים נָזְלוּ
מִפְּנֵי יְהוָה, זֶה סִינַי
מִפְּנֵי יְהוָה אֱלֹהֵי יִשְׂרָאֵל.

בִּימֵי שַׁמְגַּר בֶּן־עֲנָת,
בִּימֵי יָעֵל חָדְלוּ אֳרָחוֹת;
וְהֹלְכֵי נְתִיבוֹת יֵלְכוּ אֳרָחוֹת עֲקַלְקַלּוֹת.

THE SONG OF MIRIAM

EXODUS 15.20–21

And Miriam the prophetess, the sister of Aaron,
took a timbrel in her hand;
and all the women went out after her with timbrels
and with dances.

And Miriam answered them,
Sing ye to the LORD,
for he hath triumphed gloriously;
the horse and his rider
hath he thrown into the sea.

from The Holy Bible, Authorized (King James) Version, *1611*

THE SONG OF DEBORAH

JUDGES 5.1–31

On that day Deborah sang and Barak son of Abinoam:

When hair goes untrimmed[1] in Israel,
When people dedicate themselves—
Bless the LORD!

Hear, O kings! Give ear, O potentates!
I will sing, will sing to the LORD,
Will hymn the LORD, the God of Israel.

O LORD, when You came forth from Seir,
Advanced from the country of Edom,
The earth trembled;
The heavens rained,

Yea, the clouds rained water,
The mountains quaked—
Before the LORD, the One of Sinai,
Before the LORD, God of Israel.

In the days of Shamgar son of Anath,
In the days of Yael, caravans ceased,
And wayfarers went by roundabout paths.

1. Not cutting one's hair was a way of consecrating oneself to God.

חָדְלוּ פְרָזוֹן,
בְּיִשְׂרָאֵל חָדֵלּוּ—
עַד שַׁקַּמְתִּי, דְּבוֹרָה,
שַׁקַּמְתִּי אֵם בְּיִשְׂרָאֵל.
יִבְחַר אֱלֹהִים חֲדָשִׁים—
אָז לָחֶם שְׁעָרִים;
מָגֵן אִם־יֵרָאֶה וָרֹמַח
בְּאַרְבָּעִים אֶלֶף בְּיִשְׂרָאֵל.

לִבִּי לְחוֹקְקֵי יִשְׂרָאֵל,
הַמִּתְנַדְּבִים בָּעָם—
בָּרְכוּ יְהֹוָה!
רֹכְבֵי אֲתֹנוֹת צְחֹרוֹת,
יֹשְׁבֵי עַל־מִדִּין,
וְהֹלְכֵי עַל־דֶּרֶךְ—שִׂיחוּ!
מִקּוֹל מְחַצְצִים
בֵּין מַשְׁאַבִּים,
שָׁם יְתַנּוּ צִדְקוֹת יְהֹוָה,
צִדְקֹת פִּרְזוֹנוֹ בְּיִשְׂרָאֵל;
אָז יָרְדוּ לַשְּׁעָרִים עַם־יְהֹוָה
עוּרִי, עוּרִי, דְּבוֹרָה!
עוּרִי, עוּרִי, דַּבְּרִי־שִׁיר
קוּם, בָּרָק
וּשֲׁבֵה שֶׁבְיְךָ, בֶּן־אֲבִינֹעַם!

אָז יְרַד שָׂרִיד לְאַדִּירִים עָם,
יְהֹוָה יְרַד־לִי בַּגִּבּוֹרִים.

מִנִּי אֶפְרַיִם, שָׁרְשָׁם בַּעֲמָלֵק;
אַחֲרֶיךָ בִנְיָמִין בַּעֲמָמֶיךָ.
מִנִּי מָכִיר יָרְדוּ מְחֹקְקִים,
וּמִזְּבוּלֻן מֹשְׁכִים בְּשֵׁבֶט סֹפֵר.
וְשָׂרַי בְּיִשָּׂשכָר עִם־דְּבֹרָה,
וְיִשָּׂשכָר—כֵּן בָּרָק;
בָּעֵמֶק שֻׁלַּח בְּרַגְלָיו.

בִּפְלַגּוֹת רְאוּבֵן
גְּדֹלִים חִקְקֵי־לֵב.
לָמָּה יָשַׁבְתָּ בֵּין הַמִּשְׁפְּתַיִם
לִשְׁמֹעַ שְׁרִקוֹת עֲדָרִים?
לִפְלַגּוֹת רְאוּבֵן
גְּדוֹלִים חִקְרֵי־לֵב.
גִּלְעָד בְּעֵבֶר הַיַּרְדֵּן שָׁכֵן;
וְדָן—לָמָּה יָגוּר אֳנִיּוֹת?
אָשֵׁר יָשַׁב לְחוֹף יַמִּים
וְעַל מִפְרָצָיו יִשְׁכּוֹן.

Deliverance ceased,
Ceased in Israel,
Till you arose, O Deborah,
Arose, O mother, in Israel!
When they chose new gods
Was there a fighter in the gates?
No shield or spear was seen
Among forty thousand in Israel!

My heart is with Israel's leaders,
With the dedicated of the people—
Bless the LORD!
You riders on tawny she-asses,
You who sit on saddle rugs,
And you wayfarers, declare it!
Louder than the sound of archers,
There among the watering places
Let them chant the gracious acts of the LORD,
His gracious deliverance of Israel.
Then did the people of the LORD march down to the gates!
Awake, awake, Deborah!
Awake, awake, strike up the chant!
Arise, Barak,
Take your captives, O son of Abinoam!

Then the remnant was made victor over the mighty,
The LORD's people won my victory over the warriors.

From Ephraim they came whose roots are in Amalek;
After you, your kin Benjamin;
From Machir leaders came down,
From Zebulun bearers of the marshal's staff.
And Issachar's chiefs were with Deborah;
As Barak, so was Issachar—
Rushing after him into the valley.

Among the clans of Reuben
Were great decisions of the heart:
Why did you stay among the sheepfolds
And listen to their piping for the flocks?
Among the clans of Reuben
Were great searchings of the heart.
Gilead tarried beyond the Jordan:
And Dan—why did he linger by the ships?
Asher remained at the seacoast
And tarried at its harbors.

זְבֻלוּן — עַם חֵרֵף נַפְשׁוֹ לָמוּת.
וְנַפְתָּלִי — עַל מְרוֹמֵי שָׂדֶה.

בָּאוּ מְלָכִים, נִלְחָמוּ,
אָז נִלְחֲמוּ מַלְכֵי כְנַעַן בְּתַעְנַךְ,
עַל־מֵי מְגִדּוֹ;
בֶּצַע כֶּסֶף לֹא לָקָחוּ.
מִן־שָׁמַיִם נִלְחָמוּ,
הַכּוֹכָבִים מִמְּסִלּוֹתָם נִלְחֲמוּ עִם־סִיסְרָא.
נַחַל קִישׁוֹן גְּרָפָם,
נַחַל קְדוּמִים, נַחַל קִישׁוֹן!

תִּדְרְכִי, נַפְשִׁי, עֹז!

אָז הָלְמוּ עִקְּבֵי־סוּס
מִדַּהֲרוֹת, דַּהֲרוֹת אַבִּירָיו.

אוֹרוּ מֵרוֹז — אָמַר מַלְאַךְ יְהוָה —
אֹרוּ אָרוֹר יֹשְׁבֶיהָ!
כִּי לֹא־בָאוּ לְעֶזְרַת יְהוָה,
לְעֶזְרַת יְהוָה בַּגִּבּוֹרִים.

תְּבֹרַךְ מִנָּשִׁים יָעֵל,
אֵשֶׁת חֶבֶר הַקֵּינִי,
מִנָּשִׁים בָּאֹהֶל תְּבֹרָךְ!
מַיִם שָׁאַל — חָלָב נָתָנָה;
בְּסֵפֶל אַדִּירִים הִקְרִיבָה חֶמְאָה.
יָדָהּ לַיָּתֵד תִּשְׁלַחְנָה,
וִימִינָהּ — לְהַלְמוּת עֲמֵלִים,
וְהָלְמָה סִיסְרָא, מָחֲקָה רֹאשׁוֹ,
וּמָחֲצָה וְחָלְפָה רַקָּתוֹ.
בֵּין רַגְלֶיהָ כָּרַע, נָפַל, שָׁכָב,
בֵּין רַגְלֶיהָ כָּרַע, נָפָל;
בַּאֲשֶׁר כָּרַע — שָׁם נָפַל שָׁדוּד.

בְּעַד הַחַלּוֹן נִשְׁקְפָה וַתְּיַבֵּב
אֵם סִיסְרָא, בְּעַד הָאֶשְׁנָב:
"מַדּוּעַ בֹּשֵׁשׁ רִכְבּוֹ לָבוֹא?
מַדּוּעַ אֶחֱרוּ פַּעֲמֵי מַרְכְּבוֹתָיו?"
חַכְמוֹת שָׂרוֹתֶיהָ תַּעֲנֶינָּה,
אַף־הִיא תָּשִׁיב אֲמָרֶיהָ לָהּ:
"הֲלֹא יִמְצְאוּ יְחַלְּקוּ שָׁלָל —
רַחַם רַחֲמָתַיִם לְרֹאשׁ גֶּבֶר;
שְׁלַל צְבָעִים לְסִיסְרָא;
שְׁלַל צְבָעִים רִקְמָה,
צֶבַע רִקְמָתַיִם
לְצַוְּארֵי שָׁלָל."

Zebulun is a people that mocks at death,
Naphtali—on the open heights.

Then the kings came, they fought,
The kings of Canaan fought at Taanach,
By Megiddo's waters—
They took no spoil of silver.
The stars fought from heaven,
Fought from their courses against Sisera.
The torrent Kishon swept them away,
That raging torrent, the torrent Kishon.

March on, my soul, with courage!

Then the horses' hoofs hammered;
The galloping, galloping stallions.

"Curse Meroz," said the angel of the LORD.
"Bitterly curse the ones who dwell there
Who did not come to the help of the LORD,
To the help of the LORD over the warriors."

Most Blessed of women is Yael,
Wife of Heber the Kenite,
Most blessed of women in the tents.
He asked for water, she offered milk;
In a princely bowl she brought him curds.
Her [left] hand reached for the tent pin,
Her right for the workmen's hammer.
She struck Sisera, crushed his head,
Smashed and skewered his temple.
At her feet he sank, falling outstretched,
At her feet he sank, lay still
Where he sank; he lay there—slain.

Through the window she looked out,
Sisera's mother, looked from behind the lattice:
"Why is his chariot so long in coming?
Why so late the clatter of his wheels?"
The wisest of her ladies give answer,
And she to her own self replies:
"They must be finding, dividing the spoil:
One or two girls for each man,
Spoil of dyed cloth for Sisera,
Spoil of embroidered cloth,
Two garments of dyed embroidery
Around every neck as spoil."

כֵּן יֹאבְדוּ כָל־אוֹיְבֶיךָ, יְהוָה!
וְאֹהֲבָיו — כְּצֵאת הַשֶּׁמֶשׁ בִּגְבֻרָתוֹ.

וַתִּשְׁקֹט הָאָרֶץ אַרְבָּעִים שָׁנָה

קינות

איכה א 12–16, 19–22

א 12–16

לוֹא אֲלֵיכֶם, כָּל־עֹבְרֵי דֶרֶךְ —
הַבִּיטוּ וּרְאוּ:
אִם־יֵשׁ מַכְאוֹב כְּמַכְאֹבִי,
אֲשֶׁר עוֹלַל לִי
אֲשֶׁר הוֹגָה יְהוָה
בְּיוֹם חֲרוֹן אַפּוֹ?
מִמָּרוֹם שָׁלַח־אֵשׁ בְּעַצְמֹתַי
וַיִּרְדֶּנָּה;
פָּרַשׂ רֶשֶׁת לְרַגְלַי,
הֱשִׁיבַנִי אָחוֹר;
נְתָנַנִי שֹׁמֵמָה כָּל־הַיּוֹם דָּוָה.
נִשְׂקַד עֹל פְּשָׁעַי בְּיָדוֹ
יִשְׂתָּרְגוּ;
עָלוּ עַל־צַוָּארִי
הִכְשִׁיל כֹּחִי;
נְתָנַנִי אֲדֹנָי בִּידֵי
לֹא־אוּכַל קוּם.
סִלָּה כָל־אַבִּירַי
אֲדֹנָי בְּקִרְבִּי;
קָרָא עָלַי מוֹעֵד
לִשְׁבֹּר בַּחוּרָי;
גַּת דָּרַךְ אֲדֹנָי
לִבְתוּלַת בַּת־יְהוּדָה.

עַל־אֵלֶּה אֲנִי בוֹכִיָּה,
עֵינִי עֵינִי יֹרְדָה מַּיִם:
כִּי־רָחַק מִמֶּנִּי מְנַחֵם
מֵשִׁיב נַפְשִׁי;
הָיוּ בָנַי שׁוֹמֵמִים
כִּי גָבַר אוֹיֵב.

So may all Your enemies perish, O LORD!
But may those who love Him be like the sun rising in full strength!

And the land was calm for forty years.

from Tanakh: The Holy Scriptures, According to the Traditional Hebrew Text, *Jewish Publication Society (translation), 1985, with adaptations*

LAMENTS

LAMENTATIONS 1.12–16, 19–22

1.12–16

'Let it not come unto you, all ye that pass by!
Behold, and see
If there be any pain like unto my pain,
Which is done unto me,
Wherewith the LORD hath afflicted me
In the day of His fierce anger.
From on high hath He sent fire into my bones,
And it prevaileth against them;
He hath spread a net for my feet,
He hath turned me back;
He hath made me desolate and faint all the day.
The yoke of my transgressions is impressed by His hand;
They are knit together,
They are come up upon my neck;
He hath made my strength to fail;
The LORD hath delivered me into their hands,
Against whom I am not able to stand.
The LORD hath set at nought
All my mighty men in the midst of me;
He hath called a set time[1] against me
To crush my young men;
The LORD hath trodden as in a winepress
The virgin daughter of Judah.'

'For these things I weep;
Mine eye, mine eye runneth down with water;
Because the comforter is far from me,
Even he that should refresh my soul;
My children are desolate,
Because the enemy hath prevailed.'

1. Translation corrected according to most recent scholarship.

א 19–22

קָרָאתִי לַמְאַהֲבַי,
הֵמָּה רִמּוּנִי;
כֹּהֲנַי וּזְקֵנַי
בָּעִיר גָּוָעוּ
כִּי־בִקְשׁוּ אֹכֶל לָמוֹ
וְיָשִׁיבוּ אֶת־נַפְשָׁם.
רְאֵה, יְהוָה, כִּי־צַר־לִי
מֵעַי חֳמַרְמָרוּ
נֶהְפַּךְ לִבִּי בְּקִרְבִּי
כִּי מָרוֹ מָרִיתִי.
מִחוּץ שִׁכְּלָה־חֶרֶב,
בַּבַּיִת כַּמָּוֶת.
שָׁמְעוּ כִּי נֶאֱנָחָה אָנִי
אֵין מְנַחֵם לִי;
כָּל־אֹיְבַי שָׁמְעוּ רָעָתִי שָׂשׂוּ
כִּי אַתָּה עָשִׂיתָ:
הֵבֵאתָ יוֹם־קָרָאתָ
וְיִהְיוּ כָמוֹנִי.
תָּבֹא כָל־רָעָתָם לְפָנֶיךָ,
וְעוֹלֵל לָמוֹ
כַּאֲשֶׁר עוֹלַלְתָּ לִי
עַל כָּל־פְּשָׁעָי;
כִּי־רַבּוֹת אַנְחֹתַי
וְלִבִּי דַוָּי.

רות ונעמי

רות א 16–17, 19–21

א 16–17

וַתֹּאמֶר רוּת:
אַל־תִּפְגְּעִי־בִי לְעָזְבֵךְ
לָשׁוּב מֵאַחֲרָיִךְ;
כִּי אֶל־אֲשֶׁר תֵּלְכִי אֵלֵךְ
וּבַאֲשֶׁר תָּלִינִי אָלִין;
עַמֵּךְ עַמִּי
וֵאלֹהַיִךְ אֱלֹהָי.
בַּאֲשֶׁר תָּמוּתִי אָמוּת
וְשָׁם אֶקָּבֵר;
כֹּה יַעֲשֶׂה יְהוָה לִי — וְכֹה יוֹסִיף —
כִּי הַמָּוֶת יַפְרִיד בֵּינִי וּבֵינֵךְ.

1.19–22
'I called for my lovers,
But they deceived me;
My priests and mine elders
Perished, in the city,
While they sought them food
To refresh their souls.
Behold, O LORD, for I am in distress,
Mine inwards burn;
My heart is turned within me,
For I have grievously rebelled.
Abroad the sword bereaveth,
At home there is the like of death.
They have heard that I sigh,
There is none to comfort me;
All mine enemies have heard of my trouble, and are glad,
For Thou hast done it;
Thou wilt bring the day that Thou has proclaimed,
And they shall be like unto me.
Let all their wickedness come before Thee;
and do unto them,
As Thou hast done unto me
For all my transgressions;
For my sighs are many
And my heart is faint.'

from The Holy Scriptures, According to the Masoretic [traditional Hebrew] Text, *Jewish Publication Society, 1916*

RUTH AND NAOMI

RUTH 1.16–17, 19–21

1.16–17
And Ruth said:
Entreat me not to leave thee,
or to return from following after thee;
for whither thou goest, I will go,
and where thou lodgest, I will lodge;
thy people shall be my people,
and thy God my God.
Where thou diest, will I die,
and there will I be buried;
the LORD do so to me, and more also,
if ought but death part thee and me.

א 19–21

וַתֹּאמַרְנָה:
"הֲזֹאת נָעֳמִי?"
וַתֹּאמֶר אֲלֵיהֶן:
"אַל־תִּקְרֶאנָה לִי נָעֳמִי
קְרֶאןָ לִי מָרָא
כִּי־הֵמַר שַׁדַּי לִי מְאֹד.
אֲנִי מְלֵאָה הָלַכְתִּי
וְרֵיקָם הֱשִׁיבַנִי יְהוָה.
לָמָּה תִקְרֶאנָה לִי נָעֳמִי
וַיהוָה עָנָה בִי
וְשַׁדַּי הֵרַע לִי?"

השולמית

שיר השירים א 2–6, ב 1–7, ג 1–5, ה 2–16, ח 1–7, 14

א 2–6

יִשָּׁקֵנִי מִנְּשִׁיקוֹת פִּיהוּ!
כִּי־טוֹבִים דֹּדֶיךָ
מִיָּיִן.

לְרֵיחַ שְׁמָנֶיךָ טוֹבִים
שֶׁמֶן תּוּרַק שְׁמֶךָ
עַל־כֵּן עֲלָמוֹת אֲהֵבוּךָ.

מָשְׁכֵנִי אַחֲרֶיךָ, נָּרוּצָה!

הֱבִיאַנִי הַמֶּלֶךְ חֲדָרָיו;
נָגִילָה וְנִשְׂמְחָה בָּךְ
נַזְכִּירָה דֹדֶיךָ
מִיַּיִן.

מֵישָׁרִים אֲהֵבוּךָ.

שְׁחוֹרָה אֲנִי וְנָאוָה
בְּנוֹת יְרוּשָׁלִָם!
כְּאָהֳלֵי קֵדָר
כִּירִיעוֹת שְׁלֹמֹה.

אַל־תִּרְאוּנִי שֶׁאֲנִי שְׁחַרְחֹרֶת:
שֶׁשְּׁזָפַתְנִי הַשָּׁמֶשׁ.

1.19–21
. . . and they [the women] said,
"Is this Naomi?"
And she said unto them,
"Call me not Naomi,[1]
Call me Mara;[2]
for the Almighty hath dealt very bitterly with me.
I went out full,
And the Lord hath brought me home again empty.
Why, then, call ye me Naomi
seeing the Lord hath testified against me,
and the Almighty hath afflicted me?"

from The Holy Bible, Authorized (King James) Version, *1611*

THE SHULAMITE

SONG OF SONGS 1.2–6, 2.1–7, 3.1–5, 5.2–16, 8.1–7, 14

1.2–6
Kiss me, make me drunk with your kisses!
Your sweet loving
is better than wine.

You are fragrant,
you are myrrh and aloes.
All the young women want you.

Take me by the hand, let us run together!

My lover, my king, has brought me into his chambers.
We will laugh, you and I, and count
each kiss,
better than wine.

Every one of them wants you.

I am dark, daughters of Jerusalem,
and I am beautiful!
Dark as the tents of Kedar, lavish
as Solomon's tapestries.

Do not see me only as dark:
the sun has stared at me.

1. Meaning *pleasant.*
2. Meaning *bitter.*

בְּנֵי אִמִּי נִחֲרוּ־בִי,
שָׂמֻנִי נֹטֵרָה אֶת־הַכְּרָמִים.
כַּרְמִי שֶׁלִּי לֹא נָטָרְתִּי.

ב 1–7

אֲנִי חֲבַצֶּלֶת הַשָּׁרוֹן
שׁוֹשַׁנַּת הָעֲמָקִים.

כְּשׁוֹשַׁנָּה
בֵּין הַחוֹחִים
כֵּן רַעְיָתִי
בֵּין הַבָּנוֹת.

כְּתַפּוּחַ בַּעֲצֵי הַיַּעַר
כֵּן דּוֹדִי בֵּין הַבָּנִים;
בְּצִלּוֹ חִמַּדְתִּי וְיָשַׁבְתִּי
וּפִרְיוֹ מָתוֹק לְחִכִּי.

הֱבִיאַנִי אֶל־בֵּית הַיָּיִן
וְדִגְלוֹ עָלַי אַהֲבָה.

סַמְּכוּנִי בָּאֲשִׁישׁוֹת
רַפְּדוּנִי בַּתַּפּוּחִים!
כִּי־חוֹלַת אַהֲבָה אָנִי.

שְׂמֹאלוֹ תַּחַת לְרֹאשִׁי
וִימִינוֹ
תְּחַבְּקֵנִי:

הִשְׁבַּעְתִּי אֶתְכֶם, בְּנוֹת יְרוּשָׁלַםִ,
בִּצְבָאוֹת אוֹ בְּאַיְלוֹת הַשָּׂדֶה,
אִם־תָּעִירוּ וְאִם־תְּעוֹרְרוּ אֶת־הָאַהֲבָה
עַד שֶׁתֶּחְפָּץ.

ג 1–5

עַל־מִשְׁכָּבִי בַּלֵּילוֹת
בִּקַּשְׁתִּי אֵת שֶׁאָהֲבָה נַפְשִׁי.
בִּקַּשְׁתִּיו וְלֹא מְצָאתִיו.

אָקוּמָה נָּא וַאֲסוֹבְבָה בָעִיר
בַּשְּׁוָקִים וּבָרְחֹבוֹת
אֲבַקְשָׁה אֵת שֶׁאָהֲבָה נַפְשִׁי.
בִּקַּשְׁתִּיו
וְלֹא מְצָאתִיו.

מְצָאוּנִי הַשֹּׁמְרִים
הַסֹּבְבִים בָּעִיר.
״אֵת שֶׁאָהֲבָה נַפְשִׁי
רְאִיתֶם?״

My brothers were angry with me,
they made me guard the vineyards.
I have not guarded my own.

2.1–7
I am the rose of Sharon,
the wild lily of the valleys.

Like a lily in a field
of thistles,
such is my love
among the young women.

And my beloved among the young men
is a branching apricot tree in the wood.
In that shade I have often lingered,
tasting the fruit.

Now he has brought me to the house of wine
and his flag over me is love.

Let me lie among vine blossoms,
in a bed of apricots!
I am in the fever of love.

His left hand beneath my head,
his right arm
holding me close.

Daughters of Jerusalem, swear to me
by the gazelles, by the deer in the field,
that you will never awaken love
until it is ripe.

3.1–5
At night in my bed I longed
for my only love.
I sought him, but did not find him.

I must rise and go about the city,
the narrow streets and squares, till I find
my only love.
I sought him everywhere
but I could not find him.

Then the watchmen found me
as they went about the city.
"Have you seen him? Have you seen
the one I love?"

כִּמְעַט שֶׁעָבַרְתִּי מֵהֶם
עַד שֶׁמָּצָאתִי אֵת שֶׁאָהֲבָה נַפְשִׁי.
אֲחַזְתִּיו וְלֹא אַרְפֶּנּוּ
עַד־שֶׁהֲבֵיאתִיו אֶל־בֵּית אִמִּי
וְאֶל־חֶדֶר הוֹרָתִי.

הִשְׁבַּעְתִּי אֶתְכֶם, בְּנוֹת יְרוּשָׁלַםִ,
בִּצְבָאוֹת אוֹ בְּאַיְלוֹת הַשָּׂדֶה,
אִם־תָּעִירוּ וְאִם־תְּעוֹרְרוּ אֶת־הָאַהֲבָה
עַד שֶׁתֶּחְפָּץ.

ה 2–16

אֲנִי יְשֵׁנָה וְלִבִּי עֵר.
קוֹל דּוֹדִי דוֹפֵק—

פִּתְחִי־לִי, אֲחֹתִי רַעְיָתִי
יוֹנָתִי תַמָּתִי!
שֶׁרֹּאשִׁי נִמְלָא־טָל
קְוֻצּוֹתַי רְסִיסֵי לָיְלָה.

פָּשַׁטְתִּי אֶת־כֻּתָּנְתִּי
אֵיכָכָה אֶלְבָּשֶׁנָּה?
רָחַצְתִּי אֶת־רַגְלַי
אֵיכָכָה אֲטַנְּפֵם?

דּוֹדִי שָׁלַח יָדוֹ מִן־הַחֹר
וּמֵעַי
הָמוּ עָלָיו.

קַמְתִּי אֲנִי לִפְתֹּחַ לְדוֹדִי
וְיָדַי נָטְפוּ־מוֹר,
וְאֶצְבְּעֹתַי מוֹר עֹבֵר
עַל כַּפּוֹת הַמַּנְעוּל.

פָּתַחְתִּי אֲנִי לְדוֹדִי
וְדוֹדִי חָמַק עָבָר.
נַפְשִׁי יָצְאָה בְדַבְּרוֹ!

בִּקַּשְׁתִּיהוּ
וְלֹא מְצָאתִיהוּ.
קְרָאתִיו
וְלֹא עָנָנִי.

מְצָאֻנִי הַשֹּׁמְרִים
הַסֹּבְבִים בָּעִיר.
הִכּוּנִי פְצָעוּנִי
נָשְׂאוּ אֶת־רְדִידִי מֵעָלַי,
שֹׁמְרֵי הַחֹמוֹת.

I had just passed them when I found
my only love.
I held him, I would not let him go
until I brought him to my mother's house,
into my mother's room.

Daughters of Jerusalem, swear to me
by the gazelles, by the deer in the field,
that you will never awaken love
until it is ripe.

5.2–16
I was asleep but my heart stayed awake.
Listen!
my lover knocking:

"Open, my sister, my friend,
my dove, my perfect one!
My hair is wet, drenched
with the dew of night."

"But I have taken off my clothes,
how can I dress again?
I have bathed my feet,
must I dirty them?"

My love reached in for the latch
and my heart
beat wild.

I rose to open to my love,
my fingers wet with myrrh,
sweet flowing myrrh
on the doorbolt.

I opened to my love
but he had slipped away.
How I wanted him when he spoke!

I sought him everywhere
but could not find him.
I called his name
but he did not answer.

Then the watchmen found me
as they went about the city.
They beat me, they bruised me,
they tore the shawl from my shoulders,
those watchmen of the walls.

הִשְׁבַּעְתִּי אֶתְכֶם, בְּנוֹת יְרוּשָׁלַם,
אִם־תִּמְצְאוּ אֶת־דּוֹדִי
מַה־תַּגִּידוּ לוֹ
שֶׁחוֹלַת אַהֲבָה אָנִי.

מַה־דּוֹדֵךְ מִדּוֹד
הַיָּפָה בַּנָּשִׁים?
מַה־דּוֹדֵךְ מִדּוֹד
שֶׁכָּכָה הִשְׁבַּעְתָּנוּ?

דּוֹדִי צַח וְאָדוֹם
דָּגוּל
מֵרְבָבָה.

רֹאשׁוֹ כֶּתֶם פָּז
קְוֻצּוֹתָיו תַּלְתַּלִּים
שְׁחֹרוֹת כָּעוֹרֵב.

עֵינָיו כְּיוֹנִים עַל־אֲפִיקֵי מָיִם
רֹחֲצוֹת בֶּחָלָב
יֹשְׁבוֹת עַל־מִלֵּאת.

לְחָיָו כַּעֲרוּגַת הַבֹּשֶׂם
מִגְדְּלוֹת מֶרְקָחִים,
שִׂפְתוֹתָיו שׁוֹשַׁנִּים
נֹטְפוֹת מוֹר עֹבֵר.

יָדָיו גְּלִילֵי זָהָב מְמֻלָּאִים בַּתַּרְשִׁישׁ,
מֵעָיו עֶשֶׁת שֵׁן
מְעֻלֶּפֶת סַפִּירִים,
שׁוֹקָיו עַמּוּדֵי שֵׁשׁ
מְיֻסָּדִים עַל־אַדְנֵי־פָז.

מַרְאֵהוּ כַּלְּבָנוֹן
בָּחוּר כָּאֲרָזִים!

חִכּוֹ מַמְתַקִּים וְכֻלּוֹ מַחֲמַדִּים.

זֶה דוֹדִי
וְזֶה רֵעִי,
בְּנוֹת יְרוּשָׁלָם.

Swear to me, daughters of Jerusalem!
If you find him now
you must tell him
I am in the fever of love.

How is your lover different
from any other, O beautiful woman?
Who is your lover
that we must swear to you?

My beloved is milk and wine,
he towers
above ten thousand.

His head is burnished gold,
the mane of his hair
black as the raven.

His eyes like doves
by the rivers
of milk and plenty.

His cheeks a bed of spices,
a treasure
of precious scents, his lips
red lilies wet with myrrh.

His arm a golden scepter with gems of topaz,
his loins the ivory of thrones
inlaid with sapphire,
his thighs like marble pillars
on pedestals of gold.

Tall as Mount Lebanon,
a man like a cedar!

His mouth is sweet wine, he is all delight.

This is my beloved
and this is my friend,
O daughters of Jerusalem.

ח 1–7
מִי יִתֶּנְךָ כְּאָח לִי
יוֹנֵק שְׁדֵי אִמִּי!
אֶמְצָאֲךָ בַחוּץ אֶשָּׁקְךָ
גַּם לֹא־יָבֻזוּ לִי.

אֶנְהָגְךָ אֲבִיאֲךָ אֶל־בֵּית אִמִּי
תְּלַמְּדֵנִי.
אַשְׁקְךָ מִיַּיִן הָרֶקַח
מֵעֲסִיס רִמֹּנִי.

שְׂמֹאלוֹ תַּחַת רֹאשִׁי
וִימִינוֹ
תְּחַבְּקֵנִי.

הִשְׁבַּעְתִּי אֶתְכֶם, בְּנוֹת יְרוּשָׁלָם,
מַה־תָּעִירוּ וּמַה־תְּעֹרְרוּ אֶת־הָאַהֲבָה
עַד שֶׁתֶּחְפָּץ.

מִי זֹאת
עֹלָה מִן־הַמִּדְבָּר
מִתְרַפֶּקֶת עַל־דּוֹדָהּ!

תַּחַת הַתַּפּוּחַ
עוֹרַרְתִּיךָ —
שָׁמָּה חִבְּלַתְךָ אִמֶּךָ
שָׁמָּה חִבְּלָה יְלָדַתְךָ.

שִׂימֵנִי כַחוֹתָם עַל־לִבֶּךָ
כַּחוֹתָם עַל־זְרוֹעֶךָ

כִּי־עַזָּה כַמָּוֶת אַהֲבָה
קָשָׁה כִשְׁאוֹל קִנְאָה;
רְשָׁפֶיהָ רִשְׁפֵּי אֵשׁ
שַׁלְהֶבֶתְיָה.

מַיִם רַבִּים לֹא יוּכְלוּ לְכַבּוֹת אֶת־הָאַהֲבָה,
וּנְהָרוֹת לֹא יִשְׁטְפוּהָ.

אִם־יִתֵּן אִישׁ אֶת־כָּל־הוֹן בֵּיתוֹ
בָּאַהֲבָה,
בּוֹז יָבוּזוּ לוֹ.

ח 14
בְּרַח דּוֹדִי!
וּדְמֵה־לְךָ לִצְבִי אוֹ לְעֹפֶר הָאַיָּלִים
עַל הָרֵי בְשָׂמִים.

8.1–7
If only you were a brother
who nursed at my mother's breast!
I would kiss you in the streets
and no one would scorn me.

I would bring you to the house of my mother
and she would teach me.
I would give you spiced wine to drink,
my pomegranate wine.

His left hand beneath my head,
his right arm
holding me close.

Daughters of Jerusalem, swear to me
that you will never awaken love
until it is ripe.

Who is that
rising from the desert,
her head on her lover's shoulder!

There, beneath the apricot tree,
your mother conceived you,
there you were born.
In that very place, I awakened you.

Bind me as a seal upon your heart,
a sign upon your arm,

for love is as fierce as death,
its jealousy bitter as the grave.
Even its sparks are a raging fire,
a devouring flame.

Great seas cannot extinguish love,
no river can sweep it away.

If a man tried to buy love
with all the wealth of his house,
he would be despised.

8.14
Hurry, my love! Run away,
my gazelle, my wild stag
on the hills of cinnamon.

tr. Ariel Bloch and Chana Bloch, The Song of Songs, *1995*

מדרש ויקרא רבה

[צורת הוולד כיצד]

מדרש ויקרא רבה, יד, ח

צורת הוולד כיצד—תחילת ברייתו דומה לרשון
שתי עיניו כשתי טיפין של זבוב
שתי אזניו כשתי טיפין של זבוב
שני זרועותיו כשני חוטין של זהורית,
פיו משוך כשערה, גוייתו כעדשה.
אם היתה נקיבה גוייתה כשעורה לאורכה.
....
כיזה צד הולד שרוי במעי אמו?
מקופל מונח כפינקס, ראשו מונח לו בין ברכיו,
שתי ידיו על שני צלעיו, שני עקיביו על שני עגבותיו
פיו סתום, טיבורו פתוח.
ואוכל מה שאמו אוכלת,
ושותה מה שאמו שותה
ואינו מוציא רעי שמא יהרג את אמו.
יצא לאויר העולם
נסתם הפתוח, ונפתח הסתום.

תלמוד בבלי

[ואמר אביי: אמרה לי אם]

שבת דף סו עמוד ב

ואמר אביי: אמרה לי אם:
לאשתא בת יומא—לישקול זוזא חיוורא
וליזיל למלחתא וליתקול מתקליה מילחא,
ולציירִיה בחללא דבי צואר בנירא ברקא.

שבת דף קלד עמוד א

ואמר אביי, אמרה לי אם:
האי ינוקא דלא מייץ—מיקר דקר פומיה,
מאי תקנתיה—
ליתו כסא גומרי, ולינקטיה ליה להדי פומיה דחיים פומיה ומייץ

ואמר אביי, אמרה לי אם:
האי ינוקא דלא מנשתיה
לינפפיה בנפוותא ומנשתיה

MIDRASH LEVITICUS RABBAH

"UNBORN"

Leviticus Rabbah 14:8
An unborn child is shaped like a locust
two eyes like the excrement of a fly
two ears like the excrement of a fly
two arms like two reddish threads from the madder root
mouth thin as a hair, torso a lentil.
If it is a female, it is split like a grain of barley.
. . . .
How does the unborn lie in its mother?
Folded like a writing tablet, head between knees,
hands at the sides of the forehead, heels on the buttocks,
mouth closed, navel open.
It eats what its mother eats,
drinks what its mother drinks
and does not excrete so as not to kill her.
When it leaves her for the air of the world
what is open closes, what is closed opens.

tr. Shirley Kaufman with Galit Hasan-Rokem

BABYLONIAN TALMUD

"LORE FOR HEALING"

Shabbat 66b
And Abaye said, Mother told me:
go to the salt-pool for a one-day fever,
weigh a new coin with a measure of salt,
wrap it in hair, around your throat.

Shabbat 134a
And Abaye said, Mother told me:
a baby that cannot suck has a mouth that's cold.
How do you treat it?
Bring close to its lips a cup of coals.

And Abaye said, Mother told me:
A baby who does not breathe
should be fanned with a sieve.

עירובין דף כט עמוד ב

ואמר אביי, אמרה לי אם:
האי מאן דאית ליה חולשא דליבא
לייתי בישרא
דאטמא ימינא דדיכרא,
ולייתי כבויי
דרעיתא דניסן.

יומא דף עח עמוד ב

דאמר אביי, אמרה לי אם:
רביתיה דינוקא—מיא חמימי ומשחא.
גדל פורתא—ביעתא בכותחא,
גדל פורתא—תבורי מאני.

[ואמר אביי, אמרה לי אם]

כתובות דף לט עמוד ב

אמר אביי, אמרה לי אם:
כמיא חמימי
על רישיה דקרחא.

רבא אמר,
אמרה לי בת רב חסדא:
כי ריבדא דכוסילתא.

רב פפא אמר:
אמרה לי בת אבא סוראה:
כי נהמא אקושא בחינכי.

Eruvin 29b

And Abaye said, Mother told me:
For a weak heart
  take meat
from the right loin of a stag,
  take dung
from the flocks that graze in April.

Yoma 78b

And Abaye said, Mother told me:
A growing child needs oil and hot water;
a little older, egg with sour milk;
older still, dishes to break.

tr. Shirley Kaufman with Galit Hasan-Rokem

"THE FIRST NIGHT"

Ketubot 39b

Abaye said, Mother told me:
  Like hot water
on a bald man's head.

Raba said,
  the daughter of Rab Hisda[1] told me:
Like the prick of bloodletting.

Rav Papa said,
  the daughter of Aba of Sura[2] told me:
Like hard bread for the gums.

tr. Shirley Kaufman with Galit Hasan-Rokem

1. Raba's wife.
2. Rav Papa's wife.

[אמר רבא: נשי דשכנציב אמרן]

מועד קטן, דף כח עמוד ב

אמר רבא: נשי דשכנציב אמרן הכי:

ויי לאזלא
ויי לחבילא

....

גוד גרמא מככא
ונמטי מיא לאנטיכי

....

עטוף וכסו טורי
דבר רמי ובר רברבי הוא

....

שייול אצטלא דמלתא
לבר חורין דשלימו זוודיה

....

רהיט ונפיל אמעברא
ויזופתא יזיף

....

אחנא תגרי
אזבזגי מיבדקו

....

מותא כי מותא
ומרעין חיבוליא

"SONGS FOR THE DEAD"

Moed Katan 28b

Raba said: The women of Shkanziv say:

[I. Suffering]
Woe for his leaving,
woe for our grieving.

[II. The Ritual Cleansing]
Take the bones out of the pot;
we'll need all the kettles we've got.

[III. Lineage]
Shroud yourselves mountains, be veiled:
his line was noble, his ancestors hailed.

[IV. Preparations for Burial]
Borrow a fine Milesian gown.
He's free who had none of his own.

[V. The Ferry]
He made it aboard by a hair,
and he'll have to borrow the fare.

[VI. Credentials]
Our brother's a merchant
whose goods are his virtue.

[VII. Accounts]
Whatever death you get,
the suffering settles your debt.

tr. Peter Cole

מדרש איכה רבה

[באותה שעה קפצה רחל אמנו לפני הקב"ה]

איכה רבה, פתיחתא כד

"רבונו של עולם! גלוי לפניך, שיעקב עבדך אהבני אהבה יתירה, ועבד בשבילי לאבא שבע שנים. וכשהשלימו אותן שבע שנים, והגיע זמן נשואי לבעלי, יעץ אבי להחליפני לבעלי בשביל אחותי. והוקשה עלי הדבר עד מאד, כי נודעה לי העצה; והודעתי לבעלי ומסרתי לו סימן, שיכיר ביני ובין אחותי, כדי שלא יוכל אבי להחליפני. ולאחר כן נחמתי בעצמי וסבלתי את תאותי, ורחמתי על אחותי, שלא תצא לחרפה. ולערב חלפו אחותי לבעלי בשבילי, ומסרתי לאחותי כל הסימנין שמסרתי לבעלי, כדי שיהא סבור שהיא רחל. ולא עוד, אלא שנכנסתי תחת המטה שהיה שוכב עם אחותי, והיה מדבר עמה והיא שותקת, ואני משיבתו על כל דבר ודבר, כדי שלא יכיר לקול אחותי. וגמלתי חסד עמה, ולא קנאתי בה ולא הוצאתיה לחרפה. ומה אני, שאני בשר ודם, עפר ואפר, לא קנאתי לצרה שלי ולא הוצאתיה לבושה ולחרפה; ואתה, מלך חי וקיים רחמן, מפני מה קנאת לעבודה זרה, שאין בה ממש, והגלית בני ונהרגו בחרב ועשו אויבים בם כרצונם!"

אשתו של דונש בן לברט

[היזכור יעלת החן ידידה]

הֲיִזְכּוֹר יַעֲלַת הַחֵן יְדִידָהּ
בְּיוֹם פֵּירוּד וּבִזְרוֹעָהּ יְחִידָהּ
וְשָׂם חוֹתַם יְמִינוֹ עַל שְׂמֹאלָהּ
וּבִזְרוֹעוֹ הֲלֹא שָׂמָה צְמִידָהּ

בְּיוֹם לָקְחָה לְזִכָּרוֹן רְדִידוֹ
וְהוּא לָקַח לְזִכָּרוֹן רְדִידָהּ—
הֲיִשָּׁאֵר בְּכָל אֶרֶץ סְפָרַד
וְלוּ לָקַח חֲצִי מַלְכוּת נְגִידָהּ?

late 10th century

MIDRASH LAMENTATIONS RABBAH

"RACHEL STANDS BEFORE THE HOLY ONE"

Lamentations Rabbah, Proem 24

"Creator of the World, it is clear to you that your servant Jacob loved me greatly and worked seven years for my father so he could have me. And when seven years had passed and it was time for our marriage, my father tricked him with my sister. It was hard on me, since I knew about the trick. And I told my husband, gave him signs so that he could tell the difference between my sister and me and my father would not succeed in switching us. But then I was sorry and suffered my desire and protected my sister, pitied her shame. At evening, when they sent my sister to my husband in my place, I taught her all the signs I'd given my husband so he would think she was Rachel. What's more, I crept under the bed where he lay with my sister, and spoke while she stayed silent, and answered all his questions so he would not hear my sister's voice. I was kind to my sister, and was not jealous of my rival, and did not shame and abuse her. You, Everlasting King—why are You jealous of useless idols, why exile my sons, why let them be killed and destroyed by their enemies?"

tr. Shirley Kaufman with Galit Hasan-Rokem

THE WIFE OF DUNASH BEN LABRAT

[WILL HER LOVE REMEMBER]

Will her love remember his graceful doe,
her only son in her arms as he parted?
On her left hand he placed a ring from his right,
on his wrist she placed her bracelet.

As a keepsake she took his mantle from him,
and he in turn took hers from her.
He won't settle in the Land of Spain,
though its prince give him half his kingdom.

tr. Peter Cole

מרזנא מגירונה

[מי ברוך נורא ואדיר]

זמר זה עשתה אשת חיל הגבירה מרת מרזנא הרבנית מגירונה

מִי בָּרוּךְ נוֹרָא וְאַדִּיר
  תּוֹרָה שַׂמְתָּ בְּיִשְׂרָאֵל
אַשְׁרֵי כָּל חוֹסֵי בָךְ תַּאְדִּיר
  וְלֹא יִשְׁכְּחוּ מַעַלְלֵי אֵל.

רָחֵ(ו)ק מֵרְשָׁעִים הַיְשׁוּעָה
  לָהֶם תּוֹרָתְךָ נוֹדָעָה
יָשִׂישׂוּ הַזּוֹרְעִים בְּדִמְעָה
  הַבּוֹטְחִים בְּשֵׁם יָדָם לָאֵל.

זֹאת הָלְכָה בִּרְחָבָה
  מְהֵרָה שַׁדַּי רִיבִי רִיבָה
אֲשֶׁר אוֹמְרִים הָב הָבָה
  כִּי מִי יִחְיֶה מִשֻּׂמוֹ אֵל.

נָאֶה, מוֹחֵץ וְגַם רוֹפֵא
  מַקְדִּים רְפוּאָה לְנִצְפֶּה
מַתִּישׁ הֶחָזָק וְהָרָפֶה
  תַּעֲלֶה אֲרוּכָה לְיִשְׂרָאֵל.

אַעֲלֶה נָא הַכֹּל מִפִּי
  דִּבְרֵי אֱמֶת אָשִׁיב חוֹרְפִי
הָסֵר מִפִּי דְּבַר דּוֹפִי
  וְשִׂים שָׁלוֹם עַל יִשְׂרָאֵל.

mid-15th century

MERECINA OF GERONA

[BLESSED, MAJESTIC AND TERRIBLE]

This song was made by "a woman of virtue"—the lady Merecina, the Rabbiness from Gerona[1]

Blessed, majestic and terrible
you established the Torah in Israel;
happy are they who seek your shelter,
they do not forget the Lord's will.

Salvation is far from the evil...
though they've known of your Learning and Law;
the sowers in tears will soon exult
they trust in Him who enables.

It has spread abroad—
quickly plead, O Lord, my cause
with those who say from Gehenna: Give...
Our God determines who will prevail.

He is seen, he strikes, and then heals,
applies the balm before what comes;
exhausts alike the weak and strong,
and restores well-being to Israel.

I will say what I must, and tell
the truth to him who taunts me.
Keep slander far away from me;
Grant peace to the people of Israel.

tr. Peter Cole

1. This poem draws on several biblical passages: line 3, Psalms 2.12; line 4, Psalms 68.7; line 5, Psalms 119.155; line 7, Psalms 126.5; line 10, Psalms 119.154; line 11, according to Midrashic tradition and ancient interpretations of Proverbs 30.15; line 12, Numbers 24.23; line 13, Deuteronomy 32.9; line 14, according to *Shir Hashirim Rabbah*, ch. 3; line 15, Numbers 13.18; line 16, Jeremiah 30.17; line 18, Proverbs 27.11; line 20, Numbers 6.26 and Psalms 125.5.

אסנת ברזאני

מכתבה של אסנת

שמעו החכמים מלי
ונמנים יאזינו אלי
צירי מחלתי אשמיע
אולי ישוב כחי חילי
על תורה אזעק אנאקה
כי נעדרה מכל גבולי
נתכסה ניצוץ מאיר תוך
ענן מעון מקהלי
אפסו מושכי עיון אישי
חכמה מעמקי מושכלי
נסגרו שערי הבינה
לא נודעו ארחי ושבילי
הדור אפל אין מוכיח
אבכה לזמני גם חדלי.
אני עמדתי במצב צרות
הקיפוני את ידי רגלי
תכנתי עמודי ארץ
אז אציב דינים בפלילי
גם סגרתי הנפרצות
מדרש ותפלה בגלילי
הטרידו שכלי במבוכת
הרבות עונש שלי [ע]לי
הציגוני ריק הפשיטו
את שמלת אדר ומעילי
קראתי חנוני רעי
כי צר אללי אללי לי
ולמי מקדושים אפנה
לנדיבים רופאי מחלי
אתם חסידים חמלו נא אל
תורת אלי צורי פועלי
לא אל הודי או תועלתי
היא בכייתי או תוללי
גם לא אל צורך ביתי או
אל מלבושי ומאכלי
אך אל קיום המדרשות
שלא יפיץ מני חילי.

ASENATH BARZANI

ASENATH'S PETITION

Listen, sages, to my words
  and wise ones hear me out,
I'll tell you of my misfortunes
  and perhaps my strength will return;
I'll speak for the Learning and moan
  for its vanishing from my land,
for the brilliant spark in a cloud of heaven
  has been hidden from my people;
the seekers of my husband's word have vanished,
  and wisdom from the valleys of my scholars,
the gates of understanding have been closed,
  my byways and paths are unknown;
this bleak generation knows no guide
  and I weep for my days in the world.
The situation was grim,
  and troubles overwhelmed me,
but the pillars of earth I kept firm
  and with my judgment I established laws;
and I passed on the prophet's vision—
  study and prayer in my region—
though they taunted me with confusion,
  to my punishment adding pain;
they left me with nothing and stripped me
  of my cloak and my mantle and robes;
I called out, "Have mercy my friends,
  for my misery is certainly great..."
To whom could I turn among the holy,
  if not to my healers, the nobles;
You who are righteous have mercy—
  for the word of the Lord, my Rock, my Master,
not for my own well-being or glory
  is my wailing and weeping before you;
not even for the needs of my household,
  not for my clothing and food—
but for the house of study's survival,
  that my strength not fail me there.

חיילים אגביר אל תורה
על זאת מתני מלאו חלחלי
אקים סוכה הנופלת
אסירה את כל מבדילי.
על זאת יחרד כל איש משכיל
גם נבון יחרד למלולי
אם עשיר אם עני ישלח
צרי אל לבי ולכסלי
אפס עוזר סומך אין
גם אח קרוב מגואלי.
אך לנדיבי ישראל אל
הרי עזרתם אשא קולי
הרבה מוטים אל ההרג
הצלתם התירו שלשלי.
שלא תכבה גחלת ה־
הר ניצוץ דולק בזך שיכלי
ולהרים קרן מדבר שמם
וחייתה נפשי בגללי
אל דמעתי אל תחשו
ישישו נא כל חלילי
אעשה חיל ארבה כי
באתי בכתב משאלי
וזכותכם נאדרת עד
רום שחק אל ראש מגדלי
שמכם יוחק במרום שחק
קרן הודכם לגדולי.
אם יפוצו תלמידי אל
תבל מה הם יומי לילי
לכן שמעו החסידים
אנשי צדק האזינו אלי...

16th century

For the Law I would gather my forces
  for this the fire within me burns,
I'd raise up the fallen building,
  and remove all that obstructs me.
Before this let every scholar tremble,
  let the wise man shudder before what I say—
it makes no difference whether rich man or poor
  send the balm to my heart and soul;
I have no one to protect me,
  no brother or next of kin to save me.
To the nobles of Israel I lift my voice,
  to the hills of their help I call:
Many facing death you have rescued—
  release me now from my chains.
Let not the mountain's ember go out—
  that spark in my purest of thoughts—
so his name will be raised in a desolate place
  and my soul in my body live on;
Hold not your peace in the face of my tears,
  and my frame will rejoice in delight;
I will work with all of my might—
  for this I write of my wishes—
and your merit's strength will reach the skies,
  up to the heights of my towers;
your names will be engraved on high,
  the measure of your glory will ascend to the mighty.
If my students are forced to disperse,
  what would my nights and days mean?
Therefore, O pious ones, listen,
  and you righteous men hear me out...

tr. Peter Cole

שרה רבקה רחל לאה הורביץ

תחינה אמהות

יָה רִבּוֹן עָלַם וְעָלְמַיָּא
אַנְתְּ בָּרָאתָ בְּשִׁית יוֹמַיָּא
שְׁמַיָּא וְאַרְעָא וְכָל יְצִיבָא
בְּעֶשֶׂר אֲמָרַיָּא.
וּבַשְּׁבִיעִי נַחְתָּ מִכּוּלְהוֹן אֲמָרַיָּא
וּפָקַדְתָּ(א) לְעַמָּא קַדִּישָׁא
דִלְהוֹן נַחְתָא מִכָּל דִּבְרַיָּא
בְּרַם יַתְהוֹן עַסְקִין
בְּחָפְצֵי שְׁמַיָּא וְרָזֵי סִתְרַיָּא.
וְעַמַיָּא דְאַרְעָא וּנְשַׁיָּא
יְהוֹן עַסְקִין בְּדָרֵיהוֹן בְּלִישְׁנָא קְלִילַיָּא
מַה דְחַיְיבִין בְּפִקּוּדַיָּא.

וְכֵן יְהַבְתָּ לָן מוֹעֲדַיָּא לְשִׂמְחַיָּא
וְיַרְחַיָּא לְדוּכְרָנַיָּא
וְכַד הֲוֵינָה בִּירוּשָׁלַיִם קַרְתָּא דְשׁוּפְרַיָּא
אֲתַר בֵּית מוּתְבָנָא דְאִמְנָא שְׁכִינְתָּא דְכָל שׁוּפְרַיָּא
וְעֵינֵי הָעֵדָה הֲוִין מְקַדְשִׁין לְפִי רְאוּת עֵנַיָּא.
וּבְעִידְנָא דְגָלִינָא
לָא אִשְׁתָּאַר לָן בְּרַם לְבָרֵךְ יַרְחַיָּא.
וְעֵת לְחָנְנָה כִּי בָא מוֹעֵד לְבָרֵךְ יַרְחַיָּא.
אֲנַן מְפָרְשִׂין כַּפַּיָּא לְאָבוּנָא רַחֲמָנָא דְבִשְׁמַיָּא
תִּיב לָן כִּימֵי קֶדֶם
כִּי כָשַׁל כֹּחַ הַסַבָּל לְגַדְיָא רְכִיכָא
כְּחוֹם צַהֲרַיָּא.
שָׁבַת מְשׂוֹשֵׂינוּ חַגֵינוּ וְחָדְשֵׁנוּ.
אֲנַן כְּיַתְמֵי בְּלָא אָבוּהָ
וּכְעָנָא בְּלָא רַעֲיָא

יָדוֹ פָּרַשׂ צַר עַל כָּל מַחֲמַדֵּי עַיִן
וְאֵין אוֹמֵר הָשֵׁב!
אֵל נְקָמוֹת יְיָ הוֹפִיעַ מֵהַר פָּארָן!
מַאן דְעָנָה לְאַבְהָתָנָא

SARAH REBECCA RACHEL LEAH HOROWITZ

THE *TKHINE* OF THE MATRIARCHS

God, Lord of all the worlds,
You created in six days
Heaven and earth and all that is firmly planted
By means of ten sayings.
And on the seventh day, you rested from all those sayings,
And you commanded the holy people
To rest from all words,
Except as they occupy themselves
With the business of heaven and the secret mysteries.
And ignorant folk and women
Should busy themselves in their homes, in the easy language,[1]
With what they are obligated to do according to the commandments.

And thus you have given us festivals for joy
And new moons for remembrance;
And when we were in Jerusalem, city of beauty,
The seat of the dwelling house of our Mother the Shekhinah, of all beauty,
The heads of the community would consecrate [the new moon]
  according to eyewitnesses.[2]
But in this era of exile
Nothing is left to us except the blessing of the new moon.
And it is a time appropriate for supplication, when the appointed
  time has come to bless the new moon.
We spread out our hands to our merciful Father in heaven:
Cause us to return as in days of yore,
For the endurance of the tender young kid[3] is failing
As in the noon-day heat.
Our joy, our festivals, and our new moons have ceased.
We are like orphans without a father
And like sheep without a shepherd.

The enemy has stretched out his hand over all that is precious,
And there is none to say, Restore!
God of vengeance, shine forth from Mt. Paran!
He who answered our fathers

1. I.e., Yiddish.
2. During the time of the Sanhedrin, the beginning of each month would be declared according to the reports of eyewitnesses who had seen the new moon. This procedure is described in the Mishnah, Rosh Hashanah 2:5–7.
3. I.e., the children of Israel.

הוּא יַעֲנֶה אוֹתָנָא בְּיַרְחַיָא דָא
בִּזְכוּתָא דְהַרְרֵי קֶדֶם וּגְבָעוֹת.

שָׂרָה דְפַקִידַת עָלֶיהָ אַל תִּגְעוּ בִּמְשִׁיחָי: כֵּן צֶאֱצָאֶיהָ כָּל דָּנָגַע בְּהוּ יִדְּמוּ.
רִבְקָה דְגָמַרְתְּ לָן בִּרְכָתָא: בַּעֲגָלָא תִּתְקַיֵּם כֵּן.
רָחֵל דְּאַבְטַחֲתָא וְשׁוּבוּ בָנִים לִגְבוּלָם: הָשֵׁב שְׁבוּתֵינוּ מַהֵר בְּדִילָה.
לֵאָה דְהַווֹן עֵינַיָא רַכִּיכָא
דְלָא תִּפּוֹל בְּגוֹרָלָא דְרַשִׁיעַיָא:
בִּזְכוּתָא הָאִיר עֵינַיָא
מֵחֲשׁוֹכָא דְגָלוּתָא
יוֹנָה פוּתָּה[1] בְּחֶרֶב רַוְתָה
כָּל הַיּוֹם רְצוּצָה וַחֲמוּסָה.

בַּת אַבְרָהָם אָבִינוּ בְּרַתָּא דְגָלוּתָא דְנַחֲתָא
בַּת אַבְרָהָם אָבִינוּ יוֹשֶׁבֶת תַּחַת בְּעָלִים קָשִׁים: זֶה אוֹמֵר הַדְּ וְזֶה אוֹמֵר אַף אֲנִי
כָּמוֹהוּ.
הֶרֶב כַּבְּסֵנוּ כִּי כְּבָר לָקִינוּ כִּפְלַיִם בְּמֶרְיֵינוּ.
וְחַדֵּשׁ וְהָבֵא לָן חוֹדֶשׁ הַזֶּה לְחֶדְוָה
יוֹמַיָא יַרְחַיָא דְמִתְהַפְּכִין מִבִּישָׁא לְטָבָא.
גָּאוֹן עוּזֵינוּ הָרֵם קַרְנֵינוּ
הַב לָן מוֹהַר מַתְּנָתָא טַבְתָא בְּלִי צָרָה וְעַקְתָא
בִּזְכוּת יַעֲקֹב בְּחִיר שֶׁבָּאָבוֹת
בִּזְכוּתוֹ הַטּוֹבָה לְרַבּוֹת.

סְגוּלָתִי קָרָאתָ לָן
וַאֲנַן קָרְאָן לָךְ דּוֹדִי
וְלָךְ אֲנַן מַצְלִין צְלוֹתָא תֵיתַב לָן
וּלְכָל מוֹרָנָא מֵחַבְרַיָא סִפְרַיָא קַדִּישַׁיָא
וּמְסַדְרִין צְלוֹתַיָא וּבְעוּתַיָא
בְּנִין דוּכְרִין מֵעָלְמָא דִדְכוּרָא מִסִּיטְרָא דִימִינָא חַכִּימַיָא בְּאוֹרַיְתָא
וְנֶעֶבְדִין רְעוּתָא דַאֲהָבוּתָא דִבִשְׁמַיָא
בִּדְחִילָא וּרְחִימָא עִילָאָה דְעִילָאָה כְּמֹשֶׁה רַעְיָא מְהֶמְנַיָא
בְּרָא רְחִימָא דְאַבָּא דְאִימָא עִילָאִי.
אָמֵן כֵּן יְהִי רָצוֹן.

early 18th century

1. בדפוס כתוב פיתה, אך כנראה יש להגיה.

He will answer us on this new moon,
And that by the merit of the ancient mountains and hills.

SARAH,[4] for whose sake you commanded, "Touch not my anointed ones."
So may it be for her descendants; may all who touch them be destroyed.
REBECCA, who caused the blessing [to come] to us; may it soon be fulfilled for us.
RACHEL, whom you promised, "and your children will come back to their own country;" cause us to return quickly for her sake.
LEAH, whose eyes were weak for fear she would fall to the lot
of the wicked one,[5] for the sake of her merit, cause our eyes
to shine out of the darkness of exile. The foolish dove
has had her fill of the sword; all the day she is crushed and violated.

The DAUGHTER OF Abraham our father is under the law of the exile which degrades her;
The daughter of Abraham dwells under harsh masters; this one says,
Strike! and his fellow says, Let me be like him.
Wash us THOROUGHLY, for we have already suffered double in our rebellion.
And renew and bring this month upon us for joy;
Days, months which change from evil to good.
PRIDE of our power, exalt our horn;[6]
Give us our bride-price, a good gift wihout trouble and distress,
By the merit of JACOB, the chosen one among the Patriarchs,
May you multiply his good merit.

You have called us "MY PECULIAR TREASURE [*SEGULATI*],"
And we have called you "my beloved".
To you we pray that you give to us,
And to all our teachers, the authors of holy books,
And [to] those who order prayers and supplications,
Male children, from the Male World,[7] the Right Side,[8] wise in the Torah,
And obeying the will of their Father in heaven,
In most supernal fear and love, like Moses the Faithful Shepherd,
The beloved son of the supernal Father and Mother.
Amen, so may it be His will.

tr. Chava Weissler

4. The acrostic of the author's name begins with this word. The original text highlights all the components of her name by typographical position; they are capitalized in translation.
5. I.e., Esau. According to the Babylonian Talmud, Baba Batra 123a, Leah's soft or weak eyes (Gen. 29.17) were caused by her incessant weeping, based on her assumption that as the older daughter of Laban, she was destined for Isaac's firstborn, Esau.
6. Idiomatic expression in Hebrew for *honor.*
7. Kabbalistic terminology.
8. Kabbalistic terminology.

פריחא בת אברהם בר-אדיבא

[פעמי הרימה יה מצילי]

פְּעָמַי הָרִימָה, יָהּ מַצִּילִי,
אֵלְכָה אֶל אַרְצִי בְּטוּב טַעַם.
רְדָפַנִי אוֹיֵב גּוֹי אֱוִילִי
וַיִּגְעַר בִּי בְּקוֹל רַעַם.

חִישׁ הוֹבִילֵנִי אֶל הַר גְּלִילִי
וְשַׁלַּח בָּם עֶבְרָה וָזַעַם.
אֶרְאֶה שָׁם אוֹרְךָ, אֶחְבּוֹשׁ כְּלִילִי,
אֲזַי אוֹמַר: אָמוּתָה הַפַּעַם.

late 18th century

בוקר ותשמע קולי

פְּנֵה אֵלֵינוּ בְּרַחֲמִים;
בִּזְכוּת אַבְרָהָם תָּמִים,
רַחֵם עָלֵינוּ מִמְּרוֹמִים,
הָאֵל גּוֹאֲלִי.
בֹּקֶר וְתִשְׁמַע קוֹלִי.

רַחֵם עַל עַם סְגֻלָּתֶךָ,
כִּי הֵם עַמְּךָ וְנַחֲלָתֶיךָ;
מַהֵר קַבֵּץ קְהִלָּתֶךָ
אֶל הַר גְּלִילִי.
בֹּקֶר וְתִשְׁמַע קוֹלִי.

יָחִיד נִשָּׂא וְנֶעֱלָם,
פְּדֵה בִנְךָ כְּשֶׂה נֶאֱלָם,
וּבְנֵה דְּבִיר וְאוּלָם,
וּתְמוֹךְ גּוֹרָלִי.
בֹּקֶר וְתִשְׁמַע קוֹלִי.

חוּס וַחֲמוֹל עָלֵינוּ
וּלְצִיּוֹן הַעֲלֵינוּ,
וְהָקֵם דְּבִירְךָ אֵלֵינוּ,
צוּרִי וְגוֹאֲלִי.
בֹּקֶר וְתִשְׁמַע קוֹלִי.

FREYHA BAT AVRAHAM BAR-ADIBA

[LIFT UP MY STEPS]

Lift up my steps, O Lord, my savior,
   I'd go to my country with a placid joy;
an ignorant people pursues me now,
   and taunts me with a thunderous noise.

Take me, quickly, to a Galilee mountain,
   and send your anger across their skies;
there I'll see your light, my crown,
   and say: Now I can die.

tr. Peter Cole

HEAR MY VOICE IN THE MORNING

By Abraham's virtue and merit,
turn toward us with compassion;
from on high have mercy upon us,
   my Lord, and my redemption:
Hear my voice in the morning.[1]

Have mercy on the people you've chosen,
for they are your nation and share;
hurry and gather your congregation
   upon the distant mountain:
Hear my voice in the morning.

Alone, exalted, and not to be seen,
redeem your son like a lamb gone dumb;
then build a shrine and hall,
   and resurrect my fortune:
Hear my voice in the morning.

Have pity upon us, and spare us,
and bring us up toward Zion—
establish your shrine there for us,
   my Rock and my Redemption:
Hear my voice in the morning.

1. Psalms 5.4.

אֵלִי, שְׁמַע תְּחִנָּתִי,
אָדוֹן בּוֹחֵר רִנָּתִי,
הָאֵל מָגִנִּי וּמְנָתִי,
כּוֹסִי וְחֶבְלִי.
בֹּקֶר וְתִשְׁמַע קוֹלִי.

בַּת־יוֹסֵף מְיַחֶלֶת,
הַטּוֹב מִמְּךָ שׁוֹאֶלֶת,
מַהֵר אַרְצָהּ תְּהִי נוֹחֶלֶת
מִיָּד הַיִּשְׁמְעֵלִי.
בֹּקֶר וְתִשְׁמַע קוֹלִי.

אָבִי, בְּרוֹב רַחֲמֶיךָ
הָחֵשׁ מוֹשִׁיעַ עַמֶּךָ,
וַעֲשֵׂה לְמַעַן שְׁמֶךָ,
כָּל חֵטְא מְחוֹל לִי.
בֹּקֶר וְתִשְׁמַע קוֹלִי.

בּוֹרְאִי, רַחֵם יְחִידָתִי,
צוּרִי, חַזֵּק קְהִלָּתִי,
וְהַעֲלֵנִי לְאֶרֶץ חֶמְדָּתִי
וְאַקְטִר כְּלִילִי.
בֹּקֶר וְתִשְׁמַע קוֹלִי.

בְּתוֹךְ רַבִּים אֲהַלְלֶנּוּ,
דִּגְלוֹ יָרִים בְּאָהֳלֵינוּ.
הַפְלֵא חַסְדְּךָ אֵלֵינוּ,
וּרְצֵה חֵן זֶה קוֹלִי.
בֹּקֶר וְתִשְׁמַע קוֹלִי.

late 18th century

Hear, my God, my supplication.
Choose, Lord, my song.
My shield, Lord, my portion—
  my cup, my destination:
Hear my voice in the morning.

The daughter of Yosef longs,
seeks goodness from you alone;
soon her land will be given,
  restored from the Ishmaelites' hand:
Hear my voice in the morning.

Father, in all your compassion,
let your people's savior be hastened;
and act for your Name alone.
  Pardon all my transgression:
Hear my voice in the morning.

Pity my soul, my salvation,
strengthen, my Rock, my congregation.
Carry me to the land of my yearning
  where I'll bring a perfect offering:
Hear my voice in the morning.

Among the many I'll praise Him;
we'll raise his banner over our tents;
astonish me in your compassion.
  Desire my voice's blessing:
Hear my voice in the morning.

tr. Peter Cole

רחל מורפורגו

ואלה דברי רחל בבוא לאזניה כי שמה נזכר לתהילה במכתבי עתים

אוֹי לִי תֹּאמַר נַפְשִׁי, כִּי מַר לִי מָר,
טָפַח רוּחִי עָלַי[1] וָאֶתְיַמָּר.
שָׁמַעְתִּי קוֹל אוֹמֵר: שִׁירֵךְ נִשְׁמָר,
מִי כְמוֹתֵךְ רָחֵל לוֹמֶדֶת שִׁיר?

רוּחִי יָשִׁיב אֵלַי: רֵיחִי נָמַר,
גּוֹלָה אַחַר גּוֹלָה, עוֹרִי סָמַר,
טַעְמִי לֹא עָמַד בִּי, כַּרְמִי זֻמַּר,
מִכְּלִמּוֹת אֶפְחָד, לֹא עוֹד אָשִׁיר.

אֶפְנֶה צָפוֹן דָּרוֹם קֵדְמָה וָיָמָּה.
דַּעַת נָשִׁים קַלָּה, לָזֹאת הוּרָמָה.[2]
אַחַר כַּמָּה שָׁנִים, הֵן עַתָּה לָמָּה

יִזְכֹּר מִכֶּלֶב מֵת כָּל־עִיר כָּל־פֶּלֶךְ?
הִנֵּה הָעֵד יָעִיד תּוֹשָׁב וָהֵלֶךְ
אֵין חָכְמָה לָאִשָּׁה כִּי אִם בַּפֶּלֶךְ.

נֵפֶל אֵשֶׁת יעקב מורפורגו

1847

[עד לא זקנתי]

עַד לֹא זָקַנְתִּי, עֵת לֹא יָשַׁנְתִּי
הַסְכֵּן הִסְכַּנְתִּי, לֵאמֹר שִׁירָה.
עִם לָבָן גַּרְתִּי, לָכֵן אֵחַרְתִּי
אָמוֹר אָמַרְתִּי, תִּכְלֶה צָרָה.

בָּחוֹן בָּחַנְתִּי, סִפְרִי טָמַנְתִּי
הָעֵט צָפַנְתִּי, לֵאמֹר סוּרָה.

אָמְנָם רָאִיתִי, לַשָּׁוְא צִפִּיתִי
עֵת כִּי חָזִיתִי, דּוֹבֵר סָרָה.
גַּם כִּי עָנִיתִי, יוֹם יוֹם אִוִּיתִי
קַוֹּה קִוִּיתִי, מֵאֵל עֶזְרָה:

1861

1. תלמוד ירושלמי יבמות פרק יב הלכה ו.
2. עולה למעלה כמשפט כל הגופות הקלים.

RACHEL MORPURGO

ON HEARING SHE HAD BEEN PRAISED IN THE JOURNALS

My soul sighs, fate brings only trouble,
my spirit was lifted[1] and I grew bold;
I heard a voice: "Your poem is gold.
Who like you has learned to sing, Rachel?"

My spirit in turn replies: I've lost my savor.
Exile after exile has soured my skin;
my taste has faded, my vineyard long gone thin.
For fear of shame, now, I sing no longer.

I've looked to the north, south, east, and west:
a woman's word in each is lighter than dust.[2]
Years hence, will anyone really remember

her name, in city or province, any more
than a dead dog. Ask: the people are sure:
a woman's wisdom is only in spinning wool.

Wife of Jacob Morpurgo, stillborn.

tr. Peter Cole

[BEFORE I'D GROWN OLD]

Before I'd grown old, when I wasn't sleeping
I was in the habit of offering song.
I lived with Laban and was therefore late
thinking an end to sorrow would come.

I took stock and hid my book,
my pen, and said: go away.

In fact I observed that I waited in vain—
seeing the man who betrayed with his word;
and because I suffered, daily I longed:
How I hoped for help from my Lord.

tr. Peter Cole

1. Palestinian Talmud, *Yevamot*, chapter 12, *halakha* 6.
2. It rises up as all light bodies do.

[אנסה אך הפעם]

אֲנַסֶּה אַךְ הַפָּעַם
אִם אוּכַל לָשִׁיר,
מֵאֵצֶל הַסִּיר
רָחַקְתִּי מֵרֹב זָעַם:

מָאַסְתִּי הוֹן וָהֶבֶל
וְלָצֵאת מִסֵּבֶל
יִכּוֹנוּ רַגְלָי
צוּרִי יִגְמֹל עָלָי:

בִּרְכוֹתָיו יִרְעֲפוּן
אֶל טוּב הַצָּפוּן
אֲקַוֶּה אֶל הַחֶבֶל

הִנֵּה יוֹצֵר הָרִים
מַתִּיר אֲסוּרִים
יַתִּיר לִי מִכָּל־חֶבֶל.

וּבְיוֹם מִיתָתִי,   הוּא יוֹם שִׂמְחָתִי
בִּמְקוֹם קִינָה   גִּילָה רִנָּה
וּתְמוּר שַׂקִּים   לִבְשׁוּ נָאִים
גַּם אֶל מָחוֹל   מָחוֹל אֶמְחוֹל
כִּי גֵרוּשַׁי   הֵם נִשּׂוּאָי

1866

שרה שפירא

זכר אחוז קרן

חוּשׁוּ הַצִּילוּ, מַלְּטוּ עֲנִיָּה!
צָעֲקָה שִׁפְחָה אַחַת עִבְרִיָּה,
אֲנָשִׁים רַחֲמָנִים, הָהּ הוֹשִׁיעוּ!
פַּלְּטוּנִי מִמְּרוּצַת הָאַיִל,
הָרָץ אִתִּי בְּכֹחַ וָחַיִל,
אָנָּא מִקַּרְנָיו יָדַי הוֹצִיאוּ!

כֵּן צָעֲקָה הָאִשָּׁה עַל שֶׁבֶר,
כִּי בָא אַיִל כַּבִּיר כֹּחַ כְּגֶבֶר,
וַיִּתְחַדֵּר בַּחֲדַר הַמְּבַשֶּׁלֶת;
לֶאֱכֹל הַמּוּכָן לִבְעָלֶיהָ,
וְהִיא לְבַדָּהּ אֵין אִישׁ בִּלְעָדֶיהָ,
וַתֹּאחֵז בְּקַרְנָיו מְבֹהֶלֶת,

AGAIN I'LL TRY

Again I'll try
   to offer song,
I've left the kitchen
   behind in anger—

I'm tired of vanity
   and hope for release
from suffering: for grace
   from my Lord I linger.

His blessings amass
   for the hidden goodness—
I hope for the share to come;

the creator of mountains
   and freer of slaves
from bondage will bring me to freedom.

And the day of my death   will be my delight
   and in place of a dirge   there'll be gladness;
and instead of a sackcloth   elegant dress,
   and I'll dance   to his forgiveness

—for in my divorce is my marriage . . .

tr. Peter Cole

SARAH SHAPIRA

REMEMBER THE HORN

Quick! Help! Save a poor girl!
A Hebrew servant girl screamed:
Help me, merciful people, hurry
and save me from this racing stag
who runs with such a fury.
Free my hands from his horns!

The woman screamed about her doom
because a stag as strong as a man
had entered the kitchen, and dared
consume what the cook had prepared
for her master. No one but she,
in fear, alone, took hold of his horns.

הָאַיִל רָץ, וְקַרְנָיו בְּיָדֶיהָ,
וּבְמַהֲרוֹ תְּמַהֵרְנָה רַגְלֶיהָ,
וּבְרוּצוֹ עוֹד יוֹסִיף לְהַלְאוֹתָהּ;
וַיַּרְא אִישׁ וַיֹּאמֶר אֵלֶיהָ:
מֵהַקֶּרֶן לָסוּר יָדֶיהָ,
וְלֹא יוֹסִיף עוֹד הָאַיִל לְעַנּוֹתָהּ;

אַךְ הִיא לֹא הִטְּתָה אֹזֶן לְעֵצָה,
לַעֲזֹב הַקֶּרֶן לֹא חָפֵצָה,
וַתְּצַפֶּה לִישׁוּעָה — וָאָיִן;
הָאַיִל רָץ — עוֹבְרִים צָחָקוּ,
לָעֲגוּ לְאֵידָהּ, מֶנּוּ רָחָקוּ,
וְכָכָה נִתְעַלְּמוּ מִנִּי עָיִן.

נִתְעַלְּמוּ — וּתְמוּנַת הָאַיִל,
מֶנִּי חָלָפָה כַּחֲזוֹן לָיִל;
וְעֵת תֶּרֶב בְּבַת יְהוּדָה תַאֲנִיָּה,
עַל "פַּרְנָס" רָשָׁע סוֹבֵא וְזוֹלֵל,
אֶזְכֹּר הָאַיִל וְאֵלְכָה שׁוֹלָל,
וְאָנוּד לְהָאִשָּׁה הָעִבְרִיָּה!

1886

אלישבע

שארית

זֶה שֶׁנִּשְׁאַר לִי לְעֵת זִקְנָתִי:
שָׁעָה לִפְנוֹת־עֶרֶב. אוּלַם בֵּית־קָפֶה.
שִׂיחָה מְמֻשֶּׁכֶת, וּבֶן־שִׂיחָתִי —
אֵינֶנּוּ צָעִיר וְאֵינֶנּוּ יָפֶה.

רֵיק הָאוּלָם. בִּשְׁבִיל שְׁנֵינוּ בִּלְבַד
כִּנּוֹר וּפְסַנְתֵּר מְנַגְּנִים בַּפִּנָּה.
נִגּוּן בֵּית־מַרְזֵחַ — הוּא חַי עֲדֵי־עַד,
וּמָה רַב הַיָּגוֹן בְּקוֹלוֹת־הַנְּגִינָה!

כָּל זֶה הָיָה — בֶּעָבָר, בַּדִּמְיוֹן,
בַּחֲרוּז מְשׁוֹרֵר, בְּתוֹחֶלֶת־כָּזָב...
מִבְּעַד לְחֹל שִׂיחָתֵנוּ — כְּעֵין זִכָּרוֹן:
דְּבַר־מָה הָיָה — וְהָלַךְ — וְלֹא שָׁב.

הָבָה נִשְׁתֶּה, וְאֵין צֹרֶךְ לִתְפֹּשׂ
אֶת הַצֵּל הַמַּשְׁלֶה שֶׁפָּרַח בָּאֲוִיר.
יָד נֶעְלֶמֶת תִּמְזֹג אֶל הַכּוֹס
יֵין־זִכְרוֹנוֹת — הוּא מָתוֹק וְקָרִיר.

1926

The stag ran, his horns in her hands,
her legs were racing along with his,
exhausted more and more as he ran.
Someone who watched called out to her:
Loosen your hands, let go if you can,
so the horn of the stag won't harm you.

But she didn't listen to his advice,
didn't want to let go of the horn,
waited for help, and there was none.
The stag kept running, the people laughed
and jeered at her plight, and went their way
and finally vanished from her sight.

Vanished—and the shape of the stag
dissolved in my mind like a dream at night.
But whenever a Jewish girl laments
her fate with a drunken master,
I remember the stag, how I was betrayed,
and I pity the Hebrew woman.

tr. Shirley Kaufman

ELISHEVA

WHAT'S LEFT

This is what's left to me in my old age:
an hour before twilight, a café,
and idle talk with a companion
neither handsome nor young.

The room is empty. In a corner,
a violin and piano play for us alone
a café melody that lives forever.
How great is the sadness of its song!

All this happened in the past, in the mind,
false hope in a poet's rhyme...
Apart from our mundane talk, a kind of memory:
something that was, left, and did not return.

So let's drink. There is no need to grasp
the illusory shadow that flowered in the air.
An invisible hand will pour into a glass
the wine of remembrance, sweet and cold.

tr. Robert Friend

אל ארצי

לֹא שַׁרְתִּי לָךְ, אַרְצִי,
וְלֹא פֵּאַרְתִּי שְׁמֵךְ
בַּעֲלִילוֹת גְבוּרָה,
בִּשְׁלַל קְרָבוֹת;
רַק עֵץ — יָדַי נָטְעוּ
חוֹפֵי יַרְדֵּן שׁוֹקְטִים.
רַק שְׁבִיל — כָּבְשׁוּ רַגְלַי
עַל פְּנֵי שָׂדוֹת.

אָכֵן דַּלָּה מְאֹד —
יָדַעְתִּי זֹאת, הָאֵם,
אָכֵן דַּלָּה מְאֹד
מִנְחַת בִּתֵּךְ;
רַק קוֹל תְּרוּעַת הַגִּיל
בְּיוֹם יִגַּהּ הָאוֹר,
רַק בְּכִי בַּמִּסְתָּרִים
עֲלֵי עָנְיֵךְ.

1926

רחל

הֵן דָּמָהּ בְּדָמִי זוֹרֵם,
הֵן קוֹלָהּ בִּי רָן —
רָחֵל הָרוֹעָה צֹאן לָבָן,
רָחֵל — אֵם הָאֵם.

וְעַל כֵּן הַבַּיִת לִי צַר
וְהָעִיר — זָרָה,
כִּי הָיָה מִתְנוֹפֵף סוּדָרָהּ
לְרוּחוֹת הַמִּדְבָּר;

וְעַל כֵּן אֶת דַּרְכִּי אֹחֵז
בְּבִטְחָה כָּזֹאת,
כִּי שְׁמוּרִים בְּרַגְלַי זִכְרוֹנוֹת
מִנִּי אָז, מִנִּי אָז!

1926

RAHEL

TO MY COUNTRY

I have not sung you, my country,
not brought glory to your name
with the great deeds of a hero
or the spoils a battle yields.
But on the shores of the Jordan
my hands have planted a tree,
and my feet have made a pathway
through your fields.

Modest are the gifts I bring you.
I know this, mother.
Modest, I know, the offerings
of your daughter:
Only an outburst of song
on a day when the light flares up,
only a silent tear
for your poverty.

tr. Robert Friend

RACHEL

Rachel, Mother of mothers,
who shepherded Laban's sheep—
it is her blood that flows in my blood,
her voice that sings in me.

Therefore is my house narrow
and the city strange,
because her scarf once fluttered
in the desert wind.

Therefore do I make my way
unswervingly
because my feet remember
her path of then, of then.

tr. Robert Friend

נִיב

יוֹדַעַת אֲנִי אִמְרֵי נוֹי לְמַכְבִּיר,
מְלִיצוֹת בְּלִי סוֹף.
הַהוֹלְכוֹת הָלוֹךְ וְטָפוֹף
מִבָּטָן יָהִיר.

אַךְ לִבִּי לַנִּיב הַתָּמִים כְּתִינוֹק
וְעָנָו כֶּעָפָר.
יָדַעְתִּי מִלִּים אֵין מִסְפָּר —
עַל כֵּן אֶשְׁתֹּק.

הֲתִקְלֹט אָזְנְךָ אַף מִתּוֹךְ שְׁתִיקָה
אֶת נִיבֵי הַשַּׂח?
הֲתִנְצְרֵהוּ כְּרֵעַ, כְּאָח,
כְּאֵם בְּחֵיקָהּ?

1926

גַּנֵּנוּ

לחנה מייזל

אַתְּ זוֹכֶרֶת? אָבִיב וּבֹקֶר
(הָאָבִיב, הַבֹּקֶר — אַיָּם?)
לְרַגְלֵי הַכַּרְמֶל — גַּנֵּנוּ,
וּמִנֶּגֶד לוֹ — כֹּחַל־הַיָּם.

אַתְּ מִתַּחַת לָעֵץ עוֹמֶדֶת
וַאֲנִי עַל בַּד, כְּצִפּוֹר;
בְּצַמֶּרֶת זַיִת מָכְסֶפֶת
עֲנָפִים מַשְׁחִירִים נִזְמֹר.

וְרִשְׁרוּשׁ מַשּׂוֹרֵךְ מִלְּמַטָּה
כֹּה קָצוּב מַגִּיעַ אֵלַי,
וַאֲנִי מִמַּעַל עָלַיִךְ
מַמְטִירָה קִטְעֵי חֲרוּזַי.

אַתְּ זוֹכֶרֶת? בֹּקֶר וְאֹשֶׁר...
זֶה הָיָה, זֶה אֵינֶנּוּ יוֹתֵר.
כְּאָבִיב הַקָּצֵר בְּאַרְצֵנוּ
כֵּן אֲבִיב־הַיָּמִים הַקָּצֵר.

1929

A WAY OF SPEAKING

I know many fancy ways to speak,
endless and elegant.
They go mincing down the street,
their glance is arrogant.

But I like a way of speaking
as innocent as a baby, as modest
as dust. I can say countless words.
So I don't say them.

Is my humble way of speaking
understood when not expressed?
Would you guard it as a brother would?
Or a mother at her breast?

tr. Shirley Kaufman

OUR GARDEN

to Chana Meisel

Spring and early morning—
do you remember that spring, that day?—
our garden at the foot of Mount Carmel,
facing the blue of the bay?

You are standing under an olive,
and I, like a bird on a spray,
am perched on the silvery tree-top.
We are cutting black branches away.

From below your saw's rhythmic buzzing
reaches me in my tree,
and I rain down from above you
fragments of poetry.

Remember that morning, that gladness?
They were—and disappeared,
like the short spring of our country,
the short spring of our years.

tr. Robert Friend

[רק על עצמי לספר ידעתי]

רַק עַל עַצְמִי לְסַפֵּר יָדַעְתִּי.
צַר עוֹלָמִי כְּעוֹלַם נְמָלָה,
גַּם מַשָּׂאִי עָמַסְתִּי כָּמוֹהָ
רַב וְכָבֵד מִכְּתֵפִי הַדַּלָּה.

גַּם אֶת דַּרְכִּי — כְּדַרְכָּהּ אֶל צַמֶּרֶת —
דֶּרֶךְ מַכְאוֹב וְדֶרֶךְ עָמָל,
יַד עֲנָקִים זְדוֹנָה וּבוֹטַחַת,
יָד מִתְבַּדַּחַת שָׁמָּה לְאַל.

כָּל אָרְחוֹתַי הֵלִיז וְהִדְמִיעַ
פַּחַד טָמִיר מִיַּד עֲנָקִים.
לָמָּה קְרָאתֶם לִי, חוֹפֵי הַפֶּלֶא?
לָמָּה כְּזַבְתֶּם, אוֹרוֹת רְחוֹקִים?

1930

עדנה

וּמוּזָר כָּל כָּךְ: הָרֹגֶז הַלָּז
וְדִבְרֵי תוֹכָחָה הַקָּשִׁים
כְּמוֹ הֵשִׁיבוּ רוּחַ מֻפְלָא וָעָז
בִּשְׁבִיבֵי עֶדְנָה לוֹחֲשִׁים.

וְלֹא עוֹד אִשָּׁה וְגֶבֶר בַּקְּרָב,
זֶה הַקְּרָב הָעַתִּיק, קַטְלָן —
כִּי הָיִיתָ לְאָח לִי, לְאָח נֶאֱהָב
כִּי הָיִיתָ לִבְנִי הַקָּטָן!...

1931

[I HAVE ONLY KNOWN]

I have only known how to tell of myself.
My world is like the ant's, my pack
just as much a burden to me,
too heavy for my frail back.

My way, like hers to the top of the tree,
is a way of pain and struggle, mocked
by a contemptuous giant hand
and maliciously blocked.

All my paths twist, are wet with tears
because of my fears of a giant hand.
Distant beacons, you have deceived me.
Why did you beckon, miraculous land?

tr. Robert Friend

TENDERNESS

How strange: those hard words of rebuke
were suddenly gone, those words of bitterness,
as if a miraculous wind had blown
into the whispering embers of tenderness.

No longer locked in that ageless, murderous
war between a woman and a man,
you became like a brother to me,
or a beloved son.

tr. Robert Friend

שלומית קלוגאי

איזבל

חָלְפוּ חַיַּי, כַּעֲרָפֶל נָמַסּוּ,
וְלֹא אֵדַע עַל מָה, וְלֹא אֵדַע מָתַי.
רָחֲקוּ מִמֶּנִּי בַּעַל וְעַשְׁתֹּרֶת,
וְרָחֲקָה מְלוּכָה, וְרָחֲקוּ אוֹיְבַי.

לֹא אֲצַפֶּה, סְגוּרָה וּמְסֻגֶּרֶת,
לֹא אֲצַפֶּה לְאִישׁ — כִּי מִי יָבוֹא הֲלוֹם?
אֶל אַרְמוֹנִי אֵין בָּא וְאֵין מַגִּיעַ
עוֹרֵב מִנַּחַל כְּרִית, וּבְפִיו בִּרְכַּת שָׁלוֹם.

חֲלוֹם הַכֹּל — אִי צוֹר, חֲצַר אֶתְבַּעַל,
חֲלוֹם בּוֹאִי תּוֹךְ חוֹמוֹתַיִךְ, הַשּׁוֹמְרוֹן,
חֲלוֹם נְבִיאַי, חֲלוֹם נְבִיאֵי אֱלֹהַּ,
פִּרְאֵי מַרְאֶה, מַמְרִים, קְשֵׁי עֹרֶף, קְשֵׁי חָרוֹן.

הַכֹּל תִּמְרוֹת עָשָׁן, חֲלוֹם וָהֶבֶל —
שִׁלְטוֹן וְאַהֲבָה, בָּנִים, אַחִים,
חַיֵּי אַחְאָב, מוֹתוֹ, חַיֵּי אִיזֶבֶל,
מַלְכַּת שׁוֹמְרוֹן, גֵּאָה, מְפֹאֶרֶת, בַּת מְלָכִים.

וּכְמוֹ לֵיל קַיִץ זֶה קָרֵב לַשַּׁחַר,
כֵּן מִתְקָרֵב לַקֵּץ חֲלוֹם חַיַּי.
הֵן רָחֲקוּ מִמֶּנִּי בַּעַל וְעַשְׁתֹּרֶת,
וְרָחֲקָה מְלוּכָה, וְרָחֲקוּ אוֹיְבַי.

שָׁקֵט, חָשֵׁךְ כְּקֶבֶר לֵיל הַקַּיִץ.
רַק בַּמָּרוֹם מֵעַל יָנוּדוּ כּוֹכָבִים.
קְרִיאַת נוֹטֵר, רִשְׁרוּשׁ עֲלֵי הַזַּיִת,
וּנְבִיחָה קְצָרָה, נְבִיחַת כְּלָבִים. כְּלָבִים...

1941

SHULAMIT KALUGAI

JEZEBEL

The days of my life pass by, dissolve like mist.
I don't know the what and when; I don't know the who.
Baal and Astarte have grown alien to me.
My kingdom and my foes grow alien, too.

I don't expect the arrival of anyone.
For who would come to me in my time of drouth?
No one is coming here. Not even a crow
from the river Krit with a greeting in his mouth.

Everything is dream—the islands of Tyre,
Baal's court, my self-enclosure inside Samaria's walls—
a dream, my prophets; a dream, the prophets of god,
whom—wild, rebellious, stiff-necked—nothing appalls.

All is vanity—pillars of smoke and dream—
sons, brother, sovereignty and love—all things!
Ahab's life and death, the life of Jezebel,
the Queen of Samaria, proud daughter of kings.

And as this summer night approaches dawn,
so does the dream, my life, approach its close.
And Baal and Astarte grow far and dim.
as does Samaria, as do my foes.

Silent the summer night, dark as the grave.
A few stars shine, clouds wander in the air.
A watchman's call, the rustle of olive leaves,
a dog's short bark, dogs barking everywhere...

tr. Robert Friend

אסתר ראב

[אני תחת האטד]

אֲנִי תַּחַת הָאָטָד
קַלָּה, זֵידוֹנָה,
קוֹצָיו צוֹחֶקֶת
לִקְרָאתְךָ זָקַפְתִּי;
אוֹר מַכֶּה עַל הַמֶּרְחָב,
כָּל קִפּוּל בְּשִׂמְלָתִי
לִי יִלְחַשׁ:
לִקְרַאת מָוֶת
לְבָנָה וּמְחוֹלֶלֶת
אַתְּ יוֹצְאָה.
אַתָּה מוֹפִיעַ—
וַאֲנִי קַלָּה צוֹהֶלֶת
מְנִיפָה חֶרֶב נוֹצֶצֶת
וּבְעֶצֶם צָהֳרַיִם
בִּשְׂדוֹת לְבָנִים מֵאוֹר
אֶת דִּינֵנוּ גָּזַרְתִּי
בְּאֶחָת!

1922

[סבתות קדושות בירושלים]

סַבְתּוֹת קְדוֹשׁוֹת בִּירוּשָׁלַיִם,
זְכוּתְכֶן תָּגֵן עָלַי:
רֵיחַ סְמָדַר וּפַרְדֵּסִים פּוֹרְחִים
עִם חֲלֵב אֵם הֶשְׁקֵיתִי;
כַּפּוֹת רַגְלַיִם
רַכּוֹת כְּיָדַיִם
בְּחוֹל לוֹהֵט מְמַשְׁשׁוֹת;
וְאֶקָלִיפְּטִים פְּרוּעִים
טְעוּנֵי צְרָעוֹת וּדְבוֹרִים
שִׁיר עֶרֶשׂ לִי דּוֹבְבוּ;
שֶׁבַע אֶטְבֹּל בְּיָם תִּיכוֹן
לִקְרַאת דָּוִד אַלּוּפִי הַמֶּלֶךְ
וְאַעַל אֵלָיו בְּהַרְרֵי־יְרוּשָׁלַיִם
אֲיֻמָּה־הֲדוּרָה.
וְעִם דְּבוֹרָה תַּחַת הַתֹּמֶר
אֵשְׁתְּ קַהֲנָה וַאֲשׂוֹחֵחַ
עַל הֲגָנָה וּמִלְחָמָה.

ESTHER RAAB

[I'M UNDER THE BRAMBLE]

I'm under the bramble,
at ease, wicked,
I point thorns
laughing at you.
Light strikes the landscape,
every fold of my dress
whispers to me:
"You're going out
to death
dancing and white."
You appear
and I'm at ease. Rejoicing,
I brandish a glittering sword.
And at high noon
in fields white with light
all at once
I seal our fate!

tr. Kinereth Gensler

[HOLY GRANDMOTHERS IN JERUSALEM]

Holy grandmothers in Jerusalem,
may your virtue protect me.
Scent of grape buds and blossoming orchards
I sipped with my mother's milk.
Feet
soft as hands
fumble in burning sand,
and untamed eucalyptus
heavy with wasps and bees
murmur a lullaby to me.
I will dip sevenfold in the Mediterranean
to be ready for my beloved David, the King,
and I will climb to him in awesome majesty
up to the mountains of Jerusalem.
I will drink coffee and discuss
security and war with
Deborah, under the palm tree.

סַבְתּוֹת קְדוֹשׁוֹת בִּירוּשָׁלַיִם,
זְכוּתְכֶן תָּגֵן עָלַי.
עָלָה רֵיחַ בִּגְדֵיכֶן בְּאַפִּי,
רֵיחַ נֵרוֹת־שַׁבָּת וְנַפְטָלִין.

1930

שועלה

בִּשְׂדוֹת לֵילִיִּים שׁוּעָלָה רְעֵבָה
תּוֹקַעַת בָּדָד.
תְּקִיעָה אַחַת — וָדֹם.
כְּדָם נִגָּר קוֹלָהּ לְתוֹךְ הַלַּיִל.
לֹא יַחַד כְּבוֹדָהּ בֵּין אוֹרְחִים וְתוֹבְעִים —
עֲצוּבָה הִיא תּוֹקַעַת,
רַק פַּעַם — וָהַס.
עוֹנִים לָהּ בְּאֵלֶם מֶרְחֲבֵי הַלַּיִל.
חָלָב אַחֲרוֹן יָמֹץ הַגּוּר,
תּוּגַת־עוֹלָם יִרְוֶה אָז קוֹלָהּ.
גּוּשׁ אֹרֶן זוֹמֵם, מְאַיֵּם.
גְּדֵרוֹת אֲצִים זָעִים,
מֹר הַחֲרוּלִים עַל שְׂדוֹת הַבָּר
עָבֶה כַּעֲרָפֶל.
עוֹפוֹת סְפוּנִים בַּלּוּל
וַעֲדַת כְּלָבִים מִתְנַצַּחַת בֶּחָלָל —
שׁוּעָלָה רְעֵבָה נוֹשֵׂאת רֹאשׁ אֶל כִּימָה.
כּוֹכָב קַר נִשְׁקָף בְּעֵינָהּ,
אוּלַי זוֹ דִּמְעָה בְּאִישׁוֹנָהּ.
יָמֹץ הַגּוּר לְשַׁד חַיִּים נוּגֶה —
יִלְלַת שׁוּעָלִים בּוֹתֶרֶת הַלַּיִל.

1955

Holy grandmothers in Jerusalem,
may your virtue protect me.
I inhale the smell of your clothing,
the scent of Sabbath candles and naphthalene.

tr. Shirley Kaufman

SHE-FOX

In the night fields a hungry she-fox
blasts, alone.
A single horn-blast—then silence,
her voice like blood pouring into the night.
She is not one of the visitors and claimants;
sad, she blasts
just once—then a hush.
Mutely the night's vastness answers.
When the cub suckles the last milk
her voice brims with the world's grief.
A stand of pine trees schemes and threatens,
fences sweep by.
Myrrh from nettles in the open fields
is as heavy as fog.
Chickens are sheltered in the coops,
and a pack of dogs squabbles through the emptiness.
A hungry she-fox lifts her head to the Pleiades,
a cold star mirrored in her eye
could be a tear in her pupil.
The cub will suckle at life's sad marrow—
the howl of foxes splits the night.

tr. Kinereth Gensler

משאלות

אֲנִי רוֹצָה עֵצִים יָפִים —
וְלֹא מִלְחָמוֹת!
וּכְתֹנֶת־פַּסִּים
וְלֹא מַדֵּי־צָבָא
לְכָל יַקִּירַי;
אֲנִי רוֹצָה גֶּשֶׁם
וּתְלָמִים מוֹרִיקִים;
וּבָתִּים מְלֵאִים
תִּינוֹקוֹת;
לוּחַ־בְּרִיתוֹת
וְ״כִּכַּר־הָאַחֲוָה״
וְרַעַם וּבָרָק —
בַּשָּׁמַיִם;
וְגִשְׁמֵי־בְּרָכָה
עַל הָאֲדָמָה
וְכַרְכֹּם וָרֹד
בַּנְּקִיקִים;
וְאִצְטְרֻבָּלִים
עַל מַצָּע רֵיחָנִי
שֶׁל מְחָטִים —
תַּחַת אֳרָנִים;
וְצָהֳלַת בֻּלְבּוּלִים
בְּעַלְוַת־פַּרְדֵּסִים
וּמִפְרְשֵׂי־שָׁלוֹם
עַל יַם־הַתִּיכוֹן;
וְ״תִמְרוֹן סְתָו״
שֶׁל כְּרֵיזַנְטֵימוֹת לְבָנוֹת —
בַּגַּנִּים
וְכַדּוּרִים אֲדֻמִּים מִתְגַּלְגְּלִים
בַּשְּׁבִילִים
וְשַׁרְווּלֵי־תִּינוֹק
מְאוֹתְתִים שַׁלְוָה —
עַל הַחֶבֶל...

1967

REQUESTS

I want beautiful trees—
and not wars!
and a coat of many colors
and not uniforms
for all my dear ones;
I want rain
and green furrows
and houses
full of babies;
a calendar of alliances
and a "brotherhood plaza"
and lightning and thunder—
in the sky;
and bountiful rains
on earth
and a pink crocus
in the ravines;
and pinecones
on a scented bed
of pine needles—
and bulbul birds rejoicing
among leafy orchards
and sails of peace
on the Mediterranean;
and white chrysanthemums
in the parks, their fall maneuvers;
and red balls rolling
along the paths
and the sleeves
of babies' garments signaling tranquility
on clotheslines.

tr. Catherine Harnett Shaw

תפילה אחרונה

אַל תַּעֲשֵׂנִי טוֹבָה כָּל כָּךְ
וְדַלָּה וּמְרֻשֶּׁשֶׁת,
וְרֵיקָה,
"וְיוֹדַעַת לִפְנֵי מִי אַתְּ עוֹמֶדֶת"
אַל תַּאֲפִיל יָמַי הָאַחֲרוֹנִים
אַל תְּרוֹמְמֵנִי,
וְאַל תַּעֲשֵׂנִי
עֲנָוָה כָּל כָּךְ,
וְאַל תִּתְּנֵנִי
לְבָרוֹת
לְכָל חֲלֵכָה,
לְכָל זָב,
הַיְשֵׁר גֵּוִי,
וְאַמֵּץ קְרָבַי;
תֵּן לִי לִתְלֹשׁ נַרְקִיסִים
בִּשְׁמוּרַת־גַּנְּךָ
הָאֲסוּרָה,
לְזָרְקָם לָרוּחַ,
וְלוּ רַק פַּעַם אַחַת
כְּאִלּוּ עוֹד מָלֵא הָאָסָם
כָּל־טוּב;
תֵּן לִי לְהַרְגִּישׁ
בְּשַׂקֵּי־שְׁקֵדִים
מַזִּילֵי רֵיחַ רִכְפָּה
בַּמִּרְפֶּסֶת;
וּבְרֵיחַ־תִּירוֹשׁ,
בַּעֲגָלוֹת
מְלֵאוֹת־עֵנָב
בֶּחָצֵר.

1971

LAST PRAYER

Don't make me so good,
and poor, ruined,
and empty.
"And knowing before Whom you stand."[1]
Don't darken my last days,
don't exalt me.
And don't make me
so modest,
and don't give me as nourishment
to every unfortunate,
every outcast.
Straighten my back
and strengthen my guts.
Let me uproot narcissus
in the forbidden reserve
of Your garden
and throw them to the wind.
And let the barn once again
be filled to the brim,
let me feel
the almond sacks,
leaking the fragrance of mignonette
over the terrace
and the odor of new wine
from wagons full of grapes
in the courtyard.

tr. Kinereth Gensler

1. Part of the Jewish burial service. Alludes to a passage from *The Sayings of the Fathers* (*Mishna Avot*) 3:1.

לילה

לְדֹּם —
דּוּמִיַּת־אֶבֶן
עֲצִירַת־נְשִׁימָה;
סוֹד־שְׁתִיקַת־הַסֶּלַע —
בַּהֲרָרַיִךְ, דַּעַת;
לִשְׁמֹעַ:
טִפְטוּף דַּם־לִבֵּךְ —
בְּמַחֲשַׁכִּים:
כְּבֶרֶז, פְּקוּעַ־שַׁסְתּוֹם;
לְהַאֲזִין:
לְדָפְקָהּ שֶׁל מוּרְסָא
בְּפִצְעֵי־הָעִדָּן —
הַמִּתְנַפְּחִים וְזוֹעֲקִים;
לָחוּשׁ:
פִּרְפּוּרֵי־אַרְצֵךְ, הוֹמָה —
בְּמֵיתָרִים מְתוּחִים
בֵּין שָׁמַיִם וַאֲדָמָה;
מַשַּׁק כַּנְפֵי־תּוֹר
מִתְלַבֵּט, חָרֵד —
פֶּתַע:
סִיּוּט־חֲלוֹם,
בְּעַלְוַת־הָאַלּוֹן;
חַבֵּק צַלָּקוֹת יְשָׁנוֹת
וַחֲדָשׁוֹת —
וְצַפּוֹת לְקַו־אוֹר
מֵעָל;
לְצִיּוּץ־שַׁחְרוּר —
אֲחוּז־תְּנוּמָה —
עִם בֹּקֶר.

1975

NIGHT

To be still
stillness of stone
stopped breath;
knowing rock's secret silence
in your mountains;
to hear
your heart's blood dripping
in darkness
like a faucet with a broken valve;
to listen
to the throb of an abscess
in wounds of the time
swollen and screaming;
to feel
your country's convulsion, it groans
with strings pulled
between earth and heaven;
flapping of dove's wings
struggling afraid
suddenly
nightmare
in leaves of the oak.
Cling to old scars
and new ones
and wait for a ray of light
from above
for a cry of a blackbird
fast asleep
in the morning.

tr. Shirley Kaufman

בת-חמה

ליל שימורים

לִי הַלַּיְלָה לֵיל־שִׁמּוּרִים,
בְּרֶטֶט נַפְשִׁי
אֲלִיט
סוֹד הַנְּעוּרִים.

עַל מִשְׁמַרְתִּי אֶעֱמֹד:
אַל שְׁנָת, אַל תְּנוּמָה!
וּבְעוֹד אַךְ רֶגַע
הוּסְרָה הַהִינוּמָה.

כָּתֵף לָבָן נִגְלָה,
מַחְשֹׂף חָזֶה קָרָץ!
חֲסָל!
מִשְׁפָּטִי חָרוּץ.

בִּילָלָה שְׂעָרִי אָגֹז,
נְעוּרִים!
מִי הַכְּאֵב יְשַׁלֵּם
וּלְמִי הַכִּפּוּרִים?

וְלוּ אַתָּה, לַיִל,
תִּדֹּם אַתָּה,
בַּאֲפֵלָה אַל תְּגַלֶּה
חִלּוּל כְּבוֹד הַכַּלָּה...

c. 1922 (1954)

חיה גינזבורג

[למה, הה אלי]

לָמָה, הָהּ אֵלִי, הִזְמַנְתָּ
כֹּהֵן־שֶׁקֶר לְמִקְדָּשָׁהּ הַקָּטָן?
בִּמְקוֹם אֵשׁ הַקֹּדֶשׁ בָּהּ הִלְהִיב
אֵשׁ־תֹּפֶת, אֵשׁ־שָׂטָן.

הַכֹּל בִּלְבָבָהּ שִׁחֵת, וְעִכֵּר
אֱמוּנָה בַקֹּדֶשׁ וְתוֹחֶלֶת;
אַךְ עוֹד פִּנָּה בִּלְבָבָהּ לָהּ הִשְׁאִיר
מְלֵאָה אֵשׁ רַעַל וָקֶלֶס...

1915

BAT-HAMAH

THE VIGIL

The night's vigil is mine,
with my soul's tremor
I cover
youth's secret.

I stand on guard:
I neither sleep nor doze—
and in a moment more
the bridal veil is lifted.

A white shoulder is bared,
breasts exposed!
It's over!
My sentence is passed.

With a wail I crop my hair.
O Youth!
Who will pay for the pain?
For whom is the forgiveness?

If only, night,
you would be quiet,
and the darkness not reveal
the desecration of the bride's honor.

tr. Peter Cole

HAYA GINZBURG

[WHY, MY LORD]

Why, my lord, why have you summoned
  a false-priest to her humble temple?
Instead of the sacred fire he's flamed
  the fire of Satan, the fire of Hell.

All that was in her heart he destroyed,
  her faith in the holy and hope he ruined;
but there in a corner of her heart he's left her—
  the fire of poison, the fire of scorn.

tr. Peter Cole

אלה אמיתן

בצבא

עִם עֶרֶב שְׁרִיקָה. אֶת לוֹעוֹ שׁוּב יִפְתַּח
הַמַּחְסָן הַמְּיֻזָּע, וְנִצְעֲדָה בַּסָּךְ
עֲיֵפוֹת מֵחַמְסִין וּמִיּוֹם כִּי אָרַךְ:
חַיָּלוֹת עֲמֵלוֹת.

וְלָמָה תַגִּידוּ: דְּמוּיוֹת הַתְּנָךְ,
פֶּרֶק שִׁיר וּגְבוּרָה
שֶׁל יָעֵל וּדְבוֹרָה . . .
יְגֵעוֹת, שׁוּב עִם עֶרֶב נִצְעֲדָה בַּסָּךְ,
חַיָּלוֹת עֲמֵלוֹת.

1945

יוכבד בת-מרים

מתוך מטמוניות

ה

כָּזֹאת לְפָנֶיךָ, כְּמוֹת שֶׁהִנְּנִי:
לֹא כְּחָל, לֹא שָׂרָק, לֹא פִּרְכּוּס וָחֵן,
אַךְ פְּרוּעָה, סוֹרֵרָה וְרָעָה מְאֹד —
וְכָךְ לְפָנֶיךָ אֲנִי רוֹצָה לַעֲמוֹד.

כָּךְ וְכָךְ מִדָּה לְשֵׁעוּר קוֹמָתִי,
כָּךְ וְכָךְ דּוֹרִי עַל זוֹ אֲדָמָה.
מִדָּה יְתֵרָה לַעֲלִיַּת־נִשְׁמָתִי
תַּחֲרֹג מִשִּׁבְיָהּ וְתָנוּד בִּדְמָמָה.

וְלֹא יַמְרִיאֵנִי שִׂיחִי אֶל עָל —
שִׂיחִי כְּמִגְמוּג מִפַּחַד פִּתְאֹם.
הֲכָכָה, הֲכָכָה אֲדַבֵּר אֵלֶיךָ
אֲנִי הַגּוֹעַת מִיּוֹם אֱלֵי יוֹם?

מִיּוֹם אֱלֵי יוֹם יַבֶּשֶׁת וָיָם
עוֹלִים וְקוֹרְנִים כְּחֶזְיוֹן חֲלוֹם,
כִּדְרָכִים לְבָנִים מֵאַיִן לְאַיִן
מוֹשְׁכִים בִּתְכֵלֶת מְצוּלָה וָרוֹם.

ELLA AMITAN

IN THE ARMY

With evening a whistle. Again the sweating store room
opens its throat wide, and we march out in formation
worn down by the heat wave and a day so long:
hard working soldier-women.

And why should you say: biblical figures these,
verses of song and heroics
of Yael and Deborah....
Weary again, with evening we march in formation
hard working soldier-women.

tr. Rachel Tzvia Back

YOKHEVED BAT-MIRIAM

from HIDDEN TREASURES

5

Just as you see me, that's how I am:
no eye-shadow, rouge; neither makeup nor charm,
but barbaric, perverse, and extremely rude—
that's how I want to stand before you.

So and so many feet is the sum of my height,
so and so many years my lease on this earth.
An extra measure for my spirit's flight
when it bursts from its cage and wanders without word.

And my chatter won't transport me to heaven,
a chatter turned stammer with sudden dismay.
I don't know how to address you, even,
I who am dying with each passing day.

With each passing day, like a dream's illusion
both land and sea still rise and shine,
as whitewashed highways from nought to nothing
will tug at the azure of the sky and the brine.

וַאֲנִי כְּבָר לֹא אֶהְיֶה, אֵינֶנִּי מִכְּבָר,
וּמְנַפְנְפָה דַּרְכִּי מֵעֵבֶר לַגְּבוּל.
הֲמִזֶּה וּבָזֶה לֹא יְכֻפַּר הַחֵטְא,
הָעֹנֶשׁ, הַנְּקָמָה, חֲרָטָה וּגְמוּל?

וְהִנְנִי לְפָנֶיךָ כְּמוֹ שֶׁאֲנִי,
פְּרוּעָה סוֹרֵרָה וְהוֹמָה בִּמְרִי.
וּסְבִיבִי מִתְעַטֵּף בְּכִי קָשֶׁה וְעָקָר
עַל עַצְמִי שֶׁלֹּא אֶהְיֶה מִמֶּנִּי אֲנִי...

1932

מרים

עָמְדָה מוּל הַסּוּף וְהַגֹּמֶא
וְנָשְׁמָה כּוֹכָבִים וּמִדְבָּר.
עֵין אַפִּיס עֲגֻלָּה וְרוֹדֶמֶת
הֵצִיפָה כְּחוֹלָהּ הַמֻּזְהָר

עַל הַחוֹל, עַל אִוְשָׁתוֹ הַזּוֹהֶבֶת,
עַל חִיּוּךְ בַּת מְלָכִים הַנִּלְאָט,
עַל שִׂיחַ חַרְטֻמִּים עֲלֵי אֶבֶן
וְזֶמֶר הֵיכָלִים הַמֻּצְעָד.

מִנֶּגֶד, בְּדֶשֶׁן הַזֵּכֶר,
כְּשְׁפִיפוֹן בְּתַאֲוַת עוֹלָם,
אִמְּצָה גֹּשֶׁן הַנִּדְרֶכֶת
דִּמְיוֹן שְׁבָטִים מְעֻמְעָם.

—אִתָּךְ, אִתָּךְ בַּסַּעַר
גּוּפֵךְ מִשְׂתַּרְבֵּב כְּתֹף,
אִתָּךְ בִּמְחוֹלֵךְ מוּל לַהַט
רֵיחַ חוֹלוֹת וְאֵין־סוֹף,

—אֲסַפֵּר מְקַנְּאָה וּמְצֹרַעַת,
אֲסַפֵּר מַלִּינָה עַל עַצְמִי.
הִשְׁבַּעְתִּיךְ בִּנְזִירוּתֵךְ לֹא נִכְנַעַת,
בִּבְדִידוּתֵךְ הַזְּהוּרָה נָא חֲיִי!

עָמְדָה מֵהַלַּחַשׁ מְנֻדְנֶדֶת
כְּמִלֹּבֶן פַּעֲמֵי הַגַּל.
גָּחֲנָה עַל הַתִּינוֹק כְּנֵדֶר,
כְּצַו,
כִּפְדוּת,
כְּגוֹרָל.

1939

And I've already ceased to exist, long hence,
my destination waves from across the border.
Is the remission of sin, of penance, revenge,
remorse and reward not in order?

And here I'm before you, just as I am,
barbaric, perverse, fuming bitterly.
And a bare, harsh lament envelops me
for myself who won't be the I of me . . .

tr. Bernhard Frank

MIRIAM

She stood facing the reeds and papyrus
and breathed in stars and desert.
The round sleeping eye of Apis
flooded its glimmered blue

on the sand, on its golden rustle,
on the smile of a hidden princess,
on a dialogue between hieroglyphs on stone
and a marched palace song.

At a distance, in the fertile soil of memory,
like a horned viper in everlasting desire,
trampled Goshen adopted
a dim tribal imagination.

—With you, with you in the storm
your body twisting like a timbrel,
with you in your dance facing fervor
smell of dunes and infinity.

—I will speak jealous and leprous,
I will speak complaining of myself.
I adjure you in your unsurrendered monasticism
in your resplendent isolation—do live!

She stood rocked by the spell
as by the white of the wave's beats.
She bent over the baby as a vow,
as decree,
as redemption,
as fate.

tr. Ilana Pardes

הגר

אַלְמֻגֶּיהָ תָּלְתָה עַל הַלַּיִל
וַתֵּלֵךְ דַּלָּה וּדְמוּמָה.
יָרֵחַ בְּחוֹמַת הַמַּיִם
צָלַל, הִשְׁתַּקְשֵׁק וְגָוַע.

לְבַדָּהּ. רַק הִיא, הַדֶּרֶךְ,
מְנֻשֶּׁבֶת כְּמִלְּבֶן אֱלָהוּת,
כִּכְתֹבֶת קַעֲקַע מִסְתַּחְרֶרֶת
הִפְלִיגָה מִתִּינוֹק וּבְדִידוּת.

—אֵלַיִךְ לֹא אָשׁוּב, מוֹלֶדֶת,
כַּסְפִּינְכְּס בְּפֶתַח חַמָּה,
אֶשָּׁאֵר הִנֵּה כָּאן מוּל הֶדֶר
מִדְבָּר, גּוֹרָל וְתַעֲלוּמָה.

בְּדוּיָה תְּרַשְׁרֵשׁ הַצַּמֶּרֶת,
בְּאֵר לֹא־קַיֶּמֶת תְּמַלְמֵל.
תִּשְׁכּוֹן שַׁלְוָתָם הַמְהֻרְהֶרֶת
בְּמַבָּטֵי הַלַּח וּמֵצֵל.

וְעִם זֶה שֶׁנִּשְׁאַר מֵעֵבֶר,
שֶׁחָרַג וְעָבַר אֶת גְּבוּלוֹת
אַהֲבָה יְחִידָה וּמְכַכֶּבֶת
שְׁתִיקָה, פְּרִידָה וּנְגֹהוֹת—

אִתִּי, אִתִּי מֵאַפְסָיִם,
עִם עַצְמִי בִּשְׁכוֹל וּבִדְרוֹר
אִכָּנֵף לַאֲחִיזַת עֵינַיִם,
לְדִמְיוֹן מִתְעַתֵּעַ וְשִׁכּוֹר.

נוֹדֵד רְדוּף אִי־מַרְגּוֹעַ,
אֲהוּב זָהֳרֵי הַנִּמְנָע—
יְאַמְּצֵנוּ כְּהַגְשָׁמָה וּכְכֹחַ
מַמְלֶכֶת חֲלוֹמוֹ הַנִּשְׁבָּע.

מְתַח־נָא, בְּנִי, אֶת הַשֶּׁלַח.
יַעֲנֶה לַחֵץ הַהֵד—
כִּמְקַדֵּם בִּבְרָכָה מְחַלְחֶלֶת
וּמַכְתִּיר אֶת שְׁבִילֵי הָאוֹבֵד.

1941

HAGAR

Hanging her corals on the night she leaves
silent, possessing nothing.
A moon dives, a splash extinguished
in a wall of water.

Alone, just herself, the path
blown clean with white godhead
twists like a scrawled tattoo
trailing away from child and isolation.

—I won't come back, my country,
like Sphinx at the sun's door
I'll stay here to face
the fate and mystery of the desert land.

Branches rustle in imagined trees,
absent, a well burbles,
their mind-bound tranquility seeks
shelter in the moist shade of my eye,

and for him who stayed behind
who strayed and crossed the line
of a single love starred with silence,
parting and light.

With me, with me from far away
with myself bereft but free
I will be cloaked in make believe
in the drunken error of fantasy.

Wanderer, pursued by restlessness,
in love with impossible splendor,
he will gather us up forcefully to realize
the kingdom of his promised dream.

Stretch out the bow my son,
let the echo speak to the shaft,
so a quavering sound of welcome
may crown my diminishing path.

tr. Zvi Jagendorf

אנדה פינקרפלד-עמיר

[כמו כל אשה]

אֲנִי, כְּמוֹ כָּל אִשָּׁה:
שַׁיֶּכֶת.
אֲנִי, כְּמוֹ כָּל אִשָּׁה:
מְסוּרָה.

אַךְ לַעֲוִית שְׂפָתַי נִיב זָר אוֹרֵב,
אַךְ לַעֲוִית עֵינַי זִיק זָר נוֹצֵץ.

רַב־רַב אַרְכִּין רֹאשִׁי
אֲנִי, הַשַּׁיֶּכֶת, אַף לַקָּטָן בֵּין אֲהוּבָי.

וּפֶתַע, בְּהִנָּגֵן הָאָבִיב
בּוֹז אָבוּז לָכֶם
וְאֶזְדַּקֵּף.

הֵי! תֵּדְעוּ יָדֹעַ!
לֹא הִשְׁתַּיַּכְתִּי לָכֶם לְעוֹלָם
לֹא לְאֶחָד מִכֶּם!

בַּת חוֹרִין הָיִיתִי
וְאֶהְיֶה!

1932

מירי

מתוך דהרה

יֵשׁ מַלְכָּה נֶאְדָּרָה, נְסִיכָה מוֹשֶׁלֶת,
גֵּאָה בַּשִּׁלְטוֹן, יְהִירָה בִּגְבוּרָה
יֵשׁ מַלְכָּה גְּאֵיוֹנָה שֶׁבָּעֲטָה בְּכִסְאָהּ
וַתִּבֶז לְכִתְרָהּ וַתִּקְרָא: לַשֵּׁדִים!
וַתִּקְפֹּץ עַל סוּסָהּ, וַתִּדְהַר, וַתִּדְהַר . . .
. . . .

אַתְּ מַלְכָּה גְּאֵיוֹנָה,
פָּרַצְתִּי אֵלַיִךְ
אַתְּ רַעְיַת קַשְׁיוּתִי
רְאִי — הִשְׁתּוֹלַלְתִּי
הוּרַמְתִּי בַּסּוּפָה, דָּאִיתִי בַּסְּעָרָה
וָאָבֹא אֵלַיִךְ,
וָאֶשְׁקַע בִּלְבֵּךְ

ANDA PINKERFELD-AMIR

[LIKE EVERY WOMAN]

Like every woman I
  belong
Like every woman I
  am faithful

But strange speech lurks in the look of my lips,
a strange spark glitters in the look of my eyes.

For a long time I, the one who belongs,
bowed my head to the least of my loved ones;

now suddenly, sounds of spring!
I'll scorn you all
and straighten up

Oh you'll certainly know!
I never belonged to you,
not to any one of you!

  I've been a free spirit
    and I'll stay that way!

tr. Shirley Kaufman

MIRI

***from* GALLOP**

There's a wonderful queen, a sovereign known
to be proud of her reign, disdainfully bold,
a haughty queen who, kicking her throne,
scorned her crown, and cried: To the devil!
as she leaped on her horse and galloped away . . .
. . . .
Lofty queen,
I rush to meet you
spouse of my fierceness,
look! I run wild,
tempest-borne, I glide in the storm
and come to you,
sink into your heart

וָאֶצַּק בְּדָמֵךְ
אֶתְמַזְּגָה תּוֹכֵכִי,
הַבִּיטִי, קְשַׁת עֹרֶף
אָנֹכִי הַמַּלְכָּה!
אָנֹכִי אֶנָּשֵׂא כֹּה זְקוּפָה וְגֵאָה,
פְּרוּעָה וְזָרָה,
וְאַעַל לֶהָרִים, אֶתְיַצְּבָה עָלֵימוֹ,
וְאַשְׁקִיף בְּמֶרִי!
יִפְרַע הַסַּעַר אֶת רֹאשִׁי הַמּוּרָם לְמַעְלָה
וּתְנוֹפֵף שְׂעָרִי הָעַרְמוֹן בָּרוּחַ,
יִצְנֹף הַנָּחָשׁ אֶת גֵּוִי הָרַךְ וְעָנֹג
וְיִבְרֹק הַבָּרָק בְּעֵינַי הַקּוֹרְנוֹת
וְיִרְעַם הָרַעַם בִּלְבָבִי הַגּוֹעֵשׁ
תֵּתַּךְ הַשְּׁאָגָה אֶל קוֹלִי וּבְדָמִי הַלּוֹהֵט,
תִּתְלַכֵּד גְּוִיָּתִי הַגְּמִישָׁה בְּפִרְאֵי הַיְקוּם
וְאֶקְפֹּץ עַל סוּסִי, וְאֶדְהַר וְאֶדְהַר . . .

1926

לאה גולדברג

לתמונת אמא

תְּמוּנָתֵךְ כֹּה שְׁלֵוָה. אַתְּ אַחֶרֶת:
קְצָת גֵּאָה וּנְבוֹכָה עַל שֶׁאַתְּ—אִמִּי.
מְלֻוָּה בְּדִמְעָה וּבְחִיּוּךְ מְוַתֶּרֶת
וּמֵעוֹלָם אֵינֵךְ שׁוֹאֶלֶת: ״מִי?״

לֹא תָמַהְתְּ, לֹא רָגַזְתְּ, עֵת בָּאתִי אֵלַיִךְ
מִדֵּי יוֹם בְּיוֹמוֹ וְאָמַרְתִּי: ״תְּנִי!״
אֶת הַכֹּל הֵבֵאת לִי בְּמוֹ יָדַיִךְ
רַק מִפְּנֵי שֶׁאֲנִי—אֲנִי.

וְיוֹתֵר מִמֶּנִּי אַתְּ הַיּוֹם זוֹכֶרֶת
אֶת יְגוֹן־יַלְדוּתִי, וְנַפְשֵׁךְ כְּבָר פְּתָרָהּ:
עֵת תָּבוֹא אֵלַיִךְ הַבַּת הַבּוֹגֶרֶת,
הִיא תָבִיא אֶת יֵאוּשׁ תּוּגָתָהּ שֶׁבָּגְרָה.

כֵּן. אָבוֹא רְצוּצָה וְלֹא אֶשְׁאַל לִשְׁלוֹמֵךְ.
לֹא אֶבְכֶּה בְּחֵיקֵךְ, לֹא אֶלְחַשׁ: ״אִמִּי!״
אַתְּ תֵּדְעִי:
זֶה שֶׁעֲזָבַנִי הָיָה לִי יָקָר מִמֵּךְ
וְלֹא תִשְׁאָלִינִי: ״מִי?״

1933

and course like molten iron
in your veins,
until stiff-necked
I become the queen!
Erect and proud,
dishevelled and strange,
I will rise and scale mountains, defiant
and changed!
And the storm will tousle my head held high
and wave my chestnut hair in the wind,
and a snake will coil round my soft tender body
and lightning will flash from my beaming eyes
and thunder will crash in my stormy heart
and its roar will melt in my voice and my blood,
with the wide universe my body will play
as I leap on my horse and gallop away.

tr. Gabriel Levin

LEA GOLDBERG

TO MOTHER'S PICTURE

Your picture is so peaceful, a different you,
proud and a bit bewildered, you're my mother.
Joining me with a tear, giving in with a smile,
never asking who.

You weren't astonished or angry
when I came each day saying: Give!
You brought me everything with your own hands
just because it was me.

More than I, you remember today
the pain of my childhood. You worked it out:
how your daughter, older now, comes to you
bringing her grown despair and sadness.

Yes this is me, broken, and I'll not ask how you are,
won't cry on your breast, won't whisper *mother.*
You'll know it:
    He's gone who was dearer to me than you,
you won't ask who.

tr. Zvi Jagendorf

מתוך על הפריחה

ב

זְקֵנָה, כְּחֻלַּת־עֵינַיִם וְנִשְׁזֶפֶת.
עֲטֶרֶת קוֹמָתָהּ — שֵׂיבָה וָסֵבֶל.
מַכְסִיף הַדְּלִי. מִשַּׁעֲרֵי הָרֶפֶת

דָּשֵׁן וְרַעֲנָן עוֹלֶה הַהֶבֶל.
דִּין שֶׁל חַיִּים — יָדֶיהָ הַחוֹלְבוֹת.
כַּךְ סַפָּנִים שְׁקֵטִים יֹאחֲזוּ בַּחֶבֶל.

כְּנִיעַת פָּרוֹת. וּבֹקֶר לֹא־עָבוֹת.
אִשָּׁה מֵעַל לַלֹּבֶן הַשּׁוֹפֵעַ.
וְאוֹר־חֻלִּין וְסוֹד קַדְמוּת עָבֹת

וּבַעֲלַת־הָאוֹב עָלַי כְּשָׁפֶיהָ.

1941

מתוך אהבתה של תרזה די מון

תרזה די מון היתה אשה מן האצולה הצרפתית, שחיתה בסוף המאה הט״ז בסביבות אביניון שבפרובאנס. בהיותה בת ארבעים בערך התאהבה באיטלקי צעיר, ששימש מחנך לבניה, והקדישה לו כארבעים ואחת סונטות. כאשר עזב האיטלקי הצעיר את ביתה, שרפה את כל שיריה והיא עצמה פרשה למנזר. זכר שיריה נשאר רק כאגדה בפי בני דורה.

ב

אֵינִי רוֹצָה כָּל לַיְלָה בַּחֲלוֹם
לִרְאוֹת אוֹתְךָ, אֵינִי רוֹצָה לִרְעֹד
בְּהִפָּתַח דַּלְתִּי. אֵינִי רוֹצָה
לַחְשֹׁב עָלֶיךָ כָּל שְׁעוֹת הַיּוֹם.

וּבְמַבָּטָן הָעֵר שֶׁל נְעָרוֹת
בְּנוֹת־שְׁבַע־עֶשְׂרֵה אֵינִי רוֹצָה לִרְאוֹת
שְׂחוֹק־נִצָּחוֹן וּבוּז וַעֲקִיצָה.
בָּאַהֲבָה הַזֹּאת אֵינִי רוֹצָה!

אֵיכָה בְּשַׁלְוָתִי הָאֲדִישָׁה
חָיִיתִי קֹדֶם, חֲכָמָה בּוֹטַחַת,
וּבִגְרוּתִי נָשָׂאתִי בְּלִי בּוּשָׁה,

וּבַלֵּילוֹת לֹא בְּעָתַנִי פַּחַד.
אַךְ מַה מָּתְקוּ רִגְעֵי שִׁבְתֵּנוּ יַחַד —
וְצִפִּיָּה נִכְלֶמֶת לִפְגִישָׁה.

from THE FLOWERING

2

Old woman, browned by the sun, blue-eyed,
crowned with gray hair and travail.
Odors fecund and fresh rise

from the cowshed, the silvery pail.
The law of life—her milking hands
are like silent sailors, gripping a sail.

Compliance of cows in the morning light,
a woman over a flood of white:
everyday light and the sacred task

of a sorceress over her ancient craft.

tr. Shirley Kaufman

from THE LOVE OF TERESA DE MEUN

Teresa de Meun, a French noblewoman of the late 16th century, fell in love when she was about 40 years of age with the young Italian tutor of her children, and wrote 41 sonnets to him. Only the memory of these remain—a legend; for when he returned to Italy, she burned the poems and entered a nunnery.

2

I do not want to see you in my dreams
each night. I do not want to tremble when I hear
a footstep at my door. I do not want
to think of you each hour of every day.

I do not want to see
in the watchful look of girls of seventeen
stinging derision, sly triumphant smiles.
Love of this kind is not the love I want.

In what a careless calm I lived
before you came, and how secure
in wisdom, wearing my ripe years

with dignity, and free at night of fear.
Yet dear are the moments when we sit together,
or when I wait for you in shy confusion here.

ט

מֵחַלּוֹנִי וְגַם מֵחַלּוֹנֵךְ
אוֹתוֹ הַגַּן נִשְׁקָף, אוֹתוֹ הַנּוֹף,
וְיוֹם תָּמִים מֻתָּר לִי לֶאֱהֹב
אֶת הַדְּבָרִים אֲשֶׁר לִטְּפָה עֵינֵךְ.

מוּל חַלּוֹנֵךְ וְגַם מוּל חַלּוֹנִי
בַּלַּיְלָה שָׁר אוֹתוֹ זָמִיר עַצְמוֹ,
וְעֵת יַרְטִיט לִבֵּךְ בַּחֲלוֹמוֹ
אֵעוֹר וְאַאֲזִין לוֹ גַּם אֲנִי.

הָאֹרֶן הַזָּקֵן, שֶׁבּוֹ כָּל מַחַט
אֶת מַבָּטֵךְ נוֹשֵׂאת כְּטַל טָהוֹר,
עִם בֹּקֶר יְקַדְּמֵנִי בִּבְרָכָה—

דְּבָרִים רַבִּים מְאֹד אָהַבְנוּ יַחַד,
אַךְ לֹא זָרַח בְּאֶשְׁנַבֵּךְ הָאוֹר
עֵת בְּדִידוּתִי נָגְעָה בִּבְדִידוּתֵךְ.

1952

הסתכלות בדבורה

א

בְּרִבּוּעַ חַלּוֹן מוּאָר—
עַל שִׁמְשָׁה, מִבַּחוּץ,
צְלָלִית שֶׁל דְּבוֹרָה
כִּמְעַט אֵין לִרְאוֹת אֶת כְּנָפֶיהָ.

הֲפוּכָה.
גּוּף צָר.
שֵׁשׁ רַגְלַיִם דַּקּוֹת—
בְּגִלּוּי מְכֹעָר
זוֹחֶלֶת דְּבוֹרָה.

אֵיךְ נַכְתִּיר אוֹתָהּ בְּדִבְרֵי שִׁירָה?

אֵיךְ נָשִׁיר וּמָה?
יָבוֹא יֶלֶד קָטָן וְיֹאמַר:
הַמַּלְכָּה עֵירֻמָּה.

9
From your window and mine we see
the same garden, the same landscape.
And I can love all day
the things your eye has dwelt on.

Before your window and mine
the same nightingale sings at night,
making your heart flutter in its sleep,
while I awake and listen.

The pine, whose every needle
carries your glance like pure dew,
greets me with a blessing every dawn.

Together we have loved so many things,
but no light shines through your small window
when my loneliness touches yours.

tr. Robert Friend

A LOOK AT A BEE

1
On a lit-up window square,
on the pane, outside,
the silhouette of a bee—
you can hardly see her wings.

Upside-down.
Narrow body.
Six thin legs.
Her nakedness exposed,
her ugliness menacing,
she crawls.

How can we crown her
with the words of a poem?
What can we sing?
A small child will come and say:
The Queen is naked.

ב

בַּשֶּׁמֶשׁ הִיא הָיְתָה עֲלֵה זָהָב נוֹפֵל,
בַּפֶּרַח הִיא הָיְתָה טִפָּה שֶׁל דְּבַשׁ אָפֵל,
וְאֵגֶל טַל בִּנְחִיל שֶׁל כּוֹכָבִים —
וּפֹה הִיא צֵל.

מִלָּה אַחַת שֶׁל שִׁיר בַּנְּחִיל הַמְצַלְצֵל,
בְּשׁוּרַת רָצוֹן נִמְרָץ בְּתוֹךְ שָׁרָב עָצֵל,
תְּנוּעַת הָאוֹר בְּאֵפֶר דִּמְדּוּמִים —
וּפֹה הִיא צֵל.

ג

מִדִּבְשֵׁךְ? מִי יִזְכֹּר אֶת דִּבְשֵׁךְ?
הוּא שָׁם, הַרְחֵק, בַּכַּוֶּרֶת.
כָּאן, בְּשִׁמְשָׁה מוּאָרָה, גּוּפֵךְ, רֹאשֵׁךְ —
כֻּלֵּךְ עֹקֶץ, שִׂנְאָה אֵין־אוֹנִים עֲלוּבָה וְעִוֶּרֶת.
הַפַּחַד הוֹרֵג.
הִשָּׁמְרִי לְנַפְשֵׁךְ.

1962

אלי

הַשָּׁנִים פִּרְכְּסוּ אֶת פָּנַי
בְּזִכְרוֹן אֲהָבוֹת
וְעָנְדוּ לְרֹאשִׁי חוּטֵי כֶּסֶף קַלִּים
עַד יָפִיתִי מְאֹד.

בְּעֵינַי נִשְׁקָפִים
הַנּוֹפִים.
וּדְרָכִים שֶׁעָבַרְתִּי
יִשְּׁרוּ צְעָדַי —
עֲיֵפִים וְיָפִים.

אִם תִּרְאֵנִי עַכְשָׁו
לֹא תַכִּיר אֶת תְּמוֹלֶיךָ —
אֲנִי הוֹלֶכֶת אֵלַי
בְּפָנִים שֶׁבִּקַּשְׁתָּ לַשָּׁוְא
כְּשֶׁהָלַכְתִּי אֵלֶיךָ.

1962

2

In sunlight she was a falling leaf of gold,
a drop of dark honey in a flower;
she was a dew drop in a swarm of stars,
but only a shadow here.

A word of a poem in a humming swarm,
in a scorching wind a message of keen will,
a flash of light in the ashes of dusk,
but only a shadow here.

3

Your honey? Who remembers your honey?
It's there, not here, there in the hive.
Here, on the lit-up window pane, your head, your body,
all of you sting and hatred—
miserable, blind, helpless hatred.
Fear kills.
Watch out.

tr. Robert Friend

TOWARD MYSELF

The years have made up my face
with memories of love,
adorned my head
with light silver threads
and made me beautiful.

Landscapes are reflected
in my eyes,
the paths I trod
have taught me to walk upright
with beautiful, though tired, steps.

If you should see me now,
you would not recognize
the yesterdays you knew.
I go toward myself with a face
you looked for in vain
when I went toward you.

tr. Robert Friend

זלדה

כל שושנה

כָּל שׁוֹשַׁנָּה הִיא אִי
שֶׁל הַשָּׁלוֹם הַמֻּבְטָח,
הַשָּׁלוֹם הַנִּצְחִי.

בְּכָל שׁוֹשַׁנָּה מִתְגּוֹרֶרֶת
צִפּוֹר סַפִּירִית
שֶׁשְּׁמָהּ "וְכִתְּתוּ".

וְנִדְמֶה
כֹּה קָרוֹב
אוֹר הַשּׁוֹשַׁנָּה,
כֹּה קָרוֹב
נִיחוֹחָהּ,
כֹּה קָרוֹב
שֶׁקֶט הֶעָלִים,
כֹּה קָרוֹב
אוֹתוֹ אִי —
קַח סִירָה
וַחֲצֵה אֶת יָם הָאֵשׁ.

1967

פנאי

הָיָה לָנוּ אוֹצָר סָמוּי שֶׁל פְּנַאי
עָדִין כַּאֲוִיר הַבֹּקֶר,
פְּנַאי שֶׁל סִפּוּרִים, דְּמָעוֹת, נְשִׁיקוֹת
וַחֲגִים.
פְּנַאי שֶׁל אִמָּא, סַבְתָּא, וְהַדּוֹדוֹת
יוֹשְׁבוֹת בְּנַחַת בְּסִירָה
שֶׁל זִיו,
שָׁטוֹת אַט־אַט
בְּדוּגִית הַשָּׁלוֹם
עִם הַיָּרֵחַ וְעִם הַמַּזָּלוֹת.

1967

ZELDA

EACH ROSE

Each rose is an island
of the promised peace,
the eternal peace.

Inside the petals
of each rose dwells
a sapphire bird called
"And They Shall Beat Their Swords."

And it seems so
close, the light
of that rose, so close
its scent, the silence
of its leaves, so close
that island—just take
a boat and go out
into a sea of flames.

tr. Barbara Goldberg

LEISURE

We had a secret store of leisure
delicate as morning air,
a leisure of tales and tears and kisses,
and of celebrations.
A leisure of mother, grandma, and the aunts
sitting serenely in a luminous
boat,
drifting slowly
in a skiff of peace
along with the moon and the constellations.

tr. Shirley Kaufman

אשה שהגיעה לזיקנה מפלגת

אִשָּׁה שֶׁהִגִּיעָה לְזִקְנָה מֻפְלֶגֶת
וְלֹא נוֹתַר בָּהּ שָׂרִיד מִטֵּרוּף הָאֵשׁ
מֵעֲסִיס הַקַּיִץ.
בְּשָׂרָהּ הַדַּק הָפַךְ לַאֲוִיר
וּמַבְהִיק בַּחֹשֶׁךְ כְּמָשָׁל עַתִּיק—
מְעוֹרֵר סְלִידָה בַּאֲנָשִׁים מְגֻשָּׁמִים
וּבְעָלִים יְרֻקִּים שֶׁל עֵץ הַתּוּת.

1974

מקום של אש

אֲוִיר הָרִים אֲוִיר חַי
אָהוּב נוֹשֵׁב
בַּקֵּשׁ לְמַעֲנֵנוּ רַחֲמִים
מִן הָעֶלְיוֹן עַל כֹּל.
מָקוֹם שֶׁל אֵשׁ,
מָקוֹם שֶׁל בֶּכִי,
מָקוֹם שֶׁל טֵרוּף—
גַּם חָתָן וְכַלָּה
רַחֲמֵי שָׁמַיִם מְבַקְשִׁים
שֶׁלֹּא יִתְפּוֹרֵר הָאֹפֶק.
כְּלָבִים וַחֲתוּלִים נִבְהָלִים.
רַק בַּצְּמָחִים לֹא נִדְלָחִים
עֲסִיסִים
פְּסִיעָה מִן הַתְּהוֹם,
רַק בַּפְּרָחִים הַמְּתִיקוּת לֹא נְסוֹגָה
פְּסִיעָה מִן הַמָּוֶת.
כִּי הַצְּמָחִים עַם אַחֵר
מֵאִתָּנוּ,
חוּץ מֵעֲצֵי הַזַּיִת
שֶׁהֵם עֲצוּבִים וַחֲכָמִים כַּאֲנָשִׁים.
וְכַאֲשֶׁר מֶלֶךְ זָר וְאוֹיֵב
מַכְפִּישׁ שַׁיָּכוּתֵנוּ לָעִיר
שֶׁנָּבִיא אוֹהֵב
תָּלָה עַל צַוָּארָהּ
סַפִּירִים נֹפֶךְ וְכַדְכֹּד—
נִרְעָדוֹת כְּמוֹ לִבִּי צַמְּרוֹת הַכֶּסֶף,

A WOMAN WHO'S ARRIVED AT A RIPE OLD AGE

A woman who's arrived at a ripe old age
has no memories of the madness of fire
or of summer juices.
As her gossamer flesh melts into air
it shines in the dark like an ancient parable
arousing disgust in earthy men
and in green leaves of a mulberry tree.

tr. Miriyam Glazer

PLACE OF FIRE

Mountain air, living air,
breathing lover—
beg mercy for us
from the Most-High.
Place of fire,
place of weeping,
place of madness—
even bride and groom
beg the mercy of the heavens
lest the horizon crumble.
Dogs and cats are alarmed.
Only in the plants
the nectars don't darken
a step away from the abyss.
Only in the flowers
the sweetness won't retreat
a step away from death.
For the plants are a different nation
from us,
except for the olive trees
which are sad and wise
like people.
And when a foreign, enemy king
crushes our ties to the city
upon whose neck
a loving prophet hung
sapphires, turquoise, and rubies—
the silver treetops tremble
like my heart.

וְכַאֲשֶׁר מֶלֶךְ זָר וְאוֹיֵב
מַכְפִּישׁ אַהֲבָתֵנוּ הַנּוֹרָאָה
לְעִיר דָּוִד—
שׁוֹמְעִים הַשָּׁרָשִׁים
שֶׁל עֵץ הַזַּיִת אֵיךְ לוֹחֵשׁ דָּמוֹ
שֶׁל הַחַיָּל הַקָּטָן
בְּתוֹךְ הֶעָפָר:
הָעִיר רוֹבֶצֶת עַל חַיַּי.

1974

חיה ורד

שעת האפס

אַתְּ,
אֶרֶץ כֶּתֶם דָּם שֶׁבַּמַּפָּה,
אַתְּ הַבְּלוּיָה וּמִתְבּוֹסֶסֶת בְּפִיחַ וּבְאֵפֶר,
כִּבְרַת אֶרֶץ קְטַנָּה לְחַיִּים.
וְעֵדִים הַגַּלְעֵדִים
בְּכָל מִפְנֵי דְּרָכִים וּבְצִדֵּי דְרָכִים,
וְהַרְחֵק, הַרְחֵק מִדְּרָכִים.

וּבְהֵרוֹם מָסַךְ עָשָׁן,
וְאַתְּ חוֹגֶגֶת שִׁכְרוֹנוֹת וְנִצָּחוֹן,
עַד זַעַם, עַד סֵאוּב, עַד רִפְיוֹן,
עַד לֹא רָאִית כְּלָל בְּהַכּוֹת
תּוּגַת טְרָשִׁים אֶת מִישׁוֹרֵךְ
וְאַתְּ כֻּלָּךְ מַפַּח־הַלֵּב וּדְאָבוֹן.

וְהַחַיִּים שְׁקוּדִים עַל אָכוֹל וְשָׁתֹה,
נָשׂוֹא נָשִׁים וְהוֹלֵד יְלָדִים.
וְהַזְּמַן מִיָּדַיִם נִגָּר,
מִבֵּין אֶצְבָּעוֹת חַמְדָּנִיּוֹת,
וְהֵם לֹא יִרְצוּ לָדַעַת,
כִּי יֵשׁ לַחְפֹּר מִתּוֹךְ הָאֲדָמָה
אֶת הֹלֶם הַלֵּב
אֲשֶׁר מָנָה זְמַנִּים עַל חֹד שְׁנִיָּה,
וְזָכַר, זָכַר אֶת שְׁעַת הָאֶפֶס.

הַמֵּתִים,
מַדּוּעַ מַתֶּם?
מַדּוּעַ לֹא מַתֶּם לְבַדְּכֶם,
אַתֶּם, אַתֶּם בִּלְבָד?

And when a foreign, enemy king
crushes our awesome love
for the city of David—
the roots of the olive tree
hear a small soldier's blood
whispering from the dust:
The city is crouching on my life.

tr. Marcia Falk

HAYA VERED

THE ZERO HOUR

You,
blood stain of land on the map,
tired you, immersed in soot and ashes,
forever a small piece of land.
And the monuments are witnesses
at every junction and at the roadsides,
and far, far from the roads.

And when the smoke screen lifts,
you celebrate intoxication and victory,
until you are enraged, rotten and limp,
until you are blind
to the sadness of stones beating on your plain
and you are all disappointment and pain.

The living diligently eat and drink,
taking wives and making babies.
Time runs out of hands
through greedy fingers,
and they won't want to know
that a heartbeat must be dug
out of the ground
counting time in split seconds,
and remember, remember the zero hour.

The dead.
Why did you die?
Why didn't you die alone,
you, only you?

הֵן עָמֹק, עָמֹק בָּאֲדָמָה
עִם הַדְּמָמָה בְּעֵינֵיכֶם הַלּוֹחֲמוֹת וְהַחוֹלְמוֹת,
עִם הַלֵּם לְבַבְכֶם אֲשֶׁר הָיָה כֻּלּוֹ עֵינַיִם,
חֲבוּקָה בִּזְרוֹעוֹת וְרוֹטֶטֶת
טְמוּנָה הָאַהֲבָה.

הָאַהֲבָה אֲשֶׁר עַל קְצוֹת אֶצְבְּעוֹתֶיהָ הַמֵּתוֹת
נִשָּׂא מַגַּשׁ־הַכֶּסֶף,
מַגַּשׁ־כַּסְפּוֹ שֶׁל עָם:

שַׁעַר פָּתוּחַ עַל כְּחוֹל יַמֵּנוּ שֶׁלָּנוּ,
וְאַחִים
רִבּוֹאוֹת, כְּיָם נִגְרָשׁ:
פְּאוֹת תֵּימָן,
עַנְוַת חֵן יוֹצְאֵי חוֹף הֹדּוּ,
עֵינֵי הָאֵשׁ לִיהוּדֵי מָרוֹקוֹ, טוּנִיס וְאַלְגִ׳יר,
מִכְוַת הָאֵשׁ בִּזְרוֹעַ יְהוּדֵי לִיטָא, הוֹלַנְד וּפוֹלִין,
רִבּוֹאוֹת! מַפַּת עוֹלָם כֻּלָּהּ!

*

וְאֹהָלִים וְלֶחֶם־חֶסֶד,
עֵינַיִם דְּעוּכוֹת תִּקְוָה,
רָעָב בְּגֵו הַתִּינוֹקוֹת,
אֶגְרוֹפִים אֵצֶל לִשְׁכּוֹת הָעֲבוֹדָה,
הַפְגָּנוֹת,
וְדֶרֶךְ מְדִינוֹת זְקֵנוֹת בָּלוֹת
וָאֳנִיּוֹת הוֹפְכוֹת פְּנֵיהֶן הַיָּמָּה.

מַגַּשׁ הַכֶּסֶף:
לְבָבוֹת כְּמוֹ נִימֵי־עוּגָב,
רַגְלַיִם חַמּוֹת לוֹטְפוֹת לָאֶבֶן,
לַצּוּק, לִנְתִיב הַדַּרְדַּר.
נְעוּרִים
נְדִיבִים, מַעֲנִיקִים, מְבַזְבְּזִים
עַצְמָם לָדַעַת,
מִתְנַחְשְׁלִים אֶל הַמִּדְבָּר וְאֶל הָהָר וְאֶל הַיָּם,
נְעוּרִים כְּמוֹ בָּזָק, כְּמוֹ הִבְהוּב הַחֶרֶב,
כְּמוֹ שִׁבֳּלִים, כְּמוֹ דָּגָן.
כְּמוֹ תִקְוָה.

*

גִּדְמִים פּוֹסְעִים בָּרְחוֹבוֹת,
עֵינֵי אֵימָה אֶל הַפְּקִידִים,
עִוְרִים אֲשֶׁר זָכוּ בְּכֶלֶב.
וְהָעֵינַיִם הָרוֹאוֹת רוֹאוֹת אַךְ כֶּסֶף,
וְאֶצְבָּעוֹת חוֹפְרוֹת אַךְ כֶּסֶף,

Yes, deep, deep in the ground
with silence in your dreaming, warring eyes,
with your heartbeat all eyes,
encircled by arms and trembling,
love is hidden.

The love on whose dead fingertips
the silver platter is borne,
the people's silver platter:

An open gate to our own blue sea.
And brothers
tens of thousands like a raging sea:
Yemenite ear locks,
the graceful modesty of those from the Indian shore,
the fiery eyes of the Jews of Morocco, Tunis, Algiers,
the fiery brand on the arm of the Jews of Lithuania, Holland and Poland,
tens of thousands! A whole map of the world!

*

And tents and bread of charity,
eyes without hope,
hunger in infants' bodies,
fist fights at the employment offices,
demonstrations,
and like old worn-out nations
ships turn their faces toward the sea.

The silver platter:
hearts like harp strings,
warm feet caressing stone,
cliff and thorny path.
Youth
generous, giving,
wasting themselves
storming the desert, the mountains and the sea.
Youth like a flash, the glint of a sword,
like sheaves, like grain.
Like hope.

*

Amputees stalk the streets,
their eyes threaten clerks,
the blind win a dog.
Seeing eyes see only silver,
fingers dig only for silver,

וְעַל מַגַּשׁ הַכֶּסֶף:
  בְּצָלִים וְשׁוּמִים וְדוּדֵי הַבָּשָׂר,
וְעַל מַגַּשׁ הַכֶּסֶף:
  פְּרִיגִ'ידֶרִים, דֶּה־לוּכְּסִים,
  רֶקֶב וּפִגְרוֹ שֶׁל מַצְפּוּן.
וְאַתְּ,
  תִּינֹקֶת בַּת חָמֵשׁ פְּצוּעָה,
  בּוֹכָה עַל נֶפֶשׁ
  וְעַל הָרוּחַ הַמֻּכָּה בַּמִּפְרָשִׂים.

הַקַּבַּרְנִיטִים,
  הֲרָאוּ עֵינֵיכֶם בְּקֹמֶל הַיָּפֶה בִּפְרָחִים
  בְּגַן הָאַלְפַּיִם שֶׁלָּנוּ?
מַה טָּהוֹר הָיָה הַחוֹף אֵלָיו נִשֵּׂאת, סְפִינֹנֶת!
כַּמָּה עֵצִים הָיוּ יוֹקְדִים בְּצֹהַב מִדְבָּרֵךְ,
לוּ צְרַרְתָּנוּ רוּחַ בִּכְנָפֶיהָ,
רוּחַ נְעָרֵינוּ בֶּעָפָר!

הוֹ, אֶרֶץ קְטַנָּה, אֲהוּבָה וְחַיָּה
וְנוֹשֶׁמֶת שֶׁלִּי,
הַסְכִּיתִי אֶל שְׁעַת הָאֶפֶס!
כְּרִי עִמָּדִי אֶת אָזְנֵךְ אֶל הַלְמוּת הַשָּׁעוֹן וְהַלֵּב!
הַבִּיטִי עִמִּי אֶל מְחוֹג הַזַּרְחָן
וְאֶל הַזְּוָעָה שֶׁתֵּעוֹר בְּעֵינֵי יְלָדֵינוּ!
הַקְשִׁיבִי עִמָּדִי, אִמִּי שֶׁלִּי,
סְקוּלַת הַמַּטְבְּעוֹת עַד זוֹב־דָּם,
וְזַעֲקִי אֶל הַטּוֹבִים וְאֶל הָאוֹהֲבִים,
כִּי עוֹד יְשֵׁנִים.
רוּחַ מֵתַי שֶׁבֶּעָפָר,
מִן הַכּוֹכָבִים עֲלִי, עֲלִי,
וְצַנְפִינוּ צְנֵפָה, הָרוּחַ:

לַחֲרָדָה, לְאֹמֶץ־לֵב
וּלְתִקְוָה מָרָה כַּדָּם —
עַד
יָרוּם מָסַךְ עָשָׁן
וְיִמְצָאֵךְ נוֹגַהּ, זוֹהֶרֶת.
וְעִנְבְּלֵי שְׂחוֹק יְלָדַיִךְ — פַּעֲמוֹן,
וְעַל שְׁפָיִים תֵּלֵךְ הָרוּחַ,
וּבַלְּבָבוֹת תֶּהוֹם הָרוּחַ,
בְּהֹלֶם לֵב טָהוֹר אֶחָד —
וָעָם.

(1953) 1956

and on the silver platter:
   onions and garlic and pots of meat,
and on the silver platter:
   Frigidaires, luxuries,
   decay and the corpse of conscience.
And you,
   wounded five-year-old child,
   crying for a soul
   and a wind hits the sails.

Captains,
   did your eyes see the withering of the most beautiful flowers
   in our two-thousand-year-old garden?
How pure the shore where you drifted, little boat!
How many trees would have burned in the gold of your desert,
had we been wrapped in wings of the wind,
the spirit of our youth in dust!

Oh, my small beloved country, alive
and breathing,
listen to the zero hour!
Listen with me to the beat of the clock and the heart!
Look with me at the phosphorescent dial.
At the horror waking in our children's eyes!
Listen with me, mother,
stoned by coins until you bleed,
cry to the good and the loving:
they still exist.
Spirit of my dead in the dust:
rise, rise out of the crypts,
enfold us, wind:

in fear, in faith,
in hope bitter as blood—
until
the smoke screen lifts
and you will shine in sorrow.
The bell clappers of your children's laughter ring,
and the spirit will move on the high places,
and the spirit will echo in hearts,
in one pure heart beat—
and a nation.

tr. Lisa Katz

עין טור-מלכא

אזכרה

כַּפִּים בֶּהָרִים לְפָנֵינוּ
בִּדְמוּת אִמָּהוֹת שַׁכּוּלוֹת
שֶׁהֵמִירוּ מִקֶּדֶם דְּמוּתָן:
טְלָלִים לֹא יְרַוּוּן,
הַשֶּׁמֶשׁ לֹא תְּפַזֵּן.
—מַה נּוֹרָא הָאֵלֶּם
וְאָנָה נִבְרָח?—
אַזְכָּרָה: תְּפִלָּה מְאֻחֶרֶת לָרַחֲמִים.
הַבָּנִים מֵטָלִים פְּרַקְדָן
לְרֹחַב הָאֲדָמָה
וְהָאִמָּהוֹת נִצָּבוֹת:
בְּקַו הַגֶּשֶׁם הֵן מְחַלְחֲלוֹת
לְעָמְקֵי הַקְּבָרִים בַּבֶּכִי—

1972

שמחה זרמתי-עצטה

לדמותך

עִם שַׁחַר נִשְׁמַע קוֹלֵךְ
לְקוֹל הָרֵיחַיִם וְאוֹר הַנֵּר
יוֹמֵךְ הֵחֵל בְּשֶׁבַח לָאֵל
בִּכְמִיהָה בְּכֹסֶף לִשְׁלוֹם יִשְׂרָאֵל
צְעִירָה וּכְבָר אֵם לְבָנִים
מוּדַעַת לְרַצּוֹת אֶת בַּעַל הָרָצוֹן
בַּחוּץ כְּפוּפָה תַּחַת הַמַּשָּׂא
בַּבַּיִת זְקוּפָה כְּמַלְכָּה
הָעֵינַיִם נְשׂוּאוֹת עָל אֵינָן מִתְרַפְּסוֹת
אֵינֵךְ מְבַקֶּשֶׁת חֶסֶד אַךְ גּוֹמֶלֶת חֲסָדִים
הַפֶּה לֹא חָטָא בִּתְלֻנָּה
כְּיוֹנָה הוֹמִיָּה
חֶרֶשׁ מְפַכָּה תְּפִלָּה
בְּלִבֵּךְ כּוֹלְאָה הַתְּלָאָה
דִּמְעָתֵךְ מְטַהֶרֶת הַנְּשָׁמָה
נִשְׁאָר לִי לִסְגֹּד לִדְמוּתֵךְ הַסְּגוּפָה

AYIN TUR-MALKA

MEMORIAL SERVICE

Crags in the mountains facing us
are like bereaved mothers
who long ago altered their image:
dew does not slake them,
the sun does not gild them.
—How terrible their silence
and where can we flee?—
A memorial service: belated prayer for mercy.
The sons lie flat
in the wide earth
and the mothers stand tall.
In the line of rain they soak
the depths of the graves with tears.

tr. Shirley Kaufman

SIMCHA ZARMATI-ATZTA

TO YOUR IMAGE

At dawn your voice is heard
in candlelight to the sound of grindstone
your day begins praising God
longing for Israel's peace
young and already a mother
knowing you must appease his will
stooped under your load outdoors
you are upright as a queen at home
your eyes look up—not servile
you are merciful—not seeking mercy
your mouth has no complaints
flowing over with prayer
like a dove cooing
trouble is sealed in your heart
and your tears cleanse the soul
I'm left to worship your afflicted figure—

לוּ רַק דִּמִּיתִי לָךְ
אֲנִי פְּגוּעָה עֵירֻמָּה חֲשׂוּפָה
שְׂכִירַת תַּרְבּוּת בַּאֲזִיקִים כְּבוּלָה
וּבְיָדַי לֹא עֶרֶב וְלֹא מַעֲרָב

1986

ש. שפרה

גדי אחד

הַגְּדִי שֶׁלָּנוּ הָלַךְ לָמוּת
כָּל הַשְּׁכוּנָה יָדְעָה
שֶׁהַגְּדִי שֶׁלָּנוּ הוֹלֵךְ
לָמוּת. בְּיוֹם שִׁשִּׁי,
לְיַד עֶגְלַת הַקֶּרַח,
שָׁאֲלָה אוֹתִי הַשְּׁכֵנָה
שׁוֹשַׁנָּה מַה שְּׁלוֹם
הַגְּדִי. הַגְּדִי שֶׁלָּנוּ
מֵת אָמַרְתִּי וְלֹא
הִבַּטְתִּי לָהּ בָּעֵינַיִם,
כְּבָר טוֹב לוֹ, אָמְרָה
הַשְּׁכֵנָה שׁוֹשַׁנָּה, וַאֲנִי
לֹא הִבַּטְתִּי לָהּ בָּעֵינַיִם
וְחָשַׁבְתִּי שֶׁאֵין לָהּ לֵב
לְרַחֵם עַל גְּדִי לָבָן
קָטָן שֶׁמֵּת. לַמָּחֳרָת
בַּצָּהֳרַיִם בְּשַׁבָּת
מָצְאוּ אֶת הַשְּׁכֵנָה
שׁוֹשַׁנָּה תְּלוּיָה בְּצַוָּארָהּ
בְּאֻרְוַת הַסּוּסִים
שֶׁל אָבִיהָ. לוּ רַק הִבַּטְתִּי
לָהּ בָּעֵינַיִם.

(1973) 1987

if only I resembled you
but I'm vulnerable exposed undressed
culture's mercenary shackled in irons
in my hands neither East nor West

tr. Gabriel Levin

SHIN SHIFRA

GOAT

Our goat was going to die
the whole neighborhood knew
our baby goat was
dying. Friday,
near the ice-wagon,
our neighbor Shoshana
asked me how
the goat was doing.
Our goat
died I said, not
looking into her eyes.
He's better off now, said
the neighbor Shoshana, and I
didn't look into her eyes
thinking she had no heart
to feel sorry for a small white
goat that died. Next day
Saturday at noon
they found the neighbor
Shoshana hanging by her neck
in her father's stable.
If only I had looked
into her eyes.

tr. Tsipi Keller

סהרורית

הַדּוֹד יְרֹחָם כָּל־כָּךְ דָּאַג
לַדּוֹדָה מִרְיָם עַד שֶׁהָיָה
מַשְׁאִיר אוֹתָהּ לְבַדָּהּ שֶׁתֵּדַע
אֵיךְ זֶה לִישֹׁן בִּלְעָדָיו סוֹגֵר
הַדֶּלֶת עָלֶיהָ וְהִיא
בַּמִּטָּה הַגְּדוֹלָה מְפַרְפֶּרֶת
כַּיּוֹנָה אוֹטֶמֶת חַלּוֹן בִּשְׂמִיכָה נוֹעֶלֶת
פַּעֲמַיִם וָשׁוּב
מַתִּירָה מִפְּנֵי שֶׁהֵעֵזָּה בַּצָּהֳרַיִם
לְהַזְכִּיר, לֹא חָשׁוּב
מָה, אִמָּא נִחֲשָׁה שֶׁאוּלַי
הוּא פָּשׁוּט קִנֵּא לְחִיּוּתָהּ מִפְּנֵי
שֶׁלְּלֹא סִבָּה נָצְצוּ
עֵינֶיהָ בְּאוֹתוֹ בֹּקֶר בְּאוֹר
שֶׁלִּפְנֵי הַחֲתֻנָּה וְאָז קָם עָלֶיהָ
לְרַסְּנָהּ, הוֹפֶכֶת אֶת
הַבַּיִת לְקֶבֶר, צָרַח
מְלוֹא גָּרוֹן, הָיִיתִי יַלְדָּה
בְּבִקּוּר מִשְׁפַּחְתִּי בְּבֵית
הַדּוֹדָה מִרְיָם וְהַדּוֹד
יְרֹחָם, סַהֲרוּרִית מְהַלֶּכֶת
בִּשְׁנָתָהּ, הִסְבִּיר הַדּוֹד
יְרֹחָם כְּשֶׁמָּצְאוּ אֶת
הַדּוֹדָה מִרְיָם מְטַיֶּלֶת
יְחֵפָה עִם הָנֵץ
הַחַמָּה, רַק אִמָּא נִחֲשָׁה

1987

מתוך אשה שמתאמנת בלחיות

ב

אִשָּׁה שֶׁמִּתְאַמֶּנֶת בְּלִחְיוֹת יְכוֹלָה
לָלֶכֶת לַקּוֹלְנוֹעַ בְּעֶרֶב רִאשׁוֹן לַקַּיִץ, וְלֹא
הוֹלֶכֶת, יְכוֹלָה לָלֶכֶת לַתַּעֲרוּכָה
שֶׁל דַּנְצִיגֶר בְּמוּזֵיאוֹן תֵּל־אָבִיב, וְלֹא הוֹלֶכֶת, בִּמְקוֹם
כָּל אֵלֶּה הִיא מְדַבֶּרֶת עִם הַגַּנָּן
הַמְּפַקֵּד עַל בֵּית הַקְּבָרוֹת בַּטֶּלֶפוֹן.

MOONSTRUCK

Uncle Yerocham was so worried
about Aunt Miriam he would
leave her alone so she'd know
what it feels like to sleep without him
he'd shut the door on her while she
fluttered like a dove in the large bed
covered the window
with a blanket locked the door
twice and again unlocked it
and all because at noon she dared
to mention, it doesn't matter
what, Mother guessed perhaps
he was simply jealous of her spirit
because that morning for no reason
her eyes shone with the light
before the wedding and that's why he tried
to restrain her, she turns the house
into a grave, he yelled
at the top of his lungs, I was a child
on a family visit to the house
of Aunt Miriam and Uncle
Yerocham. Moonstruck, she walks
in her sleep, explained Uncle
Yerocham when they found
Aunt Miriam walking barefoot
at sunrise, only Mother guessed

tr. Tsipi Keller

from A WOMAN WHO PRACTICES HOW TO LIVE

2

A woman who practices how to live may
go to the cinema on a first summer evening,
and doesn't, may go to a Danziger exhibit
at the Tel-Aviv Museum, and doesn't, instead
she speaks on the phone with the gardener
in charge of the cemetery.

ג

לְכַסּוֹת בְּאַפְּטֶנְיָה אֶת חֶלְקָתָהּ
הַצְּמוּדָה, מַצִּיעַ הַגַּנָּן, וְהִיא מִתְחַמֶּקֶת, הוּא מַצִּיעַ בְּרוֹשׁ
בְּחֶלְקָתָהּ הַצְּמוּדָה, וְהִיא מִתְחַמֶּקֶת, לַעֲקֹר
בְּרוֹשׁ מְשֹׁרָשׁ בְּחֶלְקָתָהּ הַצְּמוּדָה בְּבֹא
הַיּוֹם, לֹא נָעִים, הִיא מְגַמְגֶּמֶת, וְהַגַּנָּן הַמְּפַקֵּד עַל בֵּית
הַקְּבָרוֹת טוֹעֶה בְּשִׁקּוּלֶיהָ, וּמַבְטִיחַ שֶׁזּוֹ סְגֻלָּה לַאֲרִיכוּת
יָמִים, עָצִיץ, הִיא מְבַקֶּשֶׁת, גָּדוֹל, וּבוּגֶנְוִילֵיאָה, עָצִיץ
אֲרָעִי שֶׁאֶפְשָׁר בְּקַלּוּת לְהַעֲבִירוֹ מִמָּקוֹם
לְמָקוֹם בְּבֹא הַיּוֹם, כְּמוֹ שֶׁחָיִיתִי, לוֹחֶשֶׁת
לְנַפְשָׁהּ אִשָּׁה שֶׁמִּתְאַמֶּנֶת.

ה

אִשָּׁה שֶׁמִּתְאַמֶּנֶת בִּלְחִיּוֹת הוֹלֶכֶת
לַשּׁוּק לִקְנוֹת דָּגִים, עוֹלָה
בְּאַפָּהּ צַחֲנַת בִּיּוּב זוֹרֵם
בְּשׁוּלֵי הַסִּמְטָא, עוֹפוֹת תְּלוּיִים עַל
מְרִישִׁים, אִישׁ מַסִּיעַ עֲגָלָה
פּוֹגֵעַ בְּקַרְסֻלָּהּ, עֵינֶיהָ טָחוֹת מֵרְאוֹת אֶת פִּירָמִידוֹת
הַתַּפּוּחִים, הָאֲגָסִים, הַמַּנְגּוֹ, בַּבַּיִת
הִיא לֹא מַצְלִיחָה לִבְלֹעַ אֶת הַדָּג
רֵיחַ הַצַּחֲנָה תָּקוּעַ בִּגְרוֹנָהּ.

1997

שולמית הראבן

חיים חדשים

יְמִימָה וּקְצִיעָה וְקֶרֶן־הַפּוּךְ
בּוֹנוֹת מִגְדָּלִים בַּחוֹל הַתָּכֹל
יְמִימָה וּקְצִיעָה וְקֶרֶן־הַפּוּךְ
בְּהִירוֹת וּזְרִזִירִיּוֹת

וְאִמָּן הָעוֹרְבִית שֶׁעַל זְרוֹעָהּ קִעְקוּעַ
סוֹרֶגֶת מִנְחָה עַל הַסַּפְסָל
יוֹם יָמִין וְיוֹם שְׂמֹאל
וְיוֹם גֶּלֶד־דֻּגְמָה,
וְקִמְטֵי שֶׁחְיָהּ שְׁחוֹרִים
וְכַפָּהּ חֲתוּכַת־צֶמֶר

3

To cover with aptenia her connecting
plot, suggests the gardener, and she's evasive, he suggests
pine in her connecting plot, and she's evasive, to uproot
a pine in her connecting plot when the time comes
doesn't feel right, she stammers, and the gardener in charge
of the cemetery, mistakes her motives, guarantees it's a good omen
for longevity, a plant, she requests, large, bougainvillea,
a temporary pot easily transported from place
to place when the time comes, as I have lived, she whispers
to herself, a woman who practices.

5

A woman who practices how to live goes
to market to buy fish, inhales the stench
of sewage flowing in the gutter
chickens hang from hooks, a man steers
a cart into her ankle, her eyes
are blurry from so many pyramids
of apples pears mangos, at home
she can't swallow the fish
the stench sticks in her throat.

tr. Tsipi Keller

SHULAMITH HAREVEN

NEW LIFE

Jemimah, Ketziah, and Keren-happuch[1]
are building castles in the blue sand
Jemimah, Ketziah, and Keren-happuch
are fair, swift as starlings

and their mother, the raven on the bench
with a tattooed arm, knits an offering
one day purl one day knit
and one day a pattern for skin.
The creases of her armpit are black
and her palm is torn by the yarn.

1. Names of Job's new daughters have been transliterated from the biblical Hebrew.

בַּעֲרוֹב הַיּוֹם הִיא רוֹאָה כְּבוֹהָה
אֶת קְצִיעָה וִימִימָה וְקֶרֶן־הַפּוּךְ
לְשׁוֹנָן זָרָה וְשׁוֹחֶצֶת
וְרֹאשָׁן בָּהִיר כְּלֹא מִשְׁפַּחְתָּהּ

כִּי אַיֵּה אֲחֵיהֶם הַבְּכוֹרִים
אַיֵּה הַנְּעָרִים שְׁחוֹרֵי־הַמְּעִיל
שֶׁיָּלְדָה בְּעוֹדָהּ יִרְאַת אֱלֹהִים
וְסָרָה מֵרַע.

1962

מלכה שקד

בושה

אֵיךְ אֲנִי מִתְבַּיֶּשֶׁת.
אִמָּא שֶׁלִּי בְּגִילִי
הָיְתָה עוֹמֶדֶת בַּמִּרְפֶּסֶת
וְצוֹרַחַת
אֶת עֶלְבּוֹן נָשִׁיּוּתָהּ
פּוֹרַעַת לְכָל רוּחַ חֶשְׁבּוֹנָהּ הַמַּר
בְּ״מיינע שוואַרצע יאָרן״
קוֹרַעַת הַשָּׁמַיִם.
״שָׁה. הִיא מְשֻׁגַּעַת
וַחֲסְרַת בּוּשָׁה״
הָיָה לוֹחֵשׁ לִי אַבָּא
וְטוֹמֵן רֹאשִׁי אֶצְלוֹ
וַאֲנִי
בָּרַע לִי
הֶאֱמַנְתִּי לוֹ.

1996

Toward evening her vision blurs
she sees Jemimah, Ketziah, and Keren-happuch:
their language alien and arrogant
and their heads fair, not her family.

Where are their older brothers
where are the black-coated boys
to whom she gave birth when she still feared God
and avoided evil.

tr. Shirley Kaufman

MALKA SHAKED

SHAME

How ashamed I am.
My mother at my age
would stand on the balcony
and scream
the outrage of being a woman,
unravel her bitter reckoning to the winds
with *maine shvartze yorn*[1]
splitting the sky.
"Sha! She's crazy,
she's got no shame."
My father would whisper to me
and hide my head in his arms
and I
to my shame
believed him.

tr. Shirley Kaufman

1. Yiddish: *my black years.*

יהודית כפרי

האשה

"באמת את מגזימה", מתוך מכתב

הָאִשָּׁה הַמֻּגְזֶמֶת הַזֹּאת
לֹא גָּזְמוּ אוֹתָהּ נָכוֹן
מוֹצִיאָה כָּל מִינֵי עֲנָפִים מוּזָרִים
שָׁרְשֵׁי מַיִם
צַעֲקוֹת צָמָא.
אֲנִי אֶהְיֶה טוֹבָה,
הִיא מַבְטִיחָה,
מָחָר יִגְזְמוּ אוֹתִי
כְּמוֹ עֵץ מְמֻשְׁמָע.
לְסַלֵּק אוֹתָהּ מֵהַנּוֹף,
אוֹמְרִים פַּקָּחֵי הַנּוֹי,
מְקַלְקֶלֶת לָנוּ אֶת הַשּׁוּרָה
מְבַזְבְּזִים עָלֶיהָ אֶת תַּקְצִיב הַמַּיִם
שֶׁל חֲצִי שְׁכוּנָה
אֲפִלּוּ נָהָר לֹא הָיָה מַסְפִּיק לָהּ.
לֹא חָשׁוּב, טוֹעֵן מִישֶׁהוּ,
בְּאַחַד הַקֵּיצִים הֲכִי שְׁחוּנִים
רָאִיתִי כַּמָּה צִפֳּרִים קְטַנּוֹת
מִתְחַבְּאוֹת בְּצֵל הָעֲנָפִים הַמּוּזָרִים הָאֵלֶּה שֶׁלָּהּ,
זֶה הָיָה הַצֵּל הַיָּחִיד בְּכָל הַסְּבִיבָה.
צֵל! יוֹרְקִים הַגַּנָּנִים בְּבוּז,
הִיא לֹא יוֹדַעַת לִהְיוֹת דֶּקֶל מְעֻגָּל
אוֹ פִיקוּס מְרֻבָּע
אוֹ בְּרוֹשׁ זָקוּף בַּדֶּרֶךְ לְבֵית־הַקְּבָרוֹת.
וַאֲנִי חוֹשֶׁבֶת . . .
לְדַעְתִּי הָאִישִׁית — אֵין לָהּ תִּקְוָה.
אֲבָל אֲנִי לֹא אוֹמֶרֶת אֶת זֶה בְּקוֹל רָם,
לֹא מְגַלָּה,
אוּלַי יִשְׁכְּחוּ.
הַגַּנָּנִים שֶׁלָּנוּ הֲרֵי
עֲסוּקִים כָּל כָּךְ.

1988

JUDITH KAFRI

THE WOMAN

"Really, you exaggerate," from a letter

This exaggerated woman
wasn't pruned right
she sprouts all sorts of odd branches
water roots
cries of thirst.
I'll be good,
she vows,
tomorrow they'll prune me
like a disciplined tree.
Remove her from the scenery,
say the superintendents of nature,
she spoils the line,
the water budget of half a neighborhood
is wasted on her
even a river wouldn't be enough for her.
It doesn't matter, someone says,
in one of the driest summers
I saw several small birds
hiding in the shade of those odd branches of hers.
it was the only shade in the whole area.
Shade! spit the gardeners with disdain,
she doesn't know how to be a rounded palm-tree
or a square ficus
or an upright cypress on the way to the cemetery.
And I'm thinking...
if you ask me she hasn't a chance.
But I don't say it out loud
don't tell
maybe they'll forget.
Our gardeners, after all,
are so busy.

tr. Tsipi Keller

דליה רביקוביץ

בובה ממוכנת

בַּלַּיְלָה הַזֶּה הָיִיתִי בֻּבָּה מְמֻכֶּנֶת
וּפָנִיתִי יָמִינָה וּשְׂמֹאלָה, לְכָל הָעֲבָרִים,
וְנָפַלְתִּי אַפַּיִם אַרְצָה וְנִשְׁבַּרְתִּי לִשְׁבָרִים
וְנִסּוּ לְאַחוֹת אֶת שְׁבָרַי בְּיָד מְאֻמֶּנֶת.

וְאַחַר כָּךְ שַׁבְתִּי לִהְיוֹת בֻּבָּה מְתֻקֶּנֶת
וְכָל מִנְהָגִי הָיָה שָׁקוּל וְצַיְּתָנִי,
אוּלָם אָז כְּבָר הָיִיתִי בֻּבָּה מִסּוּג שֵׁנִי
כְּמוֹ זְמוֹרָה חֲבוּלָה שֶׁהִיא עוֹד אֲחוּזָה בִּקְנוֹקֶנֶת.

וְאַחַר כָּךְ הָלַכְתִּי לִרְקֹד בְּנֶשֶׁף הַמְּחוֹלוֹת
אַךְ הִנִּיחוּ אוֹתִי בְּחֶבְרַת חֲתוּלִים וּכְלָבִים
וְאִלּוּ כָּל צְעָדַי הָיוּ מְדוּדִים וּקְצוּבִים.

וְהָיָה לִי שֵׂעָר שֶׁל זָהָב וְהָיוּ לִי עֵינַיִם כְּחֻלּוֹת
וְהָיְתָה לִי שִׂמְלָה מִצֶּבַע פְּרָחִים שֶׁבַּגָּן
וְהָיָה לִי כּוֹבַע שֶׁל קַשׁ עִם קִשּׁוּט דֻּבְדְּבָן.

1959

הבגד

ליצחק לבני

אַתְּ יוֹדַעַת, הִיא אָמְרָה, תָּפְרוּ לָךְ בֶּגֶד מֵאֵשׁ,
אַתְּ זוֹכֶרֶת אֵיךְ נִשְׂרְפָה אִשְׁתּוֹ שֶׁל יָאזוֹן בִּבְגָדֶיהָ?
זֹאת מֵדֵיאָה, הִיא אָמְרָה, הַכֹּל עָשְׂתָה לָהּ מֵדֵיאָה.
אַתְּ צְרִיכָה לִהְיוֹת זְהִירָה, הִיא אָמְרָה.
תָּפְרוּ לָךְ בֶּגֶד מַזְהִיר כְּמוֹ רֶמֶץ,
בּוֹעֵר כְּמוֹ גֶּחָלִים.

אַתְּ תִּלְבְּשִׁי אוֹתוֹ? הִיא אָמְרָה, אַל תִּלְבְּשִׁי אוֹתוֹ.
זֶה לֹא הָרוּחַ שׁוֹרֵק, זֶה הָרַעַל מְפַעְפֵּעַ.
אֲפִלּוּ אֵינֵךְ נְסִיכָה, מַה תַּעֲשִׂי לְמֵדֵיאָה?
אַתְּ צְרִיכָה לְהַבְחִין בְּקוֹלוֹת, הִיא אָמְרָה,
זֶה לֹא הָרוּחַ שׁוֹרֵק.

DAHLIA RAVIKOVITCH

CLOCKWORK DOLL

That night, I was a clockwork doll
and I whirled around, this way and that,
and I fell on my face and shattered to bits
and they tried to fix me with all their skill.

Then I was a proper doll once again
and I did what they told me, poised and polite.
But I was a doll of a different sort,
an injured twig that dangles from a stem.

And then I went to dance at the ball,
but they left me alone with the dogs and cats
though my steps were measured and rhythmical.

And I had blue eyes and golden hair
and a dress all the colors of garden flowers,
and a trimming of cherries on my straw hat.

tr. Chana Bloch and Ariel Bloch

A DRESS OF FIRE

For Yitzhak Livni

You know, she said, they made you
a dress of fire.
Remember how Jason's wife burned in her dress?
It was Medea, she said, Medea did that to her.
You've got to be careful, she said,
they made you a dress that glows
like an ember, that burns like coals.

Are you going to wear it, she said, don't wear it.
It's not the wind whistling, it's the poison
seeping in.
You're not even a princess, what can you do to Medea?
Can't you tell one sound from another, she said,
it's not the wind whistling.

אַתְּ זוֹכֶרֶת, אָמַרְתִּי לָהּ, אֶת הַזְּמַן שֶׁהָיִיתִי בַּת שֵׁשׁ?
חָפְפוּ אֶת רֹאשִׁי בְּשַׁמְפּוֹ וְכָכָה יָצָאתִי לָרְחוֹב.
רֵיחַ הַחֲפִיפָה נִמְשַׁךְ אַחֲרַי כְּעָנָן.
אַחַר כָּךְ הָיִיתִי חוֹלָה מִן הָרוּחַ וּמִן הַגֶּשֶׁם.
עוֹד לֹא הֵבַנְתִּי לִקְרֹא אָז טְרָגֶדְיוֹת יְוָנִיּוֹת,
אֲבָל רֵיחַ הַבֹּשֶׂם נָדַף וְהָיִיתִי חוֹלָה מְאֹד.
הַיּוֹם אֲנִי מְבִינָה שֶׁזֶּה בֹּשֶׂם בִּלְתִּי טִבְעִי.

מַה יִּהְיֶה אִתָּךְ, הִיא אָמְרָה, תָּפְרוּ לָךְ בֶּגֶד בּוֹעֵר.
תָּפְרוּ לִי בֶּגֶד בּוֹעֵר, אָמַרְתִּי, אֲנִי יוֹדַעַת.
אָז מָה אַתְּ עוֹמֶדֶת, אָמְרָה, אַתְּ צְרִיכָה לְהִזָּהֵר,
הַאִם אַתְּ לֹא יוֹדַעַת מַה זֶּה בֶּגֶד בּוֹעֵר?

אֲנִי יוֹדַעַת, אָמַרְתִּי, אֲבָל לֹא לְהִזָּהֵר.
רֵיחַ הַבֹּשֶׂם הַהוּא מְבַלְבֵּל אֶת דַּעְתִּי.
אָמַרְתִּי לָהּ: אַף אֶחָד לֹא חַיָּב לְהַסְכִּים אִתִּי
אֵינֶנִּי נוֹתֶנֶת אֵמוּן בִּטְרָגֶדְיוֹת יְוָנִיּוֹת.

אֲבָל הַבֶּגֶד, אָמְרָה, הַבֶּגֶד בּוֹעֵר בָּאֵשׁ.
מָה אַתְּ אוֹמֶרֶת, צָעַקְתִּי, מָה אַתְּ אוֹמֶרֶת?
אֵין עָלַי בֶּגֶד בִּכְלָל, הֲרֵי זֹאת אֲנִי הַבּוֹעֶרֶת.

1969

ראש ילדותי

דְּבָרִים כָּאֵלֶּה שׁוּב אֵינָם מְצַעֲרִים אוֹתִי,
לֹא בְּרִשְׁעוּת, לֹא בְּטִמְטוּם לֵבָב
וְלֹא בַּמְּזִיגָה הַנְּפוֹצָה
שֶׁיֵּשׁ בָּהּ מִשְּׁנֵיהֶם.

אַדְווֹת גַּסּוֹת עַל פְּנֵי הַמַּיִם נִרְגָּעוֹת.
אֵין רוּחַ עַל בִּצַּת הַסּוּף.
רֹאשׁ יַלְדוּתִי קָטָן מֻנָּח פֹּה עַל הַכַּר.
מִתּוֹךְ רִכּוּז עָמֹק אֲנִי רוֹאָה אוֹתוֹ.
מַה שֶּׁעוֹבֵר בֵּינֵינוּ, רֹאשׁ מוּל רֹאשׁ,
לִפְנֵי שֶׁעַפְעַפָּיו נֶעֱצָמִים,
בִּמְאוֹר פָּנָיו הַנְּעִימִים, בְּמַבַּט עַיִן
אֵין לִי רָצוֹן לְהַעֲלוֹת עַל דַּל שְׂפָתַיִם.

1986

Remember, I told her, that time when I was six?
They shampooed my hair and I went out into the street.
The smell of shampoo trailed after me like a cloud.
Then I got sick from the wind and the rain.
I didn't know a thing about reading Greek tragedies,
but the smell of the perfume spread
and I was very sick.
Now I can see it's an unnatural perfume.

What will happen to you now, she said,
they made you a burning dress.
They made me a burning dress, I said. I know.
So why are you standing there, she said,
you've got to be careful.
You know what a burning dress is, don't you?

I know, I said, but I don't know
how to be careful.
The smell of that perfume confuses me.
I said to her, No one has to agree with me,
I don't believe in Greek tragedies.

But the dress, she said, the dress is on fire.
What are you saying, I shouted,
what are you saying?
I'm not wearing a dress at all,
what's burning is me.

tr. Chana Bloch and Ariel Bloch

LITTLE CHILD'S HEAD ON THE PILLOW

Things like that don't hurt me anymore—
not what's said in meanness, or stupidity,
or the ordinary mixture
that has something of both.

The choppy surface of the water grows calm.
No wind in the swamp of reeds.
A little child's head rests here on the pillow.
Deep in concentration, I look at it.
What passes between us, one head to the other,
before his eyelids close,
in the warmth of his face, in a glance—
I do not want to say aloud.

tr. Chana Bloch and Ariel Bloch

רחיפה בגובה נמוך

אֲנִי לֹא כָּאן.
אֲנִי עַל נְקִיקֵי הָרִים מִזְרָחִיִּים
מְנֻמָּרִים פִּסּוֹת שֶׁל קֶרַח
בְּמָקוֹם שֶׁעֵשֶׂב לֹא צָמַח
וְצֵל רָחָב נָטוּשׁ עַל הַמּוֹרָד.
רוֹעָה קְטַנָּה עִם צֹאן עִזִּים
שְׁחוֹרוֹת
הֵגִיחָה שָׁם
מֵאֹהֶל לֹא נִרְאֶה.
לֹא תוֹצִיא אֶת יוֹמָהּ הַיַּלְדָּה הַזֹּאת
בַּמִּרְעֶה.

אֲנִי לֹא כָּאן.
בְּלֹעַ הַר פָּרַח כַּדּוּר אָדֹם,
עֲדַיִן לֹא חַמָּה.
בַּהֶרֶת כְּפוֹר סְמוּקָה וְחוֹלָנִית
מִתְהַפֶּכֶת בַּלֹּעַ.

וְהַקְּטַנָּה הִשְׁכִּימָה כֹּה לָקוּם אֶל הַמִּרְעֶה
גְּרוֹנָהּ אֵינוֹ נָטוּי
עֵינֶיהָ לֹא קְרוּעוֹת בַּפּוּךְ, לֹא מְשַׂקְּרוֹת
אֵינָהּ שׁוֹאֶלֶת, מֵאַיִן יָבוֹא עֶזְרִי.

אֲנִי לֹא כָּאן.
אֲנִי כְּבָר בֶּהָרִים יָמִים רַבִּים
הָאוֹר לֹא יִצְרְבֵנִי. הַכְּפוֹר בִּי לֹא יִגַּע.
שׁוּב אֵין לִי מַה לִּלְקוֹת בְּתַדְהֵמָה.
דְּבָרִים גְּרוּעִים מֵאֵלֶּה רָאִיתִי בְּחַיַּי.

אֲנִי אוֹסֶפֶת שִׂמְלָתִי וּמְרַחֶפֶת
סָמוּךְ מְאֹד אֶל הַקַּרְקַע.
מַה הִיא חָשְׁבָה לָהּ הַיַּלְדָּה הַזֹּאת?
פְּרָאִית לְמַרְאֶה, לֹא רְחוּצָה
לְרֶגַע מִשְׁתּוֹפֶפֶת בִּכְרִיעָה.
לְחָיֶיהָ רַכּוֹת כְּמֶשִׁי
פִּצְעֵי קֹר עַל גַּב יָדָהּ.
פְּזוּרַת דַּעַת, כִּבְיָכוֹל
קַשּׁוּבָה, לַאֲמִתּוֹ שֶׁל דָּבָר.

HOVERING AT A LOW ALTITUDE

I am not here.
I am on those craggy eastern hills
streaked with ice,
where grass doesn't grow
and a wide shadow lies over the slope.
A shepherd girl appears
from an invisible tent,
leading a herd of black goats to pasture.
She won't live out the day,
that girl.

I am not here.
From the deep mountain gorge
a red globe floats up,
not yet a sun.
A patch of frost, reddish, inflamed,
flickers inside the gorge.

The girl gets up early to go to the pasture.
She doesn't walk with neck outstretched
and wanton glances.
She doesn't ask, Whence cometh my help.

I am not here.
I've been in the mountains many days now.
The light will not burn me, the frost
won't touch me.
Why be astonished now?
I've seen worse things in my life.

I gather my skirt and hover
very close to the ground.
What is she thinking, that girl?
Wild to look at, unwashed.
For a moment she crouches down,
her cheeks flushed,
frostbite on the back of her hands.
She seems distracted, but no,
she's alert.

וְעוֹד נוֹתְרוּ לָהּ כָּךְ וְכָךְ שָׁעוֹת.
אֲנִי לֹא בָּעִנְיָן הַזֶּה הָגִיתִי.
מַחְשְׁבוֹתַי רִפְּדוּנִי בִּרְפִידָה שֶׁל מוֹךְ
מָצָאתִי לִי שִׁיטָה פְּשׁוּטָה מְאֹד,
לֹא מִדְרַךְ כַּף רֶגֶל וְלֹא מָעוֹף.
רְחִיפָה בְּגֹבַהּ נָמוּךְ.

אֲבָל בִּנְטוֹת צָהֳרַיִם
שָׁעוֹת רַבּוֹת
לְאַחַר הַזְּרִיחָה
עָלָה הָאִישׁ הַהוּא בָּהָר
כִּמְטַפֵּס לְפִי תֻּמּוֹ.
וְהַיַּלְדָּה קְרוֹבָה אֵלָיו מְאֹד
וְאֵין אִישׁ זוּלָתָם
וְאִם נִסְּתָה לְהִתְחַבֵּא אוֹ צָעֲקָה
אֵין מִסְתּוֹר בֶּהָרִים.

אֲנִי לֹא כָּאן
אֲנִי מֵעַל רִכְסֵי הָרִים פְּרוּעִים וַאֲיֻמִּים
בְּפַאֲתֵי מִזְרָח.
עִנְיָן שֶׁאֵין צְרִיכִים לְהִתְעַכֵּב עָלָיו.
אֶפְשָׁר בְּטַלְטֵלָה עַזָּה וּבִרְחִיפָה
לָחוּג בִּמְהִירוּת הָרוּחַ.
אֶפְשָׁר לְהִסְתַּלֵּק וּלְדַבֵּר עַל לֵב עַצְמִי:
אֲנִי דָבָר לֹא רָאִיתִי.
וְהַקְּטַנָּה עֵינֶיהָ רַק חָרְגוּ מֵחוֹרֵיהֶן
חִכָּהּ יָבֵשׁ כַּחֶרֶס,
כְּשֶׁיָּד קָשָׁה לָפְתָה אֶת שְׂעָרָהּ וְאָחֲזָה בָּהּ
לְלֹא קֶרֶטוֹב חֶמְלָה.

1986

She still has a few hours left.
But that's not what I'm thinking about.
My thoughts cushion me gently, comfortably.
I've found a very simple method,
not with my feet on the ground, and not flying—
hovering
at a low altitude.

Then at noon,
many hours after sunrise,
that man goes up the mountain.
He looks innocent enough.

The girl is right there,
no one else around.
And if she runs for cover, or cries out—
there's no place to hide in the mountains.

I am not here.
I'm above those jagged mountain ranges
in the farthest reaches of the east.
No need to elaborate.
With one strong push I can hover and whirl around
with the speed of the wind.
I can get away and say to myself:
I haven't seen a thing.
And the girl, her palate is dry as a potsherd,
her eyes bulge,
when that hand closes over her hair, grasping it
without a shred of pity.

tr. Chana Bloch and Ariel Bloch

היתה בינינו הבנה

סַבְתָּא,
הַאִם זֶה הָעוֹר הַשָּׁקוּף שֶׁל שְׁתֵּינוּ
עוֹר שֶׁאֵינוֹ מֵגֵן עַל הַבָּשָׂר
כְּלָל וְעִקָּר.
הַסִּפּוּר שֶׁלָּנוּ
יֵשׁ בּוֹ פְּרָטִים שֶׁהַשְׁתִּיקָה יָפָה לָהֶם,
מוּטָב לְהַשְׁאִיר כְּתָמֵי שִׁכְחָה עַל דְּבָרִים שֶׁאֵרְעוּ בֶּעָבָר.
אֲבָל הַדִּמְיוֹן בֵּינֵינוּ
אֵינֶנּוּ מֻטָּל בְּסָפֵק,
מַה שֶּׁהוֹלִיד הֲבָנָה לְלֹא אַהֲדָה.

כּוֹבַע פָּנָמָה וּבְגָדִים שֶׁל גְּבֶרֶת אֵירוֹפִּית
לִפְנֵי שֶׁבָּאוּ הַיָּמִים הָרָעִים
וְכֻרְסוֹת הַקַּשׁ עָמְדוּ לְהִתְפָּרֵק.
הָיִית מְבַשֶּׁלֶת לִפְעָמִים בְּעֵסֶק גָּדוֹל,
לֹא שָׁכַחְתְּ מֵעוֹלָם
לְהַזְכִּיר אֶת הַטִּרְחָה.

וְיָמִים שֶׁהָיִית מִתְוַכַּחַת עִם הָרַדְיוֹ
מִתְנַצַּחַת עִם דַּרְשָׁנֵי פָּרָשַׁת הַשָּׁבוּעַ
בְּפִלְפּוּל שֶׁלָּמַדְתְּ מִסַּבָּא שֶׁלָּךְ.
בְּכָל "בְּנוֹת צִיּוֹן" שֶׁל הָעִיר הַנִּדַּחַת בְּיַאלִיסְטוֹק
לֹא הָיְתָה עַלְמָה גַּאַוְתָנִית כָּמוֹךְ
וַאֲפִלּוּ הָיְתָה לָזֶה מִדָּה שֶׁל הַצְדָּקָה.
סַבְתָּא, אֲנִי מִתְכַּוֶּנֶת אֵלַיִךְ,
הַסַּבְתָּא הָאֵירוֹפִּית, לֹא הַסַּבְתָּא הַשְּׁנִיָּה.
אֲנִי נִזְכֶּרֶת בָּךְ לְעִתִּים לֹא קְרוֹבוֹת
וְלֹא רְחוֹקוֹת.
כְּמוֹ בְּפֶרֶק חַיִּים שֶׁחָלַף,
בְּעָצְמַת זִכָּרוֹן עָמֹק,
בְּחֶמְלָה בִּלְתִּי פְּעִילָה.
אוּלַי זֶה הָעוֹר הַשָּׁקוּף הַמְאַחֵד בֵּינֵינוּ
אַתְּ לְלֹא הֲגָנָה
אֲנִי לְלֹא הֲגָנָה.
תּוֹעֶלֶת לֹא צָמְחָה לָךְ מִזֶּה
וְאַתְּ דָּרַשְׁתְּ בְּמַפְגִּיעַ תּוֹעֶלֶת
וְעַל הַסּוֹף הַהוּא מוּטָב שֶׁלֹּא נְדַבֵּר.
סַבְתָּא, הַחַיִּים הָהֵם נִגְמְרוּ סוֹף סוֹף
וְגַם זֶה הָיָה פִּתְרוֹן.
עַכְשָׁו כְּשֶׁאֵין לָךְ עוֹד צְרָכִים שֶׁל יוֹם יוֹם
אוּלַי יִיטַב לָךְ לָדַעַת
שֶׁהָיְתָה בֵּינֵינוּ הֲבָנָה.

1986

WE HAD AN UNDERSTANDING

Grandmother,
is it the transparent skin we share
skin which doesn't protect the flesh
at all.
Our story
there are details in it better left untold,
better to leave patches of forgetfulness on what happened in the past.
But the definite resemblance
between us
produced understanding without sympathy.

Panama hat and clothes of a European lady
before the hard times set in
and the straw armchairs started to unravel.
Sometimes you would cook with great show,
you never forgot
to mention the trouble it was.

And the days you would argue with the radio
debating the weekly portion with the weekly Bible experts
in the Talmudic logic you learned from your grandfather.
From all the "Daughters of Zion" in your remote town Bialystock
there was no maiden as proud as you
and this pride was even somewhat justified.
Grandmother, I mean you,
the European grandmother, not the other.
I am reminded of you from time
to not so distant time.
As in a period of life gone by
with the intensity of deep memory,
with dormant compassion.
Perhaps it is the transparent skin that unites us
you without protection
me without protection.
No profit ever came of it for you
and you emphatically demanded profit
and about the end it's better not to speak.
Grandmother, that life finally ended
and this too was a solution.
Now that you are without everyday needs
perhaps it's better that you know
we had an understanding.

tr. Rachel Tzvia Back

שוכבת על המים

עִיר יָם תִּיכוֹנִית מַסְרִיחָה
גְּהֻרָה עַל הַמַּיִם
רֹאשָׁהּ בֵּין בִּרְכֶּיהָ
גּוּפָהּ מְזֹהָם בְּעָשָׁן וְאַשְׁפּוֹת.
מִי יָרִים מֵאַשְׁפּוֹת
עִיר יָם תִּיכוֹנִית רְקוּבָה
רַגְלֶיהָ מֻכּוֹת גָּרָב,
בָּנֶיהָ זֶה לָזֶה
גּוֹמְלִים בְּסַכִּינִים.

וְעַכְשָׁו הוּצְפָה הָעִיר אַרְגְּזֵי עֲנָבִים וּשְׁזִיפִים
דֻּבְדְּבָנִים עוֹמְדִים בַּשּׁוּק לְעֵינֵי הָעוֹבְרִים.
הַשֶּׁמֶשׁ הַשּׁוֹקַעַת וְרֻדָּה כַּאֲפַרְסֵק
מִי יוּכַל לִשְׂנֹא בִּרְצִינוּת
עִיר יָם תִּיכוֹנִית מְסֻמֶּמֶת
כְּמוֹ פָּרָה גּוֹעָה מְיַחֶמֶת
כְּתָלֶיהָ שַׁיִשׁ אִיטַלְקִי עִם חוֹל יָם מִתְפּוֹרֵר.
לְבוּשָׁהּ סְחָבוֹת עִם רִקְמָה
אֲבָל הִיא לֹא מִתְכַּוֶּנֶת,
לֹא מִתְכַּוֶּנֶת לְשׁוּם דָּבָר.
וְהַיָּם מָלֵא סָמוּךְ לְמִצְחָהּ הָעִוֵּר
וְהַשֶּׁמֶשׁ שׁוֹלֵחַ אֵלֶיהָ קַרְנַיִם שׁוֹפְעוֹת רַחֲמִים
כַּאֲשֶׁר יָפוּג זַעֲמוֹ לְעֵת הַשְּׁקִיעָה.
וְהַדִּלּוּעִים וְהַמְלָפְפוֹנִים וְהַלִּימוֹנִים הַמִּתְפַּקְּעִים מִצֶּבַע וּמִיץ
נוֹשְׁבִים עָלֶיהָ נִיחוֹחַ קַל שֶׁל בָּשְׂמֵי קַיִץ.
וְהִיא אֵינָהּ רְאוּיָה.
אֵינָהּ רְאוּיָה לְאַהֲבָה אוֹ לְחֶמְלָה.

עִיר יָם תִּיכוֹנִית מְזֹהֶמֶת
אֵיךְ נַפְשִׁי נִקְשְׁרָה בְּנַפְשָׁהּ.
בִּגְלַל מֶשֶׁךְ הַחַיִּים,
בִּגְלַל מֶשֶׁךְ הַחַיִּים.

1992

LYING UPON THE WATER

A stinking Mediterranean city
squats on the water, head between her knees,
body fouled with soot and trash.
Who would raise a rotten Mediterranean
city out of the trash,
feet covered with scabs,
sons dealing knives
to each other.

And now the city is flooded
with crates of grapes and plums,
cherries are displayed
in the market,
the setting sun is pink as a peach.
Who could seriously hate
a Mediterranean city stoned
like a cow mooing in heat,
her walls Italian marble
and crumbling sand.
Clad in embroidered rags,
she has no intention
no intention at all.
And the sea brims at her blind forehead
and the sun shines through her, flushed with compassion,
as its fury fades in the sunset.
And the pumpkins cucumbers lemons,
bursting with juice and color
exhale a light fragrance
of summer perfumes over her.
And she is not deserving.
Not deserving of pity or love.

A rotten Mediterranean city—
how my soul is bound to hers.
As life goes on
as life goes on.

tr. Tsipi Keller

אמא מתהלכת

אִמָּא מִתְהַלֶּכֶת עִם יֶלֶד מֵת בַּבֶּטֶן
הַיֶּלֶד הַזֶּה לֹא נוֹלַד עֲדַיִן.
בְּבוֹא יוֹמוֹ יִוָּלֵד הַיֶּלֶד הַמֵּת
רֹאשׁ תְּחִלָּה, גֵּו וְעַכּוּז
וְהוּא בְּיָדָיו לֹא יְנוֹפֵף
וְהוּא לֹא יִצְרַח צְרִיחָה רִאשׁוֹנָה
וְלֹא יְטַפְּחוּ לוֹ עַל אֲחוֹרָיו
וְלֹא יַזְלִפוּ טִפּוֹת לְעֵינָיו
וְלֹא יְחַתְּלוּ אוֹתוֹ
לְאַחַר רְחִיצַת הַגּוּף.
הוּא לֹא יִהְיֶה כְּמוֹ יֶלֶד חַי.
וְאִמָּא שֶׁלּוֹ לֹא תִהְיֶה רְגוּעָה וְגֵאָה אַחֲרֵי הַלֵּדָה
וְגַם לֹא תִהְיֶה דְּאוּגָה לְגַבֵּי עֲתִידוֹ,
וְלֹא תִשְׁאַל אֶת עַצְמָהּ בַּמֶּה תְּפַרְנֵס אוֹתוֹ
וְאִם יֵשׁ לָהּ דֵּי חָלָב
וְאִם יֵשׁ לָהּ דֵּי בְּגָדִים
וְאִם יֵשׁ בַּחֶדֶר מָקוֹם לְעוֹד עֲרִיסָה.
הַיֶּלֶד הַזֶּה צַדִּיק גָּמוּר,
לֹא נִבְרָא בְּטֶרֶם נִבְרָא.
וְיִהְיֶה לוֹ קֶבֶר קָטָן בִּפְאַת בֵּית הַקְּבָרוֹת
וְיוֹם זִכָּרוֹן קָטָן
וּמַזְכֶּרֶת לֹא גְדוֹלָה.
וְאֵלֶּה תּוֹלְדוֹת הַיֶּלֶד
שֶׁהָרְגוּ אוֹתוֹ בְּבֶטֶן אִמּוֹ
בְּחֹדֶשׁ יָנוּאָר 1988
בְּנְסִבּוֹת פּוֹלִיטִיּוֹת בִּטְחוֹנִיּוֹת.

1992

רות בן-דוד

מתוך יוצאת להבראה

הַגֶּרְמָנִים אִשְּׁרוּ לִי פִּצּוּיִים.
כְּשֶׁמַּצְּבֵי הוּרַע, הַגֶּרְמָנִים אִשְּׁרוּ לִי הַבְרָאָה,
הֲרֵי שֶׁאֲנִי מְאַשֶּׁרֶת לָהֶם בַּטּוֹב וּבָרָע
וּמַה יָּכוֹל כְּבָר לְהַפְרִיד בֵּינֵינוּ?
שְׁנֵינוּ נִפְגָּשִׁים בְּיַם הַמָּוֶת.

***

A MOTHER WALKS AROUND

A mother walks around with a dead child in her belly.
The child hasn't been born yet.
When his time comes, the dead child will be born,
first the head, then the rest of him,
and he won't wave his hands and cry his first cry,
and they won't slap him on the back
and put drops in his eyes,
and they won't diaper him when they've washed his body.
He won't be like a living child.
And his mother won't be calm and proud after his birth.
She won't have to worry about his future,
she won't ask herself how to support him
or if she has enough milk or clothing
or if there's room in the house for another crib.
The child is a perfect saint already,
there's never been a saint like that child.
And he'll have a small grave at the edge of the cemetery,
a small memorial day
and not much remembrance.
And this is the history of the child
who was killed in his mother's belly
in the month of January, 1988,
for reasons of state security.

tr. Chana Bloch and Ariel Bloch

RUTH ALPERN BEN-DAVID

***from* SETTING OUT FOR CONVALESCENCE**

The Germans granted me reparations.
When I became worse, the Germans granted me convalescence,
anyway they take me for granted, for better or worse,
what can separate us now?
We both meet at the Dead Sea.

***

הַמָּלוֹן מָלֵא אוֹתָם כַּמַּיִם לַיָּם.
אֲנִי מְבִינָה אֶת שְׂפָתָם, זוֹכֶרֶת עוֹד כַּמָּה מִלִּים:
רָאוּס — זֶה שָׁלוֹם. יוּדִישֶׁה שְׁוַויין — זֶה הָאַבָּא שֶׁלִּי, שַׁיְסֶה — הָיוּ יְהוּדִים.

***

אֲנִי עוֹשָׂה לָהֶם הָאֲנָשָׁה וְהֵם יוֹצְאִים לִי דֵי דוֹמִים.
בָּאִים — הוֹלְכִים,
יוֹשְׁבִים — קָמִים,
צוֹחֲקִים
וְחָסֵר רַק שֶׁהֵם גַּם בּוֹכִים לִפְעָמִים.
לוֹעֲסִים בְּשִׁינַּיִ וִיטָמִינִים, מַשְׁאִירִים בַּצַּלָּחוֹת לְמֵאָה סִינִים.

***

"אִם לֹא תֹּאכְלִי אֶת הַדַּיְסָה, תֹּאכַל אוֹתָךְ הַמְּכַשֵּׁפָה",
אִם אֵין חָלָב וְאֵין גְּרִיסִים, יֹאכְלוּ אוֹתִי הַגֶּרְמָנִים.
כָּל כָּךְ הַרְבֵּה אֹכֶל זוֹרְקִים, מַבְרִיאִים וְלוֹקְחִים פִּצּוּיִים.

***

בַּיָּמִים מַבְרִיאִים, בַּלֵּילוֹת כַּדּוּרִים.
בָּאַרְנָק שֶׁלְּיַד הַמִּטָּה, מוּכָנִים לְהַנְשִׁים, חִיּוּכֵי הַנְּכָדִים
(שֵׁם שֵׁנִי: נְקָמָה וְנֶחָמָה).
בְּשַׁבָּת מְזַמְּרִים לְבֵית אַבָּא.
יָד אַחַת חֲסֵרָה לְמִשְׂחַק הַקְּלָפִים.

***

וְיֵשׁ לִפְעָמִים שֶׁבַּלַּיְלָה,
נִפְתָּחִים מְגוּפֵי הַסְּכָרִים, בְּרָאשֵׁי הֶהָרִים הָרְחוֹקִים, שָׁם לְמַעְלָה.
קְצָרִים כַּבָּרָק הַזְּרָמִים.
סוֹחֲפִים, מְנַקִּים וְשׁוֹקְעִים
בַּמָּקוֹם הַנָּמוּךְ בְּיוֹתֵר בָּעוֹלָם,
כְּאִלּוּ רַק מָשָׁל הָיָה.

1997

The hotel is full of them like water in the sea.
I understand their language, still remember a few words:
Raus—that's hello, *jüdische Schwein*—that's my father, *Scheisse*—once there were Jews.

***

I humanize them and make us rather like each other.
Coming—going,
sitting—standing,
laughing
they should cry now and then.
Chew with their vitamin teeth, leave enough food on the plates for a hundred Chinese.

***

"If you don't eat your porridge, the witch will eat you."
If there's no milk and no barley, the Germans will eat me.
So much food is thrown out, while convalescing and taking reparations.

***

Convalescence by day, pills at night.
In the wallet beside the bed, the smiles of the grandchildren ready to resuscitate
(middle names: Revenge and Comfort).
On the Sabbath songs of home.
One hand is missing for the card game.

***

And sometimes at night
the dams open up there on top of the far hills.
Quick as flash floods
that sweep away, cleanse and sink
to the lowest place in the world,
as if it were all just a parable.

tr. Lisa Katz

יפו, יולי 1948

אִישׁ לֹא רָאָה מַה שֶּׁעָשִׂיתִי בֵּינְתַיִם לְיַד הַגָּדֵר.
אֲנָשִׁים עָסְקוּ בְּהוֹבָלַת פְּסַנְתֵּרִים, שְׁטִיחִים,
בְּהַרְתָּחַת מֵי הַשְּׁתִיָּה.
אֲנָשִׁים אֲחֵרִים הָלְכוּ עִם יָדַיִם לְמַעְלָה.
זֶה לֹא הָיָה חֲלוֹם. הָיָה לִי יָבֵשׁ בַּפֶּה
וְהַמַּיִם שֶׁהֻרְתְּחוּ עוֹד לֹא פּוּשְׁרִים, לָכֵן בֵּינְתַיִם
מִבַּעַד לַגָּדֵר אֲנִי עוֹשָׂה מִסְחָר עִם יַלְדָּה וְרֻדָּה
מַסְטִיק מִפֶּה רָטֹב לְפֶה יָבֵשׁ בְּעַד פְּרוּסָה עִם חֶמְאָה
מְלוּחָה אֲמֶרִיקָאִית, וְהַזְּבוּבִים שֶׁאָכְלוּ מֻגְלָה מֵעֵינֶיהָ
מִתְיַשְּׁבִים עַל עֵינַי.
בֵּינְתַיִם יָבוֹא יְצוֹא, בֵּינְתַיִם תַּיָּרוּת.

כָּכָה זֶה הָיָה בְּיוּלִי 1948
כְּשֶׁפִּנּוּ אֶת הַנָּשִׁים וְהַיְלָדִים מֵהֶחָזִית לְיָפוֹ הַכְּבוּשָׁה
וּמִשְּׁנֵי עֶבְרֵי הַגָּדֵר הִסְתּוֹבְבוּ פְּלִיטִים מֵהָעוֹלָם כֻּלּוֹ.

1981

כליבות

מִיָּד הֶחֱזַקְתִּי אֶת הָאִישׁ, הִדַּקְתִּי אוֹתוֹ, לָחַצְתִּי אֶת חֲלָקָיו בְּכָל שְׁרִירֵי בִּטְנִי,
כְּמוֹ נַגָּר, אַחֲרֵי שֶׁהִלְבִּישׁ אֶת כְּלִיבוֹת הַמַּתֶּכֶת עַל הָאָרוֹן שֶׁהִתְפָּרֵק פִּתְאֹם,
מַבְרִיג וּמַבְרִיג אֶת יָדִית הַמַּכְשִׁיר, וְנֶאֱנָק קְצָת עִם הִדּוּק אֵיבָרָיו הַפְּנִימִיִּים,
כָּכָה הִדַּקְתִּי אֵלַי אֶת הָאִישׁ, בַּעֲמִידָה, בְּכָל זָוִיּוֹת הַבַּרְזֶל שֶׁנִּמְצְאוּ בִּי,
כְּשֶׁהָרוֹפֵא יָצָא וְאָמַר שֶׁהַיֶּלֶד שֶׁלָּנוּ לֹא.

1990

HAMUTAL BAR-YOSEF

JAFFA, JULY 1948

No one notices what I am doing by the border fence.
In the meantime people are busy moving pianos, carpets,
boiling the drinking water.
Other people walk with their hands up.
This is not a dream. My mouth is dry
and the water not yet lukewarm, so in the meantime
through the border fence I am doing business with a thin girl,
bubble gum from wet mouth to dry, for a slice of bread
with salty American butter, and the flies on her pus-filled
eyes settle on mine.
In the meantime import, export, tourism.

That's how it was in Jaffa in July 1948
when women and children were evacuated to occupied Jaffa
and refugees from the whole world swarmed on both sides of the fence.

tr. Shirley Kaufman

VISE

Immediately I held the man, gripped him, pressed against him with all my stomach muscles, the way a carpenter, after putting the metal vise around the cupboard that has suddenly collapsed, twists and twists the handle of the tool, and groans from the clenching of his guts, that's how I clenched the man to me, standing with every angle of iron in me, when the doctor came out and said our child would not

tr. Shirley Kaufman

אסתר אטינגר

סוגר הצער

זֶה סוּגַר הַצַּעַר
פָּחוֹת אֲפִלּוּ מֵאַרְבַּע עַל אַרְבַּע, רִצְפַּת בֶּטוֹן
חֲשׂוּפָה עָלָיו הוֹלֶכֶת לְבִיאָה, מִקָּצֶה אֶל קָצֶה
מִסּוֹף אֶל סוֹף, שֵׁשׁ פְּסִיעוֹת מְתוּנוֹת וְשָׁלֹשׁ
בִּסְעָרָה וּשְׁתַּיִם בִּקְפִיצוֹת כְּאֵב.

זֶה סוּגַר הַצַּעַר
שְׁלֹשָׁה קִירוֹת מְזֻיָּנֵי בַּרְזֶל יְרַקְרַק מְכֻסֶּה טִיחַ
וְסוֹרְגִים הַמַּחְלִידִים מִדֵּי חֹרֶף, בַּעֲדָם גֶּשֶׁם וְשֶׁמֶשׁ
וְרוּחַ וְעָלִים וּפְנֵי אֲנָשִׁים חַמִּים, וּבַלַּיְלָה אוֹרוֹת.
הִיא רוֹאָה אֶת כָּל זֶה, אֲבָל עֵינֶיהָ בָּרִצְפָּה הַמְטֻיַּחַת
פַּרְסָתוֹ מְחֻסְפָּס וְזָהֹב בִּשְׁבִילָהּ
וְרַגְלֶיהָ מוֹלִיכוֹת אוֹתָהּ לַפִּנָּה, שָׁם הִיא מִתְכַּדֶּרֶת
לְפִקְעַת צֶמֶר גְּדוֹלָה וִיבֵשָׁה וּבְפִנָּה אַחֶרֶת הִיא
שׁוֹטַחַת אֶת עַצְמָהּ הֲלוּמַת יִסּוּרִים.
כִּי זֶה סוּגַר הַצַּעַר
זֶה סֵבֶר הַצַּעַר הַזּוֹרֵם בָּעוֹרְקִים הַמְכֻסִּים
בְּפַרְוָה מַשְׁחִירָה, מוֹלִיךְ מִסּוֹף אָטוּם לְסוֹף חָשׁוּךְ
פַּעַם בִּמְתִינוּת, פַּעַם בִּסְעָרָה,
וְזֶה מְזוֹנָהּ הַיְחִידִי, טֶרֶף לְבֵיתָהּ

הִיא יוֹדַעַת, גַּם רָמְזוּ לָהּ
שֶׁהַסּוֹרְגִים הֵם תַּפְאוּרָה, שֶׁהַמַּתֶּכֶת מְצֻיֶּרֶת עַל קַרְטוֹן
וּמַהוּ קַרְטוֹן בִּשְׁבִיל לְבִיאָה, וּמַהוּ בַּרְזֶל
הַכֹּל פָּתוּחַ
וְהִיא לֹא יוֹצֵאת לַדֶּשֶׁא, לַשֶּׁמֶשׁ, לַפְּרָחִים
לִפְנֵי הָאֲנָשִׁים הָרַכִּים וְהַחַמִּים הַמִּשְׁתָּאִים לָהּ
הַנִּדְחָקִים לִרְאוֹת אוֹתָהּ, הָאוֹמְרִים לָהּ עַד לְזָרָא
קוּמִי צְאִי לָךְ
טַלְטְלִי אֶת רֹאשֵׁךְ בִּתְנוּעָה סְבוּבִית עֲגֻלָּה
קוּמִי צְאִי שַׁעַטִי
מַרְבַּדֵּי מֶרְחָבִים שָׁם, עוֹלָם

1991

ESTHER ETTINGER

THE SADNESS CAGE

It's the sadness cage
not even ten by ten, a lioness
walks back and forth on a bare concrete floor—
from end to end, from side to side, six measured paces and three
wild ones and two leaps of pain.

It's the sadness cage
three walls plastered over greenish iron studs,
and rain and sun and wind and leaves, and people's hot faces,
and lights at night, through bars that rust every winter.
She sees all this, but she watches the whitewashed floor—
her rough and golden fresco
and her legs take her into the corner where she rolls up
into a big dry woolly ball and in another corner she
sprawls out pain-struck.
Because it's the sadness cage
the sugar of sadness that streams in her veins covered
in blackening fur, leads from dead end to dark end
sometimes measured, sometimes wild,
her only food *the meat of her household.*[1]

She knows, it was also suggested
that the bars are a stage set, that the metal is painted on cardboard
and what's cardboard to a lioness, and what's iron
everything's open
and she doesn't go out to the grass, the sun, the flowers
in front of the soft warm people who wonder at her
who push in to see her, who tell her ad nauseam
rise up go forth
shake your head in a circular motion
rise up go forth race
out there carpets of space, a world.

tr. Lisa Katz

1. Proverbs 31.15.

חדוה הרכבי

כאשר היא יוצאת לבדה

כַּאֲשֶׁר הִיא יוֹצֵאת, לְבַדָּהּ, בַּלֵּילוֹת

מַה הִיא רוֹצָה.
לָצוּד אֲרָיוֹת?
לַחְפֹּר אֲדָמָה?
לִשְׁמֹעַ קוֹלוֹת שֶׁאֵינָם עַל הָאָרֶץ?
לִקְלֹט מִן הַיָּם אוֹתוֹת אַזְהָרָה?

מַה הִיא רוֹצָה.
בְּנֵי אָדָם לְהַרְגִּישׁ מֵרֶגַע לְרֶגַע?
(בֵּית־קָפֶה מְאֻחָר מַזְכִּיר לָהּ קוֹצִים?)
לְאַזֵּן אֶת הַמַּיִם, זְמַן־מָה, בְּיָדֶיהָ?
לְמַלֵּא אֶת הַשֶּׁמֶשׁ עוֹפוֹת מוּזָרִים?

מַה הִיא רוֹצָה.
עֲדִינוּת הִיא דָּבָר שֶׁאֵין בּוֹ שְׂרָרָה
עַל־כֵּן הִיא הוֹלֶכֶת עַל קְצֵה אֶצְבָּעוֹת.
לִפְעָמִים הִיא עוֹמֶדֶת בְּרֹאשׁ שַׁיָּרוֹת
שֶׁל כְּלָבִים אֲדֻמִּים
שֶׁצִּיְּרָה
וְנִדְמֶה לָהּ שֶׁהִיא מְלַוָּה שַׁיָּרוֹת
לִפְעָמִים הִיא יוֹשֶׁבֶת בְּתוֹךְ חָלִיל וָרֹד
וְנִדְמֶה שֶׁהִיא מְבַקֶּשֶׁת עֵצָה
אֵין לָהּ אֲוִיר—

מַה הִיא רוֹצָה.

1981

ילדה מאושרת מאוד

כְּמוֹ שֶׁאֲנִי אוֹמֶרֶת,
הִיא הָיְתָה תָּמִיד יַלְדָּה
מְאֻשֶּׁרֶת מְאֹד, הָיְתָה תָּמִיד
יַלְדָּה קְטַנָּה, מְאֻשֶּׁרֶת
וְאִם הָיָה קַיִץ
שַׂמְנוּ אוֹתָהּ בַּגִּנָּה
עַל הָאֲדָמָה
מִתַּחַת לָעֵצִים
עַל הַשָּׁטִיחַ
וְהָיְתָה לָהּ רְצוּעַת כֶּלֶב מִכָּאן
וּרְצוּעַת כֶּלֶב מִכָּאן
וְרוּחַ אֱלֹהִים הָיְתָה מְרַחֶפֶת בַּגִּנָּה
וּכְבָשִׂים בְּנֵי שָׁנָה שׁוֹטְטוּ מִכָּל צַד וּפִנָּה

HEDVA HARECHAVI

WHEN SHE GOES OUT ALONE

Nights when she goes out alone

what does she want.
To hunt lions?
Drill the ground?
Hear unearthly voices?
Receive warning signals from the sea?

What does she want.
To feel human beings moment by moment?
(A late-night café reminds her of thorns?)
To balance water briefly in her hands?
To fill the sun with strange fowl?

What does she want.
Gentleness has no force.
That's why she walks on tiptoe.
Sometimes she commands convoys
of red dogs
she has painted
and thinks she's their escort.
Sometimes she sits in a pink flute
and thinks she's asking for help
she needs air—

what does she want.

tr. Tsipi Keller

A VERY CHEERFUL GIRL

As I say,
she was always a very cheerful girl, always
a little cheerful girl,
and summers
we'd put her in the park
on the ground
under trees
on the rug
and she had a dog-leash
here and a dog-leash there
and the spirit of God hovered over the park
and yearling lambs roamed all over

כְּמוֹ שֶׁאֲנִי אוֹמֶרֶת,
הִיא הָיְתָה תָּמִיד יַלְדָּה מְאֻשֶּׁרֶת
כַּמָּה הָיְתָה יַלְדָּה מְאֻשֶּׁרֶת
יַלְדָּה עִם דֶּרֶךְ־אֶרֶץ
שֶׁלֹּא גוֹרֶמֶת דְּאָגָה
יַלְדָּה חוֹשֶׁבֶת, מִתְחַשֶּׁבֶת, מְאֻזֶּנֶת
אַחֲרָאִית. לִפְעָמִים הָיְתָה יוֹשֶׁבֶת בְּזָוִית
עֵינֶיהָ עֲצוּמוֹת וּמְחַיֶּכֶת
וְהָיָה עֶרֶב וְהָיָה בֹּקֶר
כָּל דָּבָר וְדָבָר הָיָה בְּרֹךְ
בַּעֲדִינוּת, בְּאַהֲבָה
תָּאֵר לְעַצְמְךָ, יַלְדָּה תַּמָּה וּנְקִיָּה
מְשַׂחֶקֶת עַל הָאָרֶץ
וְכָל הָאָרֶץ שָׁרָה עַל־יָדָהּ
כְּמוֹ שֶׁאֲנִי אוֹמֶרֶת,
הִיא הָיְתָה תָּמִיד יַלְדָּה מְאֻשֶּׁרֶת
יַלְדָּה מְיֻחֶדֶת בְּמִינָהּ
חִיּוּנִית, לְבָבִית וַאֲפִלּוּ יָפָה
הָיָה לָהּ לֵב זָהָב, כְּלוֹמַר
כָּל כָּךְ קַלָּה לְשִׁנּוּיִים
מֵעוֹלָם לֹא בָּכְתָה, כְּלוֹמַר
מֵעוֹלָם לֹא עָשְׂתָה כָּךְ
כְּשֶׁהָיְתָה עִם אֲחֵרִים
לֹא קִלְקְלָה צַעֲצוּעִים
(רַק פַּעַם אַחַת. אוֹ שְׁתַּיִם)
וְלֹא דִּבְּרָה דְּבָרִים מְעֻרְפָּלִים
לֹא, לֹא נִרְאָה
שֶׁהָיִיתִי חֲסֵרָה לָהּ.
טוֹב, אָז לֹא.
(לַמְרוֹת שֶׁאֲנִי אִמָּא שֶׁלָּהּ
וְלַמְרוֹת שֶׁהִיא הָיְתָה, תָּמִיד,
הַבַּת הַקְּטַנָּה שֶׁלִּי).
אוּלַי לֹא הִכַּרְתִּי אוֹתָהּ

אֲבָל תָּמִיד הָיִיתִי הֲגוּנָה אֵלֶיהָ.
טוֹב, לֹא כָּל־כָּךְ קְרוֹבָה
אֲבָל הָיָה אִכְפַּת לִי מַה קּוֹרֶה.
זוֹ הַהַתְחָלָה.
זֶה הָרֶקַע.
אֵלּוּ הַפְּרָטִים.
אֵלֶּה הָעֻבְדּוֹת.
הִיא הָיְתָה כָּל מַה שֶּׁצִּפִּינוּ וְקִוִּינוּ:
יַלְדָּה מְאֻשֶּׁרֶת מְאֹד.

1985

as I say,
she was always a cheerful child
how cheerful she was
a girl with nice manners
who never made you worry
a thoughtful girl, considerate, balanced,
dependable. At times she would sit in a corner
eyes shut, smiling
and it was evening and morning
everything gentle
with tenderness with love
just imagine, a neat innocent child
at play on the ground
and the entire earth sings for her
as I say,
she was always a happy child
a very special girl,
lively, sweet and even pretty
she had a heart of gold, I mean
so adaptable to change
she never cried, I mean
she never did that
with others
never broke toys
(only once or twice)
never muddled her speech
no, it didn't seem as if she
needed me.
Well, so she didn't
(even though I'm her mother
even though she was always
my little daughter),
maybe I didn't know her

but I was always decent to her.
All right, not so close
but I cared about what happens.
This is the beginning.
This is the background
These are the details.
These are the facts.
She was everything we expected and hoped for:
a very cheerful girl.

tr. Tsipi Keller

נורית זרחי

הִיא יוֹסֵף

יוֹשֶׁבֶת רָחֵל בָּאֹהֶל
קְוֻצַּת שֵׂעָר אַחַר קְוֻצָּה תֵּאָסֵף
לְהַחְבִּיא תַּחַת כִּפַּת מֶשִׁי
אֶת שְׂעַר בִּתָּהּ הַקְּטַנָּה הִיא יוֹסֵף

כִּי אִם רָצִית בְּיֶלֶד
וְיָמִינְךָ קְרֵבִים לִנְטוֹת
מַה יַּעֲשֶׂה מִלְּבַד שֶׁקֶר
אֶת רְצוֹן הָאֵל לְהַטּוֹת

יוֹשֶׁבֶת הַקְּטַנָּה בָּאֹהֶל
בִּכְתֹנֶת פַּסִּים מְצֻיֶּרֶת
וּבַנִּגְלֶה הִיא נַעַר
וּבַנִּסְתָּר נַעֲרָה

עַכְשָׁו כָּל הָעוֹלָם יוֹדֵעַ
כִּי נֶאֶסְפָה חֶרְפָּתָהּ
יָלְדָה רָחֵל בֵּן יוֹרֵשׁ לְאָבִיו
וְהִיא בִּתָּהּ

וּמַבִּיטָה הָאֵם בִּשְׂעַר הַבַּת
עָתִיד קוֹרֵאת בְּאֹפֶל שְׂעָרָהּ
הַחֲלוֹמוֹת בִּתִּי יַפִּילוּךְ לַבּוֹר
וּמִשָּׁם לְחָצֵר זָרָה

יוֹשֶׁבֶת הַקְּטַנָּה בָּאֹהֶל
שׁוֹמַעַת אֶת דְּבַר אִמָּהּ
וְהִיא אֲחוּזַת קֶסֶם
וְהִיא אֲחוּזַת אֵימָה

וְרָחֵל מַמְשִׁיכָה נִרְעֶשֶׁת
לֹא תַּמּוּ הַמַּהֲלוּמוֹת
בְּבֵית כֶּלֶא תֵּחָבְשִׁי
וְתֵחָלְצִי שׁוּב מִידֵי חֲלוֹמוֹת

חֲלוֹמוֹת יַצִּילוּךְ בִּתִּי
חֲלוֹמוֹת יַפִּילוּךְ לְבוֹר
וְרָחֵל יָמֶיהָ קְצָרִים
מִכְּדֵי סוֹד בִּתָּהּ לִפְתֹּר

יוֹשֶׁבֶת הַקְּטַנָּה בָּאֹהֶל
מַקְשִׁיבָה בִּנְשִׁימָה עֲצוּרָה
וּבַנִּגְלֶה הִיא נַעַר
וּבַנִּסְתָּר נַעֲרָה

1983

NURIT ZARCHI

SHE IS JOSEPH

Rachel sits in the tent
and gathers each curl closer
to hide them under the silken cap
of her little daughter Joseph,

because if you wanted a son
and your time was running out,
what else would you do but lie
to alter what God had done.

The little one sits in the tent
in a coat of colored stripes.
Revealed to all—a boy,
a girl whose sex is hidden.

And now the whole world knows
her shame is gone. For his father
Rachel brought forth a son
and she is her mother's daughter.

And the mother reads the future
in the dark hair of her daughter:
dreams will cast you in a pit,
a foreign court soon after.

The little one sits in the tent,
she hears the words of her mother,
and she is caught in a spell,
and she is caught in horror,

while Rachel continues, stunned,
the shocks grow more extreme:
you will be locked in prison
and freed once more by dreams.

Dreams will save you, daughter,
will cast you in a pit.
But Rachel's time is short
for the riddle of her daughter.

The little one sits in the tent,
holds her breath and listens.
Revealed to all—a boy,
a girl whose sex is hidden.

tr. Shirley Kaufman

בקלילות

בְּקְלִילוּת, כְּמוֹ שֶׁהַדָּגִים הַמְצֻיָּרִים
חוֹזְרִים אֶל הַנָּהָר,
כָּךְ הַדֶּרֶךְ הַלֹּא נְכוֹנָה שֶׁבָּחַרְתִּי בַּחֲלוֹם,
כּוֹרֶכֶת אוֹתִי סְבִיב צַוָּארִי, וְחָזוֹר,
כְּמוֹ צָעִיף הַזּוֹהֵר בְּכָל צִבְעֵי הַטָּעוּת—
כְּמוֹ לֹא נִקְבַּעְתִּי גּוּף,
כְּאִלּוּ עֲלֵי הָעֵצִים אֵינָם עֲשׂוּיִים אֲוִיר,
אוֹ הַיַּלְדָּה שֶׁהִנַּחְתִּי לִישֹׁן
תַּחַת לְשׁוֹנִי, אִם תָּקוּם,
כָּל עֲבָרִי הַמְקֻפָּל יִפְרַח בָּאֲוִיר.
בִּקְלִילוּת כְּאִלּוּ מִי שֶׁהַגּוּף
עוֹמֵד לְהִלָּקַח מִמֶּנּוּ, לֹא יְוַתֵּר—
כְּאוֹתוֹ בֵּן שֶׁמִּבֶּהָלַת אָבִיו
אִשֵּׁר אֶת הַמַּלְאָךְ בְּעֵינָיו—
יוֹתֵר מִצֵּל הַמְאַשֵּׁר אֶת הַנִּרְאֶה
וּבְעֹמֶק הַפַּחַד יִפָּתַח בַּחֲרִיקָה שַׁעַר.

1994

בלוז לתינוקות נולדים

כָּכָה בְּשֶׁקֶט בְּשֶׁקֶט
בְּעֵינַיִם עֲצוּמוֹת, נוֹשְׁרִים הַתִּינוֹקוֹת לָעוֹלָם.
כְּמוֹ גַּרְגְּרֵי גֶּשֶׁם, בַּחֹשֶׁךְ, מִכַּף יָד עֲנָקִית,
לְתוֹךְ אַבּוּבִים, לְתוֹךְ אֹהֶל עַכָּבִישׁ, תַּפּוּחַ קַר.

שֶׁקֶט בָּעוֹלָם, בְּתָאֵי כַּוָּרוֹת שְׁקוּפִים הַתִּינוֹקוֹת יְשֵׁנִים,
וּמוּזָרִים לַבֹּקֶר, בְּעֵינַיִם כְּחַלְחַלּוֹת מֵחֹשֶׁךְ
מְגַשְּׁשִׁים, חֲמִימֵי שְׂפָתַיִם, מִתְמַתְּחִים, מְפַהֲקִים,
בִּזְרוֹעוֹת תַּפּוּחַ, בְּשִׁנֵּי סֻכָּר, בְּחָלָב, בָּאַהֲבָה, בַּחוֹל הַדַּקִּיק.

אֲבָל מִי בּוֹכֶה בָּעוֹלָם,
מָה אֲנִי שׁוֹמַעַת, קוֹל בְּכִי תַּמְרוּרִי.
גָּבוֹהַּ מְיַלֶּלֶת כֶּלֶב, מִצְרִיחַת שַׁחַף,
בְּכִי מֵעַל לַגַּגּוֹת בְּכִי מִתַּחַת לַכְּבִישִׁים.
אִישׁ כְּבָר לֹא יַצְלִיחַ לִישֹׁן לְעוֹלָם.

בָּרְחוֹב שָׁרָה הַמַּקְהֵלָה.
תִּינוֹקוֹת בּוֹאוּ לַסְּעוּדָה הַמַּגְדִּילָה,
וְיוֹצְאִים הַתִּינוֹקוֹת מִן הַמְּגֵרָה,
עַל עָגוּר, עַל תֵּבָה בַּנָּהָר, רוֹכְבִים עַל צַוַּאר פָּרָה,
אֲבָל הַבְּכִי מַמְשִׁיךְ וְחוֹדֵר:
זֶה הַתִּינוֹק, אֵיפֹה הוּא קָבוּר, אֵיפֹה הִנַּחְתִּי
אֵיפֹה שָׁכַחְתִּי אֶת הַתִּינוֹק, בְּלִי מַיִם אוֹ אֲוִיר?

LIGHTLY

Lightly, like painted fish
going back to the river,
the wrong way I chose in the dream
winds me around my neck, and round again
like a scarf, brilliant with all the colors of mistake—
as if I were not assigned a body,
as if tree-leaves are not made of air.
And if the girl I let sleep under my tongue
should rise, my pleated past
would dissolve in the air.
Lightly, as if the one whose body
is about to be snatched won't let go—
the way that son, on account of his father's fright,
affirmed the angel in his eyes
more than a shadow that affirms the visible—
a gate will open, creaking, at the bottom of fear.

tr. Tsipi Keller

BABY BLUES

And so quietly, quietly,
eyes shut, babies drop into the world.
Like specks of rain, in the dark, from a gigantic hand,
into shafts, into a spider's tent, a cold apple.

Silence in the universe: the babies sleep in translucent beehives,
and strange to the morning, eyes bluish with darkness,
they grope warm-lipped, stretch, yawn,
with appled arms, sugared teeth, in milk, in love, in fine sand.

But who weeps in the universe,
what do I hear, bitter wails.
More shrill than a dog's whine, a seagull's cry,
weeping above the roofs weeping under the highways.
No one will ever get to sleep.

A chorus sings in the street.
Babies, come and eat the nourishing meal.
And the babies emerge from the drawer,
riding a crane, a basket in the river, a cow's neck,
but the perverse weeping continues:
this is the baby, where is it buried, where did I put it,
where did I forget the baby, without water or air?

בּוֹאוּ לַשֻּׁלְחָן. הָאֹכֶל מִתְקָרֵר.
אֲבָל אֵיךְ לִבְלֹעַ וְהַקּוֹל בַּגָּרוֹן.
פִּתְחוּ, פִּתְחוּ קוּפְסָאוֹת חֲלוּדוֹת, קְבָרִים שֶׁלֹּא נִשְׁדְּדוּ אַף פַּעַם,
הַקְשִׁיבוּ: אֵיפֹה הוּא קָבוּר,
אֵיפֹה הִנַּחְתִּי אֵיפֹה שָׁכַחְתִּי אֶת הַתִּינוֹק בְּלִי מַיִם אוֹ אֲוִיר?

שֶׁקֶט בָּעוֹלָם,
אֵין כְּבָר לָדַעַת עַל מָה, עַל מִי.
עָלַי עָלַי, נִשְׁמָע הַקּוֹל מִן הָאֶבֶן.
זֶה הַתִּינוֹק, כְּמוֹ שִׁדְרַת עָלֶה שָׁקוּף. תִּתְכּוֹפְפוּ לְהַבִּיט,
תְּנוּ לוֹ לִשְׁתּוֹת, תְּנוּ לוֹ לֶאֱכֹל, אִם נִשְׁאַר—

1996

מתוך הלילה הוא יום חזק

1

תִּסְלַח לִי שֶׁאֲנִי מִתְפָּרֶצֶת
נִדְמֶה לִי שֶׁיָּרוּ בִּי, אֲדוֹנִי.
נִשְׁעַנְתִּי עַל אַהֲבָה בְּטָעוּת מֻחְלֶטֶת,

אֲבָל מִי מְדַבֵּר עַל דִּיּוּק
בִּזְמַן שֶׁהוֹרְגִים נְשִׂיאִים וִילָדִים?
וְשֶׁלֹּא אֶקַּח לַלֵּב אַתָּה אוֹמֵר.

יוֹתֵר מִפַּעַם אֲנִי נִשְׁמֶרֶת לְהֵרָדֵם
בְּעֵינַיִם פְּקוּחוֹת כְּמוֹ יוֹנַת הַבָּר
שֶׁבְּאֶדֶן הַחַלּוֹן הֵטִילָה לִי בֵּיצָה

וְלַמָּחֳרָת כְּלוּם, לֹא שְׁבָרִים אֲפִלּוּ,
נָסוֹגָה כְּמוֹ אוֹר שֶׁל כּוֹכָב
לְלֹא שׁוּם בְּשׂוֹרָה בִּשְׁבִילִי.
הָיָה עָלַי לְהָבִין

לָמָּה יָרִיתָ בִּי אֲדוֹנִי: שֶׁלֹּא יַפְרִיעַ לָנוּ
עוֹד חֲלוֹם בַּדֶּרֶךְ אֶל הַשֵּׁנָה.

1998

Come to the table. The food is getting cold.
But how can you swallow with the voice in your throat.
Open, open rusty cans, graves that have never been plundered.
Listen: where is it buried,
where did I put it where did I forget the baby without water or air?

Silence in the universe,
You can no longer know why, or who.
Me, me, a voice is heard from the stone.
This is the baby, like the spine of a transparent leaf. Lean over
and look, let it drink, let it eat, if anything's—

tr. Tsipi Keller

from NIGHT IS A POWERFUL DAY

1
Pardon my outburst
I think I've been shot, sir.
I held onto love, a big mistake,

but who cares about facts
when they're killing presidents and children?
Don't take it to heart you say.

More than once I fought off sleep
eyes open wide like the pigeon
who laid an egg on my window sill

and nothing the next day, no bits and pieces,
gone like starlight
and no message for me.
I should have known

why did you shoot me sir: so another dream
won't get in the way of our sleep.

tr. Lisa Katz

אנאלפאביתית

אני עוד אלפאביתית
וזה חבל מאוד.
מומחית בספונג'ולוגיה.
עושָׂה הרבה מאוד.

בת עשר התחתנתי.
גידלתי עֲשָׂרָה.
ברוך השם הצלחתי
ורק זאת הצרה.

ללמוד עוד לא הספקתי
ואין לי שום ברירה.
הנכד כבר לועג לי
מתי תדעי לכתוב?!

מה השעה? שואלת.
ומה המחיר כתוב?
כל זר ברחוב לועג לי
וזה מאוד עצוב.

אני רק אלפאביתית
ואין לי שום מזל.
ללמוד עוד לא הספקתי
וזה מאוד חבל.

וחושך בעינים
בסוּפֶּר לא אמצא.
תאמרו אני צנצנת,
מה יש פה בקופסה?

באוטובוס טעיתי
נָסַע כיוון הפוך.
רחוב של זה נִיחובסקי
היה ממש סמוך.

מכתב חשוב זרקתי
נותַּק לי החשמל.
חשבון טעות עשיתי,
איזה בושה. תשאל.

BRACHA SERRI

ILLITERATE

I'm just a poor illi'erate
its really rather sad
at cleanin' up the 'ouse tho'
I'm really not so bad

When I was 10, got married
'ad a kid each year
thank the Lord I managed
but did it cost me dear!

I never got a chance to learn
life was all a fight
now my grandchild mocks me
'cause I don't know to write

I 'ave to ask wot time it is
and wot's the price them goods
strangers burst out laughin'
and give me funny looks

I'm just a poor illi'erate
it really is a shame
I 'ad no chance to learn, see
I'm really not to blame

Shoppin' in the supermarket
gets me in a tizzy
I 'ave to ask wot's in that tin
them labels make me dizzy

on Sunday I got on a bus
that went the other way
turned out the street I wanted
was just a stop away

they cut off me electric
I couldn't read the bill
I threw it in the dustbin
so now I'm in the chill!

כולם סודות קוראים הם
ורק אני בורה.
חוכמת עולם יודעים הם
ורק דרכי סגורה.

אני רק אַלְפַאבֵּיתִית
ואין לי שום מזל.
ללמוד עוד לא הספקתי
וזה מאוד חבל.

1983

עליזה אומרת

עליזה אומרת
שכולם הלכו לתפילה
במערת המכפלה.
שכולם בוכים
על שרה
שלא נשארה עקרה.
שכולם ברחם הגדולה
הכפולה
במלחמת התאומים
על הירושה
ועל הנחלה.
אבל אני נשארתי ילדה
עם יצחק
בעקדה
ובשבילי הוא מעולם
לא קם
משם.
ונשארתי במדבר
עם הגר
ועם ילדה ישמעאל
צמאה יבשה
מחפשת באר לחי
רואי, לרוויה
להשקות את הנער.
ונשארתי שפחה
נמלטת
מהגרת
מפגרת
פילגש

All the world is in the know
they seem so wise and clever
only me is in the dark
and there I'll be forever

I'm just a poor illi'erate
it really is a shame
I 'ad no chance to learn, see
I'm really not to blame.

tr. Yaffah Berkovits Murciano

ALIZA SAYS

Aliza says
that everyone has gone to pray
at the Patriarchs' Tomb.
That everyone is weeping
for Sarah
who did not remain barren.
That everyone is in the great womb
the double womb
of the brothers' battle
for the inheritance
for the land.
But I have remained a girl
with Isaac
at the sacrifice
and for me he never
rose
from there.
And I have remained in the desert
with Hagar
and her child Ishmael
parched dry
in search of the well of the Living One
who sees me,[1] to quench thirst
to give drink to the boy.
And I have remained a servant
fleeing
migrating
lagging behind
mistress

1. Genesis 16.14.

קפואת רגש
מעונה
בלי טינה
בלי שנאה
נרדפת
בורחת
פליטה
זרה
יהודיה
בלי מהות
בלי זהות
קפואה
עקרה.

1990

סבינה מסג

אם נכון שאגמים מזדקנים

אִם נָכוֹן שֶׁאֲגַמִּים מִזְדַּקְנִים —
לֹא רוֹאִים עָלַיִךְ.
שָׁמַיִם נְמוּכִים שֶׁלִּי, אֵינְסוֹף קָטָן,
עַיִן צְלוּלָה שֶׁל צַד שֵׁנִי שֶׁל הָעוֹלָם,
הַבֹּץ הַשָּׁחוֹר
בּוֹ יָשֵׁן הַבּוּרִי.

אִם נָכוֹן שֶׁאֲגַמִּים מִזְדַּקְנִים
וְאַתְּ "תּוֹפָעָה צְעִירָה יַחֲסִית
עִם תַּהֲלִיךְ בְּלִיָּה מוּאָץ"
כְּמוֹ שֶׁקָּרָאתִי בְּ"כָל אֶרֶץ נַפְתָּלִי" —

אֲנִי אֶחְפֹּר לָךְ מֵחָדָשׁ אֶת יַם הַחוּלָה!
(שֶׁיְּסַנֵּן שׁוּב אֶת הַמַּיִם כְּמוֹ כִּלְיָה)
אֲנִי אֶסְתֹּם אֶת הַמּוֹבִיל!
אֶפְתַּח אֶת הַנְּבִיעוֹת!

אָשִׁיב לָךְ אֶת מֶלַח הַמַּיִם.

1987

of frozen feeling
tortured
without grievance
without hatred
persecuted
escaping
refugee
stranger
jew
without meaning
without identity
frozen
barren.

tr. Rachel Tzvia Back

SABINA MESSEG

IF IT'S TRUE THAT LAKES GET OLD

If it's true that lakes get old—
it doesn't show on you.
My low skies, a small infinity,
a clear eye for another side of the world,
the black mud
in which the gray mullet sleep.

If it's true that lakes get old
and you are "a relatively recent phenomenon
whose deterioration is speeding up"
as I read in "All the Land of Naphtali"—

I'll dig the Hulah Lake[1] for you once more
(to filter the water, like a kidney, again)
I'll shut down the national water carrier
and free the sources!

I'll bring the salt back to you.

tr. Shirley Kaufman

1. The Hulah Lake, drained in the fifties to provide more agricultural land, has been flooded again in recent years for ecological reasons.

אמירה הס

[גיל המעבר אלי יום]

גִּיל הַמַּעֲבָר אֱלֵי יוֹם
וַאֲנִי לֹא עוֹד תִּינֹקֶת
בְּהִוָּלְדִי
פֶּרַח נָע וָנָד בֵּין עוֹלָם לְעוֹלָם.
חָשַׁבְתִּי חוֹפֶרֶת לַחוּץ לִמְצֹא מוֹצָא
אֶל תּוֹכְכֵי יוֹם אַחֵר,
אַךְ פַּרְגּוֹד עַל פָּנִים בַּכֶּסֶף נֶחְפָּה
וְצֶבַע הָעוֹר כְּלוֹרוֹפִיל חָרוּץ.

אָז קָנִיתִי מִשְׁקָפַיִם
מִפְּנֵי הַזּוֹרֵעַ
בְּאוֹתִיּוֹת חֹשֶׁךְ, מַחֲצִית הָאוֹת
נוֹבַעַת, מַחֲצִית הָאוֹת גּוֹוַעַת
רָצִיתִי מִשְׁקָפַיִם לְהַרְכִּיב לְעֵינַי
לְהָסִיר נֹגַהּ אוֹר מְסֻיָּם
לְכַסּוֹת כְּאֵב.
מָה עוֹשִׂים אֲנָשִׁים פְּרָחִים?
אֵיךְ צוֹנְחִים עַל הַיּוֹם וְעַל לִבֵּנוּ?
סוּמִים פִּשְׁרֵי צִבְעֵי אוֹר
וְתוֹךְ רֶחֶם לֹא סַסְגּוֹנִי עָכוּר מְעַט.

1984

מתוך עת זמירים יחלפו בתהומי מצוקה

6

נִדְמֶה לִי נִהְיוּ לִי פָּנִים שֶׁל צַדִּיק
וּמִשְׁתַּמְּשִׁים בָּהֶם לִפְעָמִים
גַּם עִתִּים נֵר נְשָׁמָה הָיִיתִי
וּפְרָחִים בְּאֵיזוֹ מִרְפֶּסֶת
לֹא צְרִיכָה לֹא דֹּמֶן וְלֹא מַיִם
מִתּוֹךְ הַפָּנִים שֶׁלִּי שֶׁרֶק אֵצֵא חַמָּנִית
בְּלִי יְשִׁימוֹן—

AMIRA HESS

[MENOPAUSE TOWARD DAYLIGHT]

Menopause toward daylight
and I am no longer an infant
at my own birthing
a flower wandering among worlds.
I thought of digging to find an opening
into another day,
but a screen silvers a face
and skin is the color of golden chlorophyll.

So I bought eyeglasses
because of the sower
of darkness in letters, half the letter
flowing, half the letter dying
I wanted to wear glasses
to remove a certain luminous glow
to cover up pain.
What do the precious people do?
How do they sink into the day and our hearts?
Blind are the meanings of the colors of light
in an opaque colorless womb.

tr. Lisa Katz

from WHEN NIGHTINGALES WILL PASS THE DEPTHS OF DESPAIR

6

I think my face became a saint's face
sometimes it's useful
there were also moments I was a candle for a dead soul
and flowers on a balcony
needing neither compost nor water
if I could only emerge a sunflower
without a wilderness—

7

וְתַחַת הַשֶּׁמֶשׁ הַזֹּאת
אִם אֶפְשָׁר יְגֻדַּל נוֹרְמָלִיּוּת
בְּלִי עַצְבוּת מְרֻבֶּצֶת תּוֹרַת הוֹרִים
מִשְּׁנֵי עֵינַי וְקוֹל אִמִּי יָשִׁיר נוֹרָא מְנַקֵּר כְּתִינֹקֶת
וְתַחְשֹׁב צַעֲצוּעִים הַשָּׁדַיִם שֶׁלִּי כִּמְעַט תִּמְצֹץ מְצַיֶּצֶת
וּמַה נִּשְׁאַר לִי חָלָב לָתֵת לַיְלָדִים
בְּתוֹךְ נְשָׁמָה סְגוּרָה
חֲלוּלָה מְאֹד לְהָכִיל
וְחָל בָּהּ הַקּוֹלוֹת שֶׁל שְׁנֵינוּ
בְּדוֹ רֶה מִי—

8

וְכָל זֹאת מֵאֶדֶן הַחַלּוֹן הַהוּא
רָאִיתִי הַיּוֹנָה הַדּוֹגֶרֶת עַל הַזְּמַן
וְעֵינֶיהָ עֲגֻלּוֹת רִיסִים סְבוּכִין
וְסִבּוּכֵי גַּלְגִּלּוֹת בָּהּ
וּמְדוֹרוֹת עֶצֶב
וְגַעְגּוּעַ מִן הַפְּתָחִים הַחוּצָה—

9

וְאִמָּא שֶׁלִּי שׁוֹאֶלֶת: יֵשׁ לָךְ פְּרָחִים
בַּגִּנָּה
אֲנָשִׁים רוֹצִים לִרְאוֹת פְּרָחִים
וְשֶׁיֵּשׁ גִּנָּה בִּישִׁימוֹנֵי הַמִּחְיָה
בַּפְּרָאוּת שֶׁל הַגּ׳וּנְגֶל
הַמְהַדְהֵד שֶׁלָּךְ
אֲנִי רוֹצָה לִרְאוֹת אֶת שַׂעֲרוֹתַיִךְ
כְּמוֹ שָׂדֶה
בַּחֶדֶר שֶׁל הָאִישׁ הַהוּא
וְאֵדַע שֶׁאַתְּ בִּתִּי—

10

אֲנִי אֲמִירָה
הוֹלֶכֶת בַּשֶּׁבִי שֶׁל עַצְמִי
וְיֵשׁ אַבָּא שֶׁלִּי קָבוּר בְּהַר הַזֵּיתִים

יְשַׁתֵּף לָנוּ דֹּמִי הַדְּמָמָה בְּתוֹכִי
וּמַרְחֶשֶׁת הַשֵּׂעָר עַל צַוָּארִי
אִם עֶלֶם הָיִיתִי לוֹ
אִם נִכְבַּלְתִּי לְתוֹפְעוֹת דִּמְמָתוֹ
בְּלִי שִׁחְרוּר—

1993

7
And under that sun
if it's possible to raise normality
without the sadness in my eyes put there by parenting
and mother's voice will sing terrible and piercing like an infant
who will think my breasts are toys and almost suck twittering
and what's left for me milk for children
inside a shut soul
too vacuous to contain
and our two voices occur in it
with do re mi—

8
And all this from that windowsill
I saw a dove brooding over time
and its round eyes and matted lashes
and tangles of rollers
and tiers of sadness
and longing from the openings outwards—

9
And my mother asks: do you have flowers
in the garden
people want to see flowers
and when there's a garden in the wilderness of sustenance
in the wildness
of your echoing jungle
I want to see your hair
like a field
in that man's room
and I will know you are my daughter—

10
I am Amira
take myself into captivity
and there's Daddy buried on the Mount of Olives

the stillness of my inner silence shared between us
a vortex of hair at my throat
as if I were a boy for him
chained to the phenomena of his silence
without release—

tr. Lisa Katz

רות בלומרט

תקלות

עַתָּה אֲנִי נִתְקֶלֶת בְּכָל דֶּלֶת
שַׁרְווּלִי נִתְפָּס בַּיָּדִית
תֶּפֶר נִפְרָם
סִימָן כָּחֹל
הַמִּתְמַהְמֵהַּ לְהוֹרִיק וְלִדְהוֹת.

מִי מַכֶּה אוֹתָךְ?   שׁוֹאֵל מִי.
מִי?!
וַאֲנִי תּוֹהָה עִמּוֹ
עַל פֵּרוּשֵׁי הַתַּקָּלוֹת
בְּשִׁוּוּי מִשְׁקָל
שֶׁל כְּנִיסוֹת וִיצִיאוֹת
לֹא דְּרָמָטִיּוֹת כְּלָל
לְעֵין הַיּוֹם
לְעֵין כֹּל.

וַאֲנִי נִזְהֶרֶת יוֹתֵר,   כְּמוֹ
בְּמִשְׂחַק מַחְשֵׁב מְחֻכָּם:
לָצֵאת בַּפֶּתַח הַנֶּחְשָׁף,
לֹא לָגַעַת בַּדְּפָנוֹת אוֹ בַּסַּף.
רַק מַשֶּׁהוּ בִּי חוֹגֵג לְעַצְמוֹ,
אֵיזֶה אֶלֶקְטְרוֹן נֶאוּרוֹטִי,
אֵיזֶה נֶזֶק מֹחִי שֶׁנִּתָּן
לְפֵרוּשִׁים נוֹסָפִים.

הֲלִיכָה בַּדִּירָה
כְּמוֹ בְּמָבוֹךְ
כְּמוֹ בְּמִשְׂרָד
כְּמוֹ בָּרְחוֹב
אוֹ לְהִתְיַשֵּׁב בָּאוֹטוֹבּוּס וְלָגַעַת
בְּמִישֶׁהוּ הַנִּדְחָק קָרוֹב מִדַּי.

אָז אֲנִי מִתְכַּנֶּסֶת בְּקוֹנְכִיָּתִי
פְּנִימָה פְּנִימָה,
אֶל תּוֹךְ הַפְּנִינָה הַסּוֹפֶגֶת
אֶת גַּרְגֵּר הַחוֹל שֶׁלִּי.

1997

RUTH BLUMERT

COLLISIONS

Now I bump into doors
my sleeve caught on the handle
a seam splits
a blue mark
hesitates, turns green and fades.

Who beats you up? Anyone asks me.
Who?!
And I consider with him
the significance of collisions
of balance
of entrance and exit
not at all dramatic
in broad daylight
in plain view.

And I'm more cautious, as
in a clever computer game:
leave through the revealed doorway,
stay clear of the edges or the threshold.
Only something inside me celebrates itself
some neurotic electron,
some brain damage open
to further interpretations.

Pacing the apartment
as if in a maze
as if in an office
as if on the street,
or seated on a bus, touching
someone who crowds too close.

So I huddle into my shell
deeper deeper
into the pearl that holds
my grain of sand.

tr. Tsipi Keller

יונה וולך

אבשלום

אֲנִי מֻכְרָחָה פַּעַם נוֹסֶפֶת
לְהִזָּכֵר בִּבְנִי אַבְשָׁלוֹם
שֶׁשַּׂעֲרוֹתָיו נִתְפְּסוּ בְּרַחְמִי
וְלֹא יָצָא לִי
לִגְמֹר אֶת אַבְשָׁלוֹם בְּנִי
אֲנִי בּוֹנָה אֶת אֶפְשָׁרוּיוֹת הַרְגָּשָׁתִי
הָרַחֲמִים שׁוֹטְפִים בִּי
וְהָרַעַב הָאֶפְשָׁרִי
רְצוֹנוֹת הַתּוֹרָשָׁה
וְאַבְשָׁלוֹם שֶׁלֹּא הֻרְשָׁה
בְּגִלְגּוּל אַחֵר אַבְשָׁלוֹם יִהְיֶה
אֲהוּבִי וַאֲנִי אָחוּשׁ זִכְרָהּ
כְּשֶׁאַבְשָׁלוֹם אֲהוּבִי
תְּחוּשָׁה גּוּפָנִית אוֹ אֵיךְ בִּטְנִי
רֵיקָה מֵאַבְשָׁלוֹם בְּנִי
סִדּוּר שֶׁל כּוֹכָבִים
נוֹפְלִים וְחֶרֶב מַכָּה
בְּמַגְנֶט עַל לִבָּהּ
הַרְגָּשָׁה מְדֻיֶּקֶת:
בַּמֶּה תִּלָּחֵם
וְעַל מַה תָּנוּחַ
הָרוּחַ
לְאָן תִּשָּׁאֵף
הָרוּחַ בְּנִי.

1967

[דבה גריזילית גדלה אותי]

דֻּבָּה גְּרִיזִילִית גִּדְּלָה אוֹתִי
חֲלֵב כּוֹכָבִים הָיָה מְזוֹנִי הָעִקָּרִי
הַדָּבָר הָרִאשׁוֹן שֶׁרָאִיתִי
בִּימֵי חַיַּי כַּוָּנָתִי שֶׁאֲנִי זוֹכֵר
הָיָה אֲנִי אֵיךְ אוּכַל לִשְׁכֹּחַ

1976

YONA WALLACH

ABSALOM

One more time I must
remember my son Absalom
whose hair caught in my womb
and didn't come out for me
to finish Absalom my son
I construct the possibilities of my feeling
pity floods me
and the hunger that might be
the wills of heredity
and Absalom who wasn't allowed
in another incarnation Absalom will be
my lover and I'll sense traces of her
when Absalom my lover
is a bodily sensation or how my belly
is empty of Absalom my son
an arrangement of stars
falling and a sword that strikes
the magnet on its heart
a precise feeling:
what will you fight
and on what will the wind
rest
where will it carry you
the wind my son.

tr. Linda Zisquit

[A GRIZZLY SHE-BEAR REARED ME]

A grizzly she-bear reared me
milk-of-stars was my main nourishment
the first thing I saw
in the days of my life I mean that I remember
was me how can I forget it?

tr. Linda Zisquit

תפילין

תָּבוֹא אֵלַי
אַל תִּתֵּן לִי לַעֲשׂוֹת כְּלוּם
אַתָּה תַּעֲשֶׂה בִּשְׁבִילִי
כָּל דָּבָר תַּעֲשֶׂה בִּשְׁבִילִי
כָּל דָּבָר שֶׁרַק אַתְחִיל לַעֲשׂוֹת
תַּעֲשֶׂה אַתָּה בִּמְקוֹמִי
אֲנִי אַנִּיחַ תְּפִלִּין
אֶתְפַּלֵּל
הַנַּח אַתָּה גַּם אֶת הַתְּפִלִּין עֲבוּרִי
כְּרֹךְ אוֹתָם עַל יָדַי
שַׂחֵק אוֹתָם בִּי
הַעֲבֵר אוֹתָם מַעֲדַנּוֹת עַל גּוּפִי
חַכֵּךְ אוֹתָם בִּי הֵיטֵב
בְּכָל מָקוֹם גָּרֵה אוֹתִי
עַלֵּף אוֹתִי בִּתְחוּשׁוֹת
הַעֲבֵר אוֹתָם עַל הַדַּגְדְּגָן שֶׁלִּי
קְשֹׁר בָּהֶם אֶת מָתְנַי
כְּדֵי שֶׁאֶגְמֹר מַהֵר
שַׂחֵק אוֹתָם בִּי
קְשֹׁר אֶת יָדַי וְרַגְלַי
עֲשֵׂה בִּי מַעֲשִׂים
לַמְרוֹת רְצוֹנִי
הֲפֹךְ אוֹתִי עַל בִּטְנִי
וְשִׂים אֶת הַתְּפִלִּין בְּפִי רֶסֶן מוֹשְׁכוֹת
רְכַב עָלַי אֲנִי סוּסָה
מְשֹׁךְ אֶת רֹאשִׁי לְאָחוֹר
עַד שֶׁאֶצְוַח מִכְּאֵב
וְאַתָּה מְעֻנָּג
אַחַר כָּךְ אֲנִי אַעֲבִיר אוֹתָם עַל גּוּפְךָ
בְּכַוָּנָה שֶׁאֵינָהּ מִסְתַּתֶּרֶת בַּפָּנִים
הוֹ עַד מָה תִּהְיֶינָה אַכְזָרִיּוֹת פָּנַי
אַעֲבִיר אוֹתָם לְאַט עַל גּוּפְךָ
לְאַט לְאַט לְאַט
סְבִיב צַוָּארְךָ אַעֲבִיר אוֹתָם
אֲסוֹבֵב אוֹתָם כַּמָּה פְּעָמִים סְבִיב צַוָּארְךָ, מִצַּד אֶחָד
וּמֵהַצַּד הַשֵּׁנִי אֶקְשֹׁר אוֹתָם לְמַשֶּׁהוּ יַצִּיב
בִּמְיֻחָד כָּבֵד מְאֹד אוּלַי מִסְתּוֹבֵב
אֶמְשֹׁךְ וְאֶמְשֹׁךְ

TEFILLIN

Come to me
don't let me do anything
you do it for me
do everything for me
what I even start doing
you do instead of me
I'll put on tefillin[1]
I'll pray
you put on the tefillin for me too
bind them on my hands
play them on me
move them with delight on my body
rub them hard against me
stimulate me everywhere
make me swoon with sensation
move them over my clitoris
tie my waist with them
so I'll come quickly
play them in me
tie my hands and feet
do things to me
against my will
turn me over on my belly
and put the tefillin in my mouth
bridle reins
ride me I'm a mare
pull my head back
till I scream with pain
and you're pleasured
then I'll move them onto your body
with unconcealed intention
oh how cruel my face will be
I'll move them slowly over your body
slowly slowly slowly
around your neck I'll move them
I'll wind them several times around your neck, on one side
and on the other I'll tie them to something solid
especially heavy maybe twisting
I'll pull and I'll pull

1. Usually translated *phylacteries.* They consist of two black leather boxes containing scriptural passages that are bound by black leather strips traditionally on the left arm and on the head and worn for daily prayers by religious Jewish men.

עַד שֶׁתֵּצֵא נִשְׁמָתְךָ
עַד שֶׁאֶחְנֹק אוֹתְךָ
לְגַמְרֵי בַּתְּפִלִּין
הַמִּתְמַשְּׁכִים לְאֹרֶךְ הַבָּמָה
וּבֵין הַקָּהָל הַמֻּכֶּה תַּדְהֵמָה.

1983

עברית

בִּשְׁמוֹת מִין יֵשׁ לְאַנְגְּלִית כָּל הָאֶפְשָׁרֻיּוֹת
כָּל אֲנִי — בְּפֹעַל
הוּא כָּל אֶפְשָׁרוּת בְּמִין
וְכָל אַתְּ הִיא אַתָּה
וְכָל אֲנִי הוּא בְּלִי מִין
וְאֵין הֶבְדֵּל בֵּין אַתְּ וְאַתָּה
וְכָל הַדְּבָרִים הֵם זֶה — לֹא אִישׁ לֹא אִשָּׁה
לֹא צָרִיךְ לַחְשֹׁב לִפְנֵי שֶׁמִּתְיַחֲסִים לְמִין
עִבְרִית הִיא סֶקְסְמַנְיַאקִית
עִבְרִית מַפְלָה לְרָעָה אוֹ לְטוֹבָה
מְפַרְגֶּנֶת נוֹתֶנֶת פְּרִיבִילֶגְיוֹת
עִם חֶשְׁבּוֹן אָרֹךְ מֵהַגָּלוּת
בְּרַבִּים יֵשׁ זְכוּת קְדִימָה לָהֶם
עִם הַרְבֵּה דַּקּוּת וְסוֹד כָּמוּס
בְּיָחִיד הַסִּכּוּיִים שָׁוִים
מִי אוֹמֵר שֶׁכָּלוּ כָּל הַקִּצִּים
עִבְרִית הִיא סֶקְסְמַנְיַאקִית
רוֹצָה לָדַעַת מִי מְדַבֵּר
כִּמְעַט מַרְאֶה כִּמְעַט תְּמוּנָה
מַה שֶּׁאָסוּר בְּכָל הַתּוֹרָה
לְפָחוֹת לִרְאוֹת אֶת הַמִּין
הָעִבְרִית מְצִיצָה מִבַּעַד לְחוֹר הַמַּנְעוּל
כְּמוֹנִי לְאִמָּא שֶׁלָּךְ וְלָךְ
כְּשֶׁהֱיִיתֶן מִתְרַחֲצוֹת אָז בַּצְּרִיף
לְאִמֵּךְ הָיָה תַּחַת גָּדוֹל
אֲבָל אַף פַּעַם לֹא הִפְסַקְתִּי לַחְשֹׁב
הַיָּמִים עָבְרוּ כַּחֲלֹף הַטּוּשִׁים
נִשְׁאַרְתְּ יַלְדָּה רָזָה וּמְסֻבֶּנֶת
אַחַר כָּךְ סְתַמְתֶּן אֶת כָּל הַחוֹרִים
סְתַמְתֶּן אֶת כָּל הַפִּרְצוֹת
הָעִבְרִית מְצִיצָה לָךְ מֵחוֹר הַמַּנְעוּל
הַשָּׂפָה רוֹאָה אוֹתָךְ עֵירֻמָּה
אָבִי לֹא הִרְשָׁה לִי לִרְאוֹת
הוּא סוֹבֵב אֶת גַּבּוֹ כְּשֶׁהִשְׁתִּין
אַף פַּעַם לֹא רָאִיתִי אוֹתוֹ טוֹב מַמָּשׁ

till your soul leaves you
till I choke you
completely with the tefillin
that stretch the length of the stage
and into the stunned crowd.

tr. Linda Zisquit

HEBREW

About pronouns and sex English leaves its options open
in practice each *I*
has all the options
she is *he* when it's *you*
I doesn't have a sex
there's no difference between she-*you* and he-*you*
and all *things* are *it*—not man not woman
no need to think before relating to sex
Hebrew is a sex maniac
Hebrew discriminates for and against
forgives, gives privileges
with a big gripe from the exile
in plural men have the right of way
it's a thin line it's a big secret
in the singular chances are equal
who says it's a lost case
Hebrew is a sex maniac
wants to know who's talking
almost a mirror almost a picture
forbidden by the Torah
at least looking at sex
Hebrew peeks through the keyhole
as I did at you and your mother
when you washed in the shed
your mother had a big ass
but I never stopped thinking
the days passed like showers
you remained a thin girl, soaping herself
afterwards you women plugged all the holes
plugged all the gaps
Hebrew peeks at you through the keyhole
the language sees you naked
my father didn't let me see
he turned his back when he peed
I never really saw him

תָּמִיד הוּא הֶחְבִּיא אֶת הַמִּין
כְּמוֹ שֶׁרַבִּים מַחְבִּיא אִשָּׁה
כְּמוֹ שֶׁקָּהָל הוּא זָכָר בְּגוּפִים
כְּמוֹ שֶׁמִּלָּה הִיא זָכָר וּנְקֵבָה
אֵין כְּמוֹ אֵלּוּ דְּבָרִים מְתוּקִים
הָעִבְרִית הִיא אִשָּׁה מִתְרַחֶצֶת
הָעִבְרִית הִיא בַּת־שֶׁבַע נְקִיָּה
הָעִבְרִית הִיא פֶּסֶל שֶׁלֹּא פּוֹסֵל
יֵשׁ לָהּ נְקֻדּוֹת חֵן קְטַנּוֹת וְסִימָנֵי לֵדָה
כְּכֹל שֶׁהִיא מִתְבַּגֶּרֶת הִיא יוֹתֵר יָפָה
הַשִּׁפּוּט שֶׁלָּהּ הוּא פְּרֶהִיסְטוֹרִי לִפְעָמִים
נוֹירוֹזָה כָּזֹאת הִיא לְטוֹבָה
תַּגִּיד לִי בְּזָכָר תַּגִּיד לִי בִּנְקֵבָה
כָּל אֲנִי יַלְדוּתִי בֵּיצִית בְּטֶרֶם הַפְרָיָה
עַל מִין אֶפְשָׁר לִפְסֹחַ
עַל מִין אֶפְשָׁר לְוַתֵּר
מִי יַגִּיד מִינוֹ שֶׁל אֶפְרוֹחַ?
הָאִישׁ שֶׁהַטֶּבַע יוֹצֵר
לִפְנֵי שֶׁהֻטְבַּע בּוֹ פֹּעַל מֵטֶה.
זִכָּרוֹן הוּא זָכָר
יוֹצֵר מִינִים
תוֹלָדָה הָעִקָּר
כִּי הִיא הַחַיִּים
עִבְרִית הִיא סֶקְסְמַנְיַאקִית
וּמָה שֶׁתַּגֵּדְנָה בִּטְרוּנְיָה פֶּמִינִיסְטִיּוֹת
הַמְחַפְּשׂוֹת גֵּרוּיִים מִחוּץ לַשָּׂפָה
בְּאִינְטוֹנַצְיָה הַנּוֹתֶנֶת פֵּרוּשׁ לַדְּבָרִים
סִימָנִים רַק שֶׁל זָכָר וּנְקֵבָה בְּמִשְׁפָּט
יִתְּנוּ יְחָסִים מִינִיִּים מְשֻׁנִּים
עַל כָּל נְקֵבָה סִימָן, עַל זָכָר סִימָן אַחֵר
כְּשֶׁגַּם כָּל פֹּעַל וּבִנְיָן מְסֻמָּנִים
מָה עוֹשֶׂה הָאִישׁ לָאִשָּׁה
מַה הוּא מְקַבֵּל בִּתְמוּרָה
אֵיזֶה כֹּחַ הִיא מַפְעִילָה עָלָיו
וְאֵיזֶה סִימָן נִתַּן לָעֶצֶם
וּלְשֵׁם עֶצֶם מִפְשָׁט וְלַמִּלִּיּוֹת
נְקַבֵּל מִין מִשְׂחָק טֶבַע
הִתְרַחֲשׁוּת נַפְשִׁית כְּיַעַר צָעִיר
מִשְׂחָק שֶׁל כֹּחוֹת טֶבַע כְּלָלִיִּים
שֶׁמֵּהֶם נִגְזָרִים כָּל הַפְּרָטִים
סִימָנִים כְּלָלִיִּים לִכְלַל הָאֵרוּעִים
שֶׁאֶפְשָׁרִי שֶׁיִּקְרוּ בִּזְמַן מִן הַזְּמַנִּים
תִּרְאֶה אֵיזֶה גּוּף יֵשׁ לַשָּׂפָה וּמִדּוֹת
אֹהַב אוֹתָהּ עַכְשָׁו בְּלִי כְּסוּת לָשׁוֹן

1985

he always hid his sex
the way the Hebrew plural hides a woman
the way an audience is masculine in Hebrew
the way the word *word* in Hebrew is masculine and feminine
there's nothing like these sweet things
Hebrew is a woman bathing
Hebrew is Batsheva clean
Hebrew is an unsculpted sculpture
with tiny beauty marks and stretch marks from giving birth
the older she gets the more beautiful she is
her judgment is sometimes prehistoric
this kind of neurosis is for her own good
tell me in masculine tell me in feminine
every *I* is childlike an unfertilized egg
you can skip over sex
you can give up sex
who can tell the sex of a baby chick?
man created by nature
before a conjugated verb is planted in him.
Memory is masculine
creates sexes
the offspring are the main thing
because that's life
Hebrew is a sex maniac
and whatever you women say in a feminist complaint
searching for stimulation outside the language
with an intonation that gives meaning to things
signs just of male or female in a sentence
will change sexual relations
mark every female, a different mark for men
when every verb and verb group are marked
what does man do to a woman
what does he get in return
what power does she exert over him
and what sign given to an object
and to an abstract noun and prepositions
we'll get a sort of natural game
an emotional happening like a new forest
a game of universal natural forces
determining all the particulars
universal signs for all events
that may happen someday
look what a body language has and what proportions
love her now without cover of words

tr. Lisa Katz

שוב אינני אוהבת כל כך לפחד

הָיִיתִי מְשַׂחֶקֶת בַּפַּחַד
כְּמוֹ עִם יֶלֶד
מְנִיפָה אוֹתוֹ מוּלִי
מִסְתַּכֶּלֶת בְּפָנָיו
וְקוֹרֵאת לוֹ
פַּחַד פַּחַד בּוֹא,
הָיִיתִי קוֹרֵאת
אֶת הַדְּבָרִים
הֲכִי מַפְחִידִים,
הָיִיתִי מִתְמַכֶּרֶת לַתְּחוּשׁוֹת
כְּאִילוּ זֶה הָיָה הַדָּבָר הַיָּחִיד
וְעוֹדִי
הַפַּחַד,
פְּחָדִים קְטַנִּים לֹא עִנְיְנוּ אוֹתִי
רַק הַפַּחַד הַגָּדוֹל
סוֹחֵף הַכֹּל
כָּעֵת שׁוּב אֵינֶנִּי אוֹהֶבֶת לְפַחֵד כָּל כָּךְ
מָצָאתִי עַצְמִי יוֹשֶׁבֶת
וְקוֹרֵאת לוֹ שׁוּב בְּלַחַשׁ
כְּמֵאָז בַּיָּמִים הָהֵם
פַּחַד פַּחַד בּוֹא
בּוֹא לְשַׂחֵק אִתִּי בְּפַחַד
חָשַׁבְתִּי שֶׁזֶּה מַה
שֶּׁאֲנִי צְרִיכָה לַעֲשׂוֹת
אָז בַּיָּמִים הָהֵם
לְפַחֵד,
הָיִיתִי קוֹפֵאת מִפַּחַד
רוֹאָה דְּבָרִים אֲיֻמִּים
גַּם שׁוֹמַעַת
יוֹם אֶחָד זֶה הִתְחִיל
גִּלִּיתִי אֶת הַפַּחַד
גִּלִּיתִי עוֹד דְּבָרִים
שִׁגָּעוֹן לְמָשָׁל
אֲבָל זֶה בְּמָקוֹם אַחֵר
בְּצוּרָה דּוֹמָה,
גִּלִּיתִי אֶת הַתְּחוּשׁוֹת הָאֱנוֹשִׁיּוֹת
מָצָאתִי הֶלֶם פֵּרוּשׁ אַחֲרֵי כֵן
דְּבָרִים שׁוֹנִים הֵבַנְתִּי
וּדְבָרִים אֲחֵרִים נִמְאֲסוּ עָלַי
אֲבָל הַפַּחַד הָיָה אַחֲרוֹן
הָלַכְתִּי בְּמִסְדְּרוֹנוֹת אֲרֻכִּים
תָּמִיד מִסְדְּרוֹנוֹת אֲרֻכִּים
שֶׁל מִנְזָרִים בָּתֵּי חוֹלִים

I NO LONGER REALLY LOVE BEING AFRAID

I would play with fear
as with a child
wave it in front of me
look at its face
and call it
fear fear come,
I would read
the most frightening
things,
I would become addicted to the sensations
as if that were the only thing
still me
the fear,
small fears didn't interest me
only the large fear
sweeping everything away
now I no longer really love being afraid
I found myself sitting
and calling it again whispering
as it was then in those days
fear fear come
come play fear with me
I thought that was
what I had to do
then in those days
being afraid,
I'd freeze from fear
see terrible things
hear as well
one day it began
I discovered the fear
I discovered other things
madness for example
but that's in another place
in a similar form,
I discovered the human feelings
I found interpretation shock afterwards
different things I understood
and other things I became fed up with
but the fear was last
I walked long corridors
always long corridors
of monasteries hospitals

מִבְנֵי צִבּוּר
וְאָמַרְתִּי לִי
שֶׁמֵּרֹאשׁ הַפַּחַד וְהַשִּׁגָּעוֹן
אֲנִי יוֹצֵאת נִמְאַס לִי
שׁוּב אֵינֶנִּי אוֹהֶבֶת כָּל כָּךְ לְפַחֵד,
כָּעֵת הוּא זְמַן הָאָסִיף
אֲנִי אוֹסֶפֶת אֶת פֵּרוֹת הַפַּחַד
הַבְּאוּשִׁים בְּדֶרֶךְ כְּלָל
מַבִּיטָה בָּהֶם בְּחִיּוּךְ
לֹא בִּזְוָעָה
וְדוֹחָה אוֹתָם מִלְּפָנַי
שׁוּב אֵינִי אוֹהֶבֶת לְפַחֵד.

1985

יהודית מוסל-אליעזרוב

השמלה

בְּגִנַּת הַבַּיִת
רָחֲשׁוּ נְחָשִׁים בָּאֲפֵלָה
מְקַצְּצִים בִּנְטִיעוֹת צְעִירוֹת
אֶזְכֹּר אֵיךְ רָצְצוּ
אֶזְכֹּר צְלִיפוֹת חֲגוֹרָתְךָ עַל בְּשַׂר יַלְדָּה
בְּחִוְרוֹן חֲרוֹנְךָ מֵאֵחָר בַּנֶּשֶׁף
חַג עַצְמָאוּת.

הַמָּוֶת כְּבָר נָגַע בַּבַּיִת
נְחָשִׁים הֵרִימוּ רֹאשׁ
וַאֲנִי נִצַּלְתִּי שִׂמְלוֹתַי הַשּׁוֹנוֹת
מִשָּׁם—
לְהִתְנָאוֹת

אָז שׁוּב יָבוֹאוּ הַזְּקֵנִים, חֲרֵדִים לְבֵית אָבִי
יַצְבִּיעוּ בִּכְתוּבֵי לְךָ
כִּי מוֹרֶדֶת בִּתְּךָ
(מִנֵּיהּ וּבֵיהּ פָּרְשׂוּ הַשִּׂמְלָה)

בְּרִגְשָׁה,
נִרְעֶשֶׁת מִן הַצְּבָעִים וְהַצּוּרוֹת
לוֹפֶתֶת בְּתֵי הַתִּינֹקֶת
שִׂמְלָתִי הַפְּרוּשָׂה.

1988

public buildings
and I said to me
that from the start the fear and the madness
I'm leaving I'm fed up
I no longer really love being afraid
now is the harvesttime
I'm gathering the fruits of fear
mostly rotten
looking at them with a smile
not horror
and rejecting them from my sight
I no longer love being afraid.

tr. Linda Zisquit

JUDITH MOSSEL-ELIEZEROV

THE DRESS

In the garden
snakes rustled in the dark
slashing the young shoots
I remember how they were crushed
I remember the lash of your belt on the girl's flesh
your pale rage late in the evening
on Independence Day

death had already touched our home
snakes raised their heads
and I saved my dresses
from there—
so I could look fancy

then again the elders arrive, concerned for my father's house
they show you how rebellious
your daughter is in her writing
(right away they display the dress)

excited,
amazed by its colors and shape
my baby daughter grips
my flaunted dress.

tr. Gabriel Levin

רחל חלפי

איזו עדינות יש

אֵיזוֹ עֲדִינוּת יֵשׁ בְּגוּפֵנוּ שָׁעָה שֶׁהוּא
נוֹטֵשׁ
אוֹתָנוּ לְאַט,
חוֹשֵׁשׁ לְהַכְאִיבֵנוּ
בְּמַהֲלֻמַּת־פֶּתַע.
לְאַט   בְּעֶרְגָּה
כִּיפֵהפִיָּה נִרְדֶּמֶת־לְמֶחֱצָה
הוּא טוֹוֶה לָנוּ
קְמָטִים קְטַנִּים שֶׁל אוֹר וְשֶׁל חָכְמָה—
לֹא בְּקִיעִים שֶׁל רְעִידַת אֲדָמָה—
רֶשֶׁת אַוְרִירִית שֶׁל חֲרִיצֵי־אֵימָה.
כַּמָּה טוּב־לֵב מִצַּד גּוּפֵנוּ
שֶׁאֵינוֹ מְשַׁנֶּה אֶת פָּנֵינוּ
בְּאַחַת
שֶׁאֵינוֹ שׁוֹבֵר אֶת עַצְמוֹתֵינוּ
בְּמַכָּה

לֹא,   בִּזְהִירוּת
כְּסַהַר חִוֵּר הַשּׁוֹפֵךְ זָהֳרוֹ עָלֵינוּ
הוּא מֵאִיר אוֹתָנוּ
בְּרֶשֶׁת עֲצַבִּים עֲצֵבִים
מְקַפֵּל אֶת עוֹרֵנוּ בַּפִּנּוֹת
מַקְשֶׁה אֶת עַמּוּד הַשִּׁדְרָה שֶׁלָּנוּ—
שֶׁנּוּכַל לַעֲמֹד בְּכָל זֶה.

אֵיזֶה יֹפִי   אֵיזוֹ עֲדִינוּת יֵשׁ
בְּגוּפֵנוּ הַבּוֹגֵד בָּנוּ לְאַט
בְּנִימוּס מֵכִין אוֹתָנוּ
מְסַפֵּר לָנוּ בְּלַחַשׁ
מְעַט־מְעַט   שָׁעָה־שָׁעָה
שֶׁהוּא   הוֹלֵךְ

(1968) 1990

RAHEL CHALFI

SUCH TENDERNESS

Such tenderness in our bodies
when they abandon us
slowly
reluctant to hurt us
with a sudden jolt.
Gradually,   wistfully
like a semi-sleeping beauty
they weave for us
tiny wrinkles of light and wisdom—
not faults of an earthquake—
an airy network, cracks of horror.
How kind of our bodies
that they don't alter our faces
all at once
that they don't break our bones
with one blow.

No,   cautiously
like a pale moon bestowing its glow
they illumine us
in a net of grieving nerves
fold our skin at the edges
harden our spines
so we can withstand it all.

Such beauty   such tenderness
in our bodies that gradually betray us
graciously prepare us
tell us in whispers
little by little   hour by hour
that they   are leaving

tr. Tsipi Keller

בלוז הלכתי לעבוד בתור בת־יענה

הָלַכְתִּי לְגַן־הַחַיּוֹת לַעֲבֹד בְּתוֹר בַּת־יַעֲנָה
אָמְרוּ לִי אֵין לָךְ קְוָלִיפִיקַצְיוֹת לַעֲבֹד בְּתוֹר בַּת־יַעֲנָה
יֵשׁ לָךְ יוֹתֵר מִדַּי עֵינַיִם וּפָחוֹת מִדַּי חוֹל
תּוֹצִיאִי לָךְ מִן הָרֹאשׁ שֶׁתִּהְיִי פַּעַם בַּת־יַעֲנָה

כַּמָּה חוֹל כַּמָּה חוֹל אֲנִי צְרִיכָה
רוֹאָה הַכֹּל רוֹאָה הַכֹּל אֲנִי צְרִיכָה
וְגַם מַשְׂכֹּרֶת צְרִיכָה
לַעֲבֹד כַּמָּה מָתוֹק לַעֲבֹד בְּתוֹר בַּת־יַעֲנָה   מוּכָנָה
אֲפִלּוּ לַעֲשׂוֹת כְּתַחְבִּיב בַּת־יַעֲנָה בְּהִתְנַדְּבוּת בַּת־יַעֲנָה רַק שֶׁיִּתְּנוּ לִי
לַעֲבֹד בְּתוֹר בַּת־יַעֲנָה

אַתְּ לֹא מְבִינָה?   רָצָה רָצָה כְּמוֹ צִפֹּרֶת־עֲנָק מְשַׁסֶּפֶת חוֹל־שִׁכְחָה
וְצָרִיךְ מְשַׁסֶּפֶת רֹאשׁ,   אַתְּ לֹא מְבִינָה?

מוּכָנָה אֲפִלּוּ לַעֲשׂוֹת אֶת עַצְמִי יַעֲנִי בַּת־יַעֲנָה!
מַה זֶּה מְשַׁנֶּה שֶׁאֲנִי מוּכָנָה אִם הֵם לֹא
רוֹצִים לָתֵת לִי לִהְיוֹת בַּת־יַעֲנָה?

הַצַּוָּאר שֶׁלָּךְ זָקוּף מִדַּי הֵם אוֹמְרִים לִי בְּלִשְׁכַּת הָעֲבוֹדָה הַזּוֹאוֹלוֹגִית
הַגּוּף שֶׁלָּךְ חָצוּף מִדַּי הַמַּבָּט שֶׁלָּךְ חָשׂוּף מִדַּי אוֹמֶרֶת הָעוֹבֶדֶת
הַסּוֹצְיַאלִית שֶׁל גַּן־הַחַיּוֹת
אַתְּ לֹא מְבִינָה שֶׁעַד שֶׁלֹּא תִּתְהַפְּכִי בַּהֲפֵכָה
תַּהַפְכִי אֶת עוֹרֵךְ תְּעַקְּמִי אֶת צַוָּארֵךְ וְתִקְבְּרִי אֶת רֹאשֵׁךְ
לֹא תְקַבְּלִי עֲבוֹדָה שֶׁל בַּת־יַעֲנָה?!

אוּלַי, לְפָחוֹת, אֶלְבַּשׁ שִׂמְלָה עֲשׂוּיָה נוֹצוֹת שֶׁל בַּת־יַעֲנָה
זֶה כָּל כָּךְ חוּשָׁנִי   זֶה כָּל כָּךְ חוּשָׁנָהּ

נָא! זֶה לֹא עִנְיָן שֶׁל נוֹצוֹת, הֵם צוֹעֲקִים לִי, זֶה עִנְיָן שֶׁל הֲבָנָה!
שֶׁל חוֹל וַהֲבָנָה!!

(1974) 1986

שפת-ים תל-אביב, בחורף 74׳

עָנָן־תַּנִּין בָּלַע
עָנָן־עָנָן.
הַכֹּל סָמִיךְ
וּלְאָן הָלְכָה הַמִּלְחָמָה?
הַמֵּזַח צָבוּעַ אָדֹם וְצָהֹב
וְכָתוּב עָלָיו TEL-AVIV.
תֻּפֵּי הַתְּהוֹמוֹת אֲדִישִׁים.
בַּשָּׁמַיִם צוּרוֹת אֲפֵלוֹת
מִשְׁתּוֹלְלוֹת לְאַט. זִירַת הֵאָבְקוּת אֵינְסוֹפִית
בְּקֶצֶב מַצְלֵמָה אִטִּית.

"I WENT TO WORK AS AN OSTRICH" BLUES

I went to the zoo to work as an ostrich
they told me you're not qualified to work as an ostrich
you have too many eyes and too little sand
Stop wanting to be an ostrich

How much sand how much sand do I need
to see everything I need
and a salary too I need
to work how sweet to work as an ostrich   willing
to be an ostrich even as a hobby, a volunteer ostrich, if only they'd let me
work as an ostrich

Don't you see? Running around like a huge birdie-girl cut off from the
    sand of forgetting
what you need is your head cut off, don't you see?

Willing even to make myself a fake ostrich!
What difference does it make that I'm willing if they won't
let me be an ostrich?

Your neck should be rigid your body frigid
they tell me at the zoological unemployment agency
your gaze should fidget says the social worker at the zoo
Don't you see that until you are changed by a Change,
change your skin bend your neck and bury your head
you won't get an ostrich job?!

Maybe at least I'll wear a dress made of ostrich feathers
it's so sensual   it's so dimensual

Na! It's not a matter of feathers, they yell at me, it's a matter of savvy.
Of sand and savvy!

tr. Shirley Kaufman

TEL-AVIV BEACH, WINTER '74

A crocodile-cloud has gulped down
a cloud-cloud.
Everything is thick—layer upon layer,
and where has the war gone?
The pier is painted yellow-
red and reads TEL-AVIV.
The drums of the deep are indifferent.
In the sky dark shapes
slowly go wild. An eternal arena
of slow-motion wrestling.

מָנוֹף מִזְדַּקֵּר מֵעַל מְלוֹן סוּפֶּר־
הִילְטוֹן. וּלְאָן הָלְכָה הַמִּלְחָמָה.
עֲנַן־תַּנִּין בָּלַע עֲנַן־עָנָן. לְאָן הָלְכָה
הַמִּלְחָמָה. לְמַעְלָה בָּעֵמֶק
עֲנָנוֹת רַכּוֹת וּמְטוֹסִים מְתַנִּים אֲהָבִים.
הָאֲוִיר מְמַלֵּא אֶת הָרֵאוֹת
בְּמֶלַח חַד וּצְחוֹק.
הַשֶּׁמֶשׁ הִיא תַּצְלוּם דָּהוּי.
צִפֳּרֵי־חוֹף מְנַקְּרוֹת אֲפוֹרוֹת בַּחוֹל.
הַיָּם — שְׂרִירָיו נֶאֱנָקִים.
אִשָּׁה בּוֹדֶדֶת עִם מִטְפַּחַת נַיְלוֹן
לְרֹאשָׁהּ. מַה הִיא לְעֻמַּת
סוּפַת בְּרָקִים.
גַּם הַמִּקְפֶּצָה צְבוּעָה כָּתֹם.

אִשָּׁה זְקֵנָה, שְׂפָתֶיהָ מְנַסּוֹת:
הוּא הָיָה מַלְאָךְ
הוּא הָיָה מַלְאָךְ

1975

מלכת המים של ירושלים

מַלְכַּת הַמַּיִם שֶׁל יְרוּשָׁלַיִם
צָלְלָה לְתוֹךְ הַהִיסְטוֹרְיָה
הַהִיסְטוֹרְיָה הָיְתָה קָשָׁה וְהִיא גִּדְּלָה סְנַפִּירִים
לֹא הָיָה לָהּ אֲוִיר   וְהִיא זָמְמָה
זִימִים   חוֹתֶרֶת וְחוֹתֶרֶת זִכָּרוֹן
מַלְכַּת הַמַּיִם שֶׁל יְרוּשָׁלַיִם יֵשׁ לָהּ
בֶּגֶד יָם עָשׂוּי אִידִישׁ
מַלְכַּת הַמַּיִם שֶׁל יְרוּשָׁלַיִם מִתְפַּלֶּשֶׁת בְּחוֹף־אֲבָנִים בְּלָדִינוֹ
פּוֹחֶדֶת מֵעֲלִיַּת פְּנֵי הַמַּיִם בְּעַרְבִית
מַלְכַּת הַמַּיִם שֶׁל יְרוּשָׁלַיִם אֵין לָהּ
יָם בְּתוֹךְ יְרוּשָׁלַיִם
יֵשׁ לָהּ הִיסְטוֹרְיָה
יְהוּדִית
וְהִיא   מַחֲזִיקָה
מַחֲזִיקָה   מַחֲזִיקָה רֹאשָׁהּ מֵעַל
פְּנֵי   הַמַּיִם

1979

Over the Super Hilton Hotel, a lever
juts high. And where has the war gone?
Crocodile-cloud has swallowed cloud-cloud. Where has
the war gone? High in the deep
airplanes make love to voluptuous clouds.
Air fills the lungs
with laughter and sharp salt.
The sun is a faded photograph.
Shore birds grayly peck the sand.
The sea flexes its groaning muscles.
A lonely woman has tied a nylon kerchief
to her head. What is she
compared to a thunderstorm?
The springboard is painted orange.

An old woman's lips are trying to say:
he was an angel
he was an angel

tr. Elaine Magarrell

THE WATER QUEEN OF JERUSALEM

The Water Queen of Jerusalem
dives into history
history is hard and she grows fins
there is no air so she invents
gills rowing through memory
the Water Queen of Jerusalem owns
a bathing suit made out of Yiddish
the Water Queen of Jerusalem wallows on a stone beach in Ladino
is afraid of the rising water level in Arabic
the Water Queen of Jerusalem has no
sea in Jerusalem
she has a history
Jewish
and she holds
just holds her head
above water

tr. Tsipi Keller

גלית חזן-רוקם

[ילדי בתוכי]

יַלְדִּי בְּתוֹכִי
מְמַיֵּן אֶת קִיּוּמִי לִיסוֹדוֹת מַמָּשִׁיִּים:
דָּם וְשֶׁתֶן
סִידָן וּבַרְזֶל.
בִּשְׁנָתִי אֲנִי מַחְצֵבָה
שֶׁלְּפֶתַע מָצְאוּ בָּהּ אוֹצָרוֹת נְדִירִים.

1989

פנינים שחורות

לנעמה

דַּיֶּגֶת, לָרֶשֶׁת שֶׁלָּךְ חוֹרִים גְּדוֹלִים בִּמְיֻחָד,
אֵינֵךְ גּוֹרֶרֶת אִתָּךְ כְּלוּם מֵחוֹף הַיָּם,
מִלְּבַד אוֹר הַשֶּׁמֶשׁ־בְּעוֹרֵךְ הָאֱגוֹזִי.
בַּתַּרְמִיל שֶׁעַל כְּתֵפֵךְ אַתְּ מַסְתִּירָה נָשִׁים עַתִּיקוֹת.

רֹאשֵׁךְ חָשׂוּף, אָזְנַיִךְ מְנֻקָּבוֹת,
הַטַּבּוּר הַנִּסְתָּר מַצְמִיחַ אֶל תּוֹכֵךְ
וּמַחְשְׁבוֹתַיִךְ נִרְקָמוֹת מֶשִׁי עַל קְטִיפָה,
זָהָב וְסָגֹל, תִּיק לִתְפִלִּין וְטַלִּית.

אֲנִי רוֹצָה לַחֲרֹז לָךְ פְּנִינִים שְׁחֹרוֹת
מִן הַיָּם הַקַּר שֶׁבֵּין הַיְּרֵחִים הַמְּלֵאִים,
לְהַשְׁמִיעַ לָךְ מִן הַמּוּסִיקָה הַמְּעֻגָּלִית
שֶׁכְּלֵי נְגִינָתָהּ מְכֻוָּנִים אֶל שְׁלֵמוּת הַלְּבָנָה וּפְגִיעוּתָהּ.

1998

GALIT HASAN-ROKEM

[THIS CHILD INSIDE ME]

This child inside me
sorts my existence into elements:
blood and urine
calcium and iron.
In my sleep I am a quarry
where rare treasures are suddenly found.

tr. Kathryn Hellerstein

BLACK PEARLS

for Naama

Fisherwoman, your net has unusually big holes,
you don't haul a thing from the beach
except the sunlight in your nut brown skin.
The pack on your shoulder hides ancient women.

Your head is bare, your ears pierced,
your hidden navel deepens in you
and your thoughts are silk embroidered on velvet,
gold and purple, a bag for tefillin and tallit.[1]

I want to string for you black pearls
from the cold sea between the round moons,
and play for you some orbicular music, whose instruments
are tuned to the full moon's vulnerability.

tr. Shirley Kaufman

1. Tefillin: phylacteries for prayer; tallit: prayer shawl. Both are traditionally worn by men.

דליה פלח

חוכמת־בוגר

חָכְמַת־בּוֹגֵר, מִי צָרִיךְ אוֹתָהּ,
בּוֹגֵר־נְקֵבָה, חָכְמָתָהּ זוֹרֶמֶת מִצְּדָדֶיהָ,
מִצִּדֵּי שָׁדֶיהָ שֶׁעוֹבְרִים עַכְשָׁו פֵּרוּשׁ אַחֵר,
חֲזִיַּת־מַלְמָלָה קַלָּה, שֶׁנִּלְבֶּשֶׁת מֵעַל הָרֹאשׁ,
חֲזִיַּת־הֲנָקָה מִתְכַּפְתֶּרֶת,
חֲזִיַּת־מִקְצוֹעַ, לְקֵיצִים, בְּלִי כְּתֵפִיּוֹת,
נִלְבֶּשֶׁת מִתַּחַת לִשְׂמָלוֹת קַלּוֹת מְאֹד,
עִם קֶרֶס לְפָנִים,
חֲזִיָּה וְרֻדָּה־קְרֶם, נְשׁוֹת בְּנֵי־בְּרַק
בַּשָּׁעוֹת הַמֻּקְצוֹת לָהֶן בַּבְּרֵכָה,
וְרִידֵי־רַגְלַיִם לוֹפְפוֹת אוֹתָן כְּמוֹ סְבַךְ
שֶׁהֵן שָׁקְעוּ בּוֹ, לֹא יוּכְלוּ לְהֵעָתֵק,
אֲבָל יֵשׁ אוֹמְרִים שֶׁרוּחָן מְלֵאָה
(בְּאִמָּהוּת?)—כָּל הַזְּמַן לְחַנֵּךְ אֶת הַבָּנוֹת,
לְתַקֵּן, לְהַזְכִּיר, לִכְפּוֹת בְּלִי כְּפִיָּה,
מִכָּל מָקוֹם, שׁוּרַת הַחֲזִיּוֹת הָעֲצוּמוֹת
שֶׁמִּתְחַמְּמוֹת—זֶה גּוּמִי—בַּשֶּׁמֶשׁ שֶׁעַל שׁוּרַת וָוִים—
מָה הֵן שָׁווֹת, בְּחָכְמָתָן,
הַנָּשִׁים בְּלִי הַפֵּאוֹת, קְצוּצוֹת הַשֵּׂעָר, בְּכוֹבְעֵי הָרַחְצָה,
צִדֵּי גּוּפָן הָרְחָבִים שֶׁמַּזְרִימִים אֶת הַחָכְמָה
שֶׁלֹּא שָׁוָה, שֶׁלֹּא שָׁוָה.

1997

DAHLIA FALAH

ADULT-WISDOM

Adult-wisdom, who needs it,
adult-female, her wisdom flows from her sides,
from the sides of her breasts that are now taking on a different meaning,
a light muslin bra, to be put on over the head,
a nursing-bra with buttons,
a profession-bra, for summers, strapless,
to be worn under very light dresses,
with a hook in front,
a pinkish-beige bra, the women of Bnei-Brak[1]
in the hours allotted to them at the pool,
leg-veins enwrapping them like a thicket
they have become entangled in, they'll be unable to get out,
but some people say their spirit is full
(of motherhood?)—all the time to educate the daughters,
to correct, to remind, to coerce without coercion,
in any case, a line of enormous bras
heating up—they're rubber—in the sun on a line of pegs—
what are they worth, in their wisdom,
the women without wigs, shorn hair, in bathing caps,
the wide sides of their bodies flowing with wisdom
that is worthless, is worthless.

tr. Rachel Tzvia Back

1. Bnei-Brak is a town in the greater Tel-Aviv area with a large community of ultra-Orthodox Jews.

אגי משעול

[מואזין הטרנזיסטור]

מוּאֶזִין הַטְּרַנְזִיסְטוֹר עוֹלֶה בַּמַּטָּע—
חָסֵן יָחֵף וּמְחֻבָּר לְאַדְמָתִי
לָשׁ אֶת בְּצֵק הָעֶרֶב מִקֶּמַח יְהוּדִי
יוֹתֵר מִדַּי עָדִין יָא חָאגִ׳י—אֲנִי,
שֶׁכְּבָר עָצַמְתִּי אֶת עֵינַי הַמְמֻיָּנוֹת אַחֲרֵי יוֹם קָטִיף
שְׂפוּפָה אִתּוֹ מֵעַל לָאֵשׁ שֶׁהוּא מַבְעִיר.

אֲנַחְנוּ מִתְכַּנְּנִים אֶת הָאֲפַרְסְקִים שֶׁל מָחָר
עַל ״אֵירוֹפָּה״ וְסִיגָרִיָּה בֵּיתִית.
יָא חָאגִ׳י, כָּכָה מַגִּיחָה אַנְחָתוֹ הָעַרְבִית
נִתְמֶכֶת עַל עִצּוּרֵי שְׁמֵי הַהוּנְגָרֵי הַמְסֹרָס.

בְּדִמְדּוּמֵי הַפּוֹטוֹסִינְתֶזָה הָאֵלֶּה רָצוֹת
יָדָיו מֵעַל הַפַּח
עוֹשׂוֹת בַּפִּתָּה כְּשָׁפִים.
חָסֵן מְאַרְמֵן לִי אֲגָדוֹת
אֶלֶף לַיְלָה וְלַיְלָה מֵעֵזָּה,
גּוּפוֹ שְׁפִיפוֹן גָּמִישׁ
עֵינָיו תְּשׁוּבָה לָאֵשׁ.

1986

אחוזה

שׁוּם טַוָּסִים לֹא יִסְתּוֹבְבוּ אֶצְלִי
בֶּחָצֵר. דַּי שֶׁהַבֹּקֶר עָלִיתִי מִן הַכִּיּוֹר
אֶל טְרַפְּטִיכוֹן פָּנַי וְרֵדָה מִדַּי
לְטַעֲמִי עִם כָּל הָאָנִי בְּלוֹנְד
וְעוֹד בְּתַלְתַּלִּים אֱלֹהִים
אֵיזֶה קִיטְשׁ נִהְיֵיתִי
אָז לֹא טַוָּסִים.

וְגַם אֶרְכֹּשׁ לִי חֲזִיר
אֶרְכֹּשׁ אוֹתוֹ בִּשְׁבִיל הַיְכֹלֶת
לְהַגִּיד מִשְׁפָּטִים חֲדָשִׁים לְגַמְרֵי כְּמוֹ
לֵךְ תִּבְדֹּק מָה עִם הַחֲזִיר אוֹ
מְחִיר הַחֲזִיר
עָלָה
אֲבָל לֹא טַוָּסִים.

AGI MISHOL

[THE TRANSISTOR MUEZZIN]

The transistor muezzin rises in the orchard—
Hussein barefoot and bound to my land
kneads the evening dough from Jewish flour
too fine, *ya Hagi*—I
who already closed my sorting eyes after a day of harvest,
crouch with him over the fire he kindles.

We're planning tomorrow's peaches
over Europa[1] and a handrolled cigarette.
Ya Hagi, his Arab sigh slithers forth
supported on the consonants of my castrated Hungarian name.

In these photosynthesis twilights his hands
run over the tin
casting a spell with pita.
Hussein castles me legends
a thousand and one nights from Gaza,
his body a supple viper
his eyes an answer to the fire.

tr. Linda Zisquit

ESTATE

No peacocks will strut in my yard.
It's enough that this morning I rose from the sink
to the triptych of my face
too pink to my liking, what with the honey blonde,
and curly to boot, God,
how tacky I've become.
So no peacocks.

I'll purchase a pig,
purchase a pig so I can
speak entirely new phrases, such as
go check on the pig, or,
the price of pigs
has risen.
But no peacocks.

1. Brand name of a cheap Israeli cigarette.

אָז אֲנִי הַחֲזִיר מֵהַבַּיִת הַקּוֹדֵם
שְׁכוּבָה עַל צִדִּי בִּשְׁלוּלִית הָעֶלְבּוֹן
וּדְחוּף תַּ״שְּׁמְשׁוֹנִית שֶׁלִּי לַחְמָנִיָּה שֶׁלִּי
גְּבִינָה רַכָּה שֶׁלִּי עַגְבָנִיָּה״ כִּי לְחוּד
הַמִּלִּים וּלְחוּד אַתָּה
אֲנִי הַקִּפּוֹד הַנֶּחְמָד שֶׁתָּפַח לְדַרְבָּן
אֲנִי הַדַּרְבָּן הָאָיֹם הַמַּסְגִּיל וּמַכְפִּיל
אֶת עַצְמוֹ בְּכָל אִישׁוֹן מֵאִישׁוֹנֵינוּ
אֲנִי הַזְּבוּב הַיָּרֹק־מַתַּכְתִּי הַחוֹכֵךְ
כַּפּוֹתָיו מוּל פָּנֶיךָ וְזוֹמֵם עָלֶיךָ
רַע
גַּם אִם בָּרֶקַע מֵאֲחוֹרֵי גַּבִּי
מַתְחִילִים חַמְצִיצִים לְפַטְפֵּט אָבִיב
וּלְהַלְשִׁין עַל הַחַיִּים הָאִימְפְּרֶסְיוֹנִיסְטִיִּים שֶׁלִּי
וְעַל הַוָּרֹד הַנָּקִי שֶׁאֲנִי פּוֹעֶרֶת לָעוֹלָם
כְּשֶׁאֲנִי מְפַהֶקֶת.

1995

בהיפר

1

בְּסִמְטוֹת הַהִיפֶּר אֲנִי דּוֹחֶפֶת עֲגָלָה כְּמוֹ אִמָּן
שֶׁל שְׁתֵּי הַכְּרוּבִיּוֹת מְנַוֶּטֶת עַל פִּי שִׁירְשִׁימַת הַקְּנִיּוֹת
שֶׁיָּצָא לִי הַבֹּקֶר מֵעַל לַקָּפֶה.
כּוֹתָרוֹת הַמִּבְצָע מִתְנַפְנְפוֹת לַמְעַיְּנִים
בְּסוּגַת הָרְכִיבִים שֶׁל כְּרִיכוֹת הַמָּזוֹן וּקְלַיְדֶרְמַן
מַנְעִים לָעוֹפוֹת הַקְּפוּאִים. גַּם אֲנִי
שֶׁחַיַּי עֲשׂוּיִים רַק מֵחַיִּים, מִתְנַהֶלֶת בְּעִקּוּל הַדּוּגְלִי
אֶל מַר פְּלִינְקֶר הַמַּמְתִּיק לְתוֹךְ אָזְנִי כִּי זֶה רַק הַגּוּף
שֶׁמִּתְפּוֹרֵר אֲבָל הַנֶּפֶשׁ לָעַד הִיא צְעִירָה
תַּאֲמִינִי לִי. אֲנִי מַאֲמִינָה. אַךְ פְּנֵי לְיוֹנָתָן
וַאֲלֶכְּסַנְדֶּר
חוּשׁוּ אַחִים אֶל הַקּוּסְבָּרָה
חוּשׁוּ חוּשׁוּ אַחִים
אֲנִי מְשׁוֹרֶרֶת הַהִיפֶּרְשׁוּק
אֲשׁוֹרֵר אֶת רִשְׁרוּשׁוֹ שֶׁל הַקּוֹרְנְפְלֵייקְס
וְאֶת עַקְמוּמִית הַמְּלָפְפוֹנִים הַמּוּרְדִּים
עַד שֶׁתּוֹשִׁיט לִי הַקֻּפָּה־רוֹשֶׁמֶת
גִּרְסָה סוֹפִית וּמֻדְפֶּסֶת
שֶׁל שִׁירִי.

I am that pig from the previous stanza,
splayed on my side in a puddle of hurt.
So shove your "my tomboy my muffin
my soft cheese tomato" because
words aside and you aside
I'm the cute hedgehog swelling into a porcupine
the livid porcupine doubling
in every pupil of our pupils;
I'm the metallic green fly rubbing
its forelegs before your face scheming
malice
even though in the background behind my back
sorrel has begun to chatter spring
reporting on my impressionistic life
and on the clear pink I open wide to the world
when I yawn.

tr. Tsipi Keller

IN THE SUPERMARKET

1

Through the supermarket alleys I push a cart
as if I were the mother of two heads of cauliflower,
and navigate according to the verse-list
I improvised this morning over coffee.
Sale banners wave to shoppers
studying the genre of labels on packaged foods
as Muzak entertains the frozen birds. And I too,
whose life is made of life, stride down the dog-food aisle
toward Mr. Flinker who confides in my ear that only the body
crumbles but the spirit stays young forever, believe me.
I believe, but now let me turn to Jonathan and MacIntosh.
Hurry folks, to the coriander,
hurry hurry folks,
I'm the supermarket bard,
I'll sing the rustle of cornflakes,
the curve of mutinous cucumbers,
until the cash register will hand me
the final printed version
of my poem.

2

מְשׁוֹטֶטֶת בַּהִיפֶּר בְּתוֹךְ מַהוּת עֲקֶרֶת־הַבַּיִת שֶׁלִּי
וּפִתְאֹם אַתָּה מִתְלוֹצֵץ לִי אָגִי בָּגִי
לְיַד הַחֲמוּצִים
וְאַחַר כָּךְ רַב מְזִמּוֹת
(הוֹי יוּד)
צוֹבֵט בַּאֲחוֹרַי לְיַד הַדֶּלִיקָטֶסִים
בְּעוֹד אִשְׁתְּךָ מִתְלַבֶּטֶת
בֵּין דִּבְרֵי הֶחָלָב
תָּרָה אַחֲרֶיךָ בִּשְׁבִיל
הַקְּבִיעָה הַסּוֹפִית:
חֲמִשָּׁה אָחוּז? תִּשְׁעָה אָחוּז?

3

(בַּמַּחְלָקָה לְלִבְנֵי נָשִׁים
שָׁמַעְתִּי אַחַת: אֲנִי
יֵשׁ לִי רֶגֶל יָפָה
אֲבָל הֶחָזֶה שֶׁלִּי
עַל הַפָּנִים

אֶצְלִי
אָמְרָה הָאַחֶרֶת
דַּוְקָא הֶחָזֶה זֶה
מַשֶּׁהוּ
אֲבָל הָרַגְלַיִם שֶׁלִּי
עַל הַפָּנִים)

4

אֲנִי חִבַּקְתִּי אוֹתְךָ
וְאַתָּה חִבַּקְתָּ אֲבַטִּיחַ
אֲנִי אָהַבְתִּי אוֹתְךָ וְאַתָּה לֹא
יָדַעְתָּ מַה לַּעֲשׂוֹת
עִם הָאֲבַטִּיחַ
כִּי יָדֶיךָ שֶׁרָצוּ
לְחַבֵּק אוֹתִי
לֹא יָכְלוּ
לַעֲזֹב אוֹתוֹ
וּמִצַּד שֵׁנִי
מַה
תַּגִּיד חַכִּי
רַק אַנִּיחַ
אֶת הָאֲבַטִּיחַ?

1995

2

I stroll in the supermarket clad in the essence
of my housewifery when suddenly you kid me, "Agi-Bagi"
near the pickles,
and then deviously
pinch my ass
near the delicatessen counter
while your wife hesitates
among the dairy products
hunts for you
for the final ruling:
Non-fat? Low-fat?

3

(In the lingerie department
I hear a woman say: Me,
my legs are nice,
but my breasts
are a flop.

With me
said another
it's just the opposite. My breasts
are a knockout
but my legs
are a flop.)

4

I hugged you
and you hugged a watermelon
I loved you and you didn't
know what to do
with the watermelon
because your hands wanted
to hug me
but couldn't
let go of it
on the other hand
what
could you say, wait,
let me just put down
the watermelon?

tr. Tsipi Keller

פונה לנוח בשירי סאפפו

אֲנַחְנוּ שְׂרוּעוֹת עַל הָאֶבֶן הַקְּרִירָה
מִתַּחַת לַכּוֹכָבִים הַנּוֹצְצִים
נוֹגְסוֹת בְּתַפּוּחַ
לִכְבוֹד כָּל הָאֲהוּבוֹת
וְהָאֲהוּבִים
שֶׁבָּאוּ לָנוּחַ
בֵּין יְרֵכֵינוּ

אֲנַחְנוּ מְדַבְּרוֹת עַל אַהֲבָה
בִּפְרָטֵי פְּרָטִים

עַל הַחַיִּים הַמַּצְמִיאִים
וְשֶׁהָעֵץ הוּא מִזְרָקָה
יְרֻקָּה

רֹאשָׁהּ הַיָּפֶה סָמוּךְ לְרֹאשִׁי
תַּלְתַּלֶּיהָ בְּתַלְתַּלַּי

הִיא אוֹמֶרֶת
אֲנִי אוֹמֶרֶת
וְצִחְקוּקֵינוּ חוֹמְקִים
לְתוֹךְ הַגֶּפֶן שֶׁנִּיחוֹחָהּ
מִשְׂתָּרֵג מֵאִתָּנוּ

1995

דבורה אמיר

מה שמחלחל

בְּכָל הַתְּמוּנוֹת מִן הָאַלְבּוֹם שֶׁלָּךְ מִתְגּוֹדְדוֹת פּוֹעֲלוֹת,
רַקָּה שֶׁל אַחַת נוֹשֶׁקֶת לְרַקַּת רְעוּתָהּ.
מֵיְשִׁירוּת מַבָּט נָחוּשׁ כְּמוֹ שֶׁבִּקֵּשׁ הַצַּלָּם.
אַתְּ בַּפִּנָּה, כּוֹרַעַת בֶּרֶךְ, מְמַיֶּנֶת סֶלֶק סֻכָּר
כְּמוֹ מְסָרֶבֶת לָקַחַת חֵלֶק בְּפוֹזָה פּוֹעֲלִית.

בַּיּוֹם שֶׁהִנַּחְתִּי מַבָּט רַךְ עַל אֵיבְרֵי גּוּפֵךְ הַיָּפִים,
גִּלִּיתִי בְּשׁוֹק רַגְלֵךְ סִימָנֵי נְשִׁיכוֹת.
כָּךְ, בְּאַקְרַאי מְגַלֶּה יֶלֶד נֵתַח מִן הַצּוֹרֵב בְּהוֹרָיו.
כָּל הַשָּׁנִים אַתְּ מְהַלֶּכֶת בָּאָרֶץ הַזֹּאת—עוֹלָם זָר לִי נָעוּץ בְּרַגְלַיִךְ,
גַּן אָסוּר כִּבְיָכוֹל, בַּעַל אֲחֻזָּה אַכְזָר כִּבְיָכוֹל, כַּלְבֵי שְׁמִירָה, יַלְדָּה נִטְרֶפֶת.
וּפַעַם בְּסִמְטַת גּ׳וֹרְג׳ אֶלְיוֹט, צָמוּד לְמִנְזַר ׳הָאֲחָיוֹת שֶׁל צִיּוֹן׳
תְּקָפַנִי פַּחַד גָּדוֹל, שֶׁיִּגְרְרוּנִי וְיַלְבִּישׁוּנִי בְּגָדִים
שֶׁל יְתוֹמִים, יִכְלָאוּנִי בְּמַרְתֵּף סְפוּג רֵיחַ פִּסְלוֹנֵי הַצָּלוּב,
וּבֵין פִּתּוּלֵי גְּלִימָתוֹ שֶׁל נָזִיר שָׁחֹר, יִשְׁכוּנִי כַּלְבֵי הַשָּׂטָן.

1994

TURNING TO REST IN SAPPHO'S POEMS

We're sprawled across the cool stone
under glittering stars
bite into an apple
honoring all the loved ones
women and men
who came to rest
between our thighs

We talk about love
its smallest detail

talk about life that makes us thirsty
about the tree that is
a green fountain

her beautiful head is next to mine
her curls in mine

she says
I say
and our giggles escape
into the vine whose scent
spreads out from us

tr. Tsipi Keller

DEVORAH AMIR

WHAT SINKS IN

Every photo in your album has women workers crowded
so close together their temples touch each other,
staring straight ahead, as the photographer wanted.
You in the corner, kneeling, sorting sugar beets,
as if refusing to take part in the proletarian pose.

The day I looked gently at your beautiful legs, I discovered teeth marks
on your calf. That's how a child discovers by chance a scrap
of her parent's torment. All the years you walked around this country—
a world foreign to me was driven into your legs, a forbidden garden,
as it were, a cruel landlord, watch dogs, a girl attacked.
And once in George Eliot Lane, close to the Sisters of Zion convent,
I was overwhelmed by fear they'd drag me in, put me in orphan's clothes,
lock me in a cellar soaked in the odor of crucifixes, and from the folds
of a monk's black robe, Satan's dogs would bite me.

tr. Shirley Kaufman

מאיה בז'נרו

עיבוד נתונים 60

הַפָּנִים שֶׁלִּי יָפִים כְּשֶׁמְּבִינִים אוֹתִי;
מַשֶּׁהוּ בְּכוּר פְּנִימִיּוּתִי פּוֹנֶה
אֶל מַעֲמַקִּים שָׁקוּעַ בְּאַפְלוּלִית
מִתְעוֹרֵר לְחַיִּים וְאַט אַט מְרַחֵף
מַלְאַךְ פְּרָטִיּוּתִי, מַלְעַף רוּחִי
מוֹשִׁיט אֶת אֶצְבָּעוֹ לְזוּלָתִי — פְּנֵי אָדָם מֵעָלַי
כִּי הַהֲבָנָה הִיא הַפְרָיָה
נְגוּעַת הַשְׁרָאָה וְיֹפִי חַשְׁמַלִּי
דּוֹמִים אָז לְכֵלִים זוֹהֲרִים עֲצוּמִים
הָעֲצָמִים מִסָּבִיב רוֹקְדִים, יָכוֹל לִהְיוֹת
מְדַבְּרִים אֶת הַתֶּדֶר הֲכִי אִישִׁי שֶׁלָּהֶם נֹאמַר
קוֹד הַסְּתָרִים נִבְקַע נִפְתַּח בָּהֶם —
אֲנַחְנוּ מְבִינִים אֶת הַמִּבְנֶה הַפְּנִימִי
וְהֵם נַעֲשִׂים יָפִים כֶּפֶל כִּפְלַיִם
כָּךְ אוּלַי הַפָּנִים הֵם הַפְשָׁטָה
כְּמוֹ שֶׁנֶּאֱמַר,
אַחֲרֵי שֶׁהֵם הַקְּרָבָה — קֹדֶם לָכֵן
מַקְרִיבִים אֶת לֶחֶם הַפָּנִים
קְרִי:
הַמֵּצַח הַפֶּה וְהָאַף לְחָיַיִם, עֵינַיִם
סַנְטֵר וְשֵׂעָר
קְחוּ אֶת לֶחֶם הַפָּנִים וּבִצְעוּ אוֹתוֹ לִבְצָעִים —
הֵן תֵּעָלַמְנָה הַפָּנִים, תֵּקְרַבְנָה
וּבִמְקוֹמָן נִשְׁאֶרֶת הַחִידָה הַמֵּפְשֶׁטֶת:
מַה מִּסְתַּתֵּר מֵאֲחוֹרֵי הַפָּנִים הָאֵלֶּה,
שֶׁצְּרִיכָה לְהִתְבַּהֵר;
לִתְפֹּשׂ נְקֻדָּה בֶּחָלָל וּלְבָקְעָהּ
וְאַחַר כָּךְ כְּמוֹ בְּמַעֲשֶׂה שִׁבּוּץ
יִכָּנְסוּ הָאַף וְהַפֶּה הָעֵינַיִם וְהַמֵּצַח
חֲזָרָה לִמְקוֹמָם הַיְחִידִי
בְּתוֹךְ הַמִּסְגֶּרֶת הַנֶּחֱרֶצֶת
מִסְגֶּרֶת הַיֹּפִי וְהַהֲבָנָה.

הַפָּנִים שֶׁלִּי יָפִים כְּשֶׁמְּבִינִים אוֹתִי
הֵם מִתְעַצְּמִים לִמְמַדֵּי שַׁעַר גָּדוֹל
בְּמֵאוֹת גְּוָנִים שֶׁל צְבָעִים בַּנְּיָר
בְּזָוִיּוֹת הַחֹמֶר וְחִתּוּכָיו.

1983

MAYA BEJERANO

DATA PROCESSING 60

My face is beautiful when I am understood;
something in my innermost core turns
to the depths, sunk in darkness,
awakens to live and very slowly
the angel of my privacy, my privangelic spirit hovers
stretching its finger outward—a human face above me
because understanding is germination
touched by inspiration and electric beauty.
Surrounding objects dance resembling
vast glowing vessels, perhaps
speaking their most personal frequency as if
a secret code has been cracked, opened up in them.
We grasp the internal structure
and it multiplies in its beauty.
Perhaps the face is an abstraction too,
as it is said in Scripture
from the moment it's offered—first
one sacrifices the showbread,[1]
which means:
the forehead, the mouth and the nose, cheeks, eyes,
chin and hair.
Take the showbread and break it into pieces—
then the face will disappear, will be sacrificed,
and what will remain in its place is only the abstract riddle.
What is hiding behind that face
that needs clarifying? Needs
to grab some point in outer space and split it apart
so that later, as in a mosaic,
nose, mouth, eyes and forehead will return
to their places fixed
in the incised framework,
the framework of beauty and understanding.

My face is beautiful when I am understood,
it expands to the size of a broad gate
in hundreds of shades of color on the paper
in the clay's angles and cuts.

tr. Miri Kubovy

1. Consecrated unleavened bread ritually placed by the Jewish priests of ancient Israel on a table in the sanctuary of the Tabernacle on the Sabbath.

הסיב האופטי

וַיְּהִי וַיְּהִי וַיְּהִי
בְּמַחֲצִית בְּמַחֲצִית דַּרְכִּי
אֶל כּוֹכַב הַנֶּפֶשׁ, רְכוּבָה
עַל סִיב אוֹפְּטִי שָׁקוּף,
הָיִיתִי קֶרֶן אוֹר קַלָּה, תֶּדֶר קוֹל—
מִסְפָּר בִּינַארִי; וּבְחֻבִּי מִלָּה
וְעוֹד מִלָּה וְעוֹד מִלָּה
כִּפְעִימוֹת אוֹר חֹשֶׁךְ מִלֵּב חַשְׁמַלִּי,
הַמְשַׁדֵּר אוֹתוֹת מַרְטִיטִים, גַּלִּים, רַצֵּי גַּלִּים כְּסוּפָה
מִקְצֵה הָאָרֶץ עַד סוֹפָהּ;
וְשָׁם בִּקְצֵה הָאָרֶץ יַחֲזֹר הַמִּסְפָּר הַמְכֻשָּׁף
יִהְיֶה מִסְפָּר רָגִיל תּוֹךְ חֶלְקִיקֵי שְׁנִיָּה,
וּמִן הַסִּיב הָאוֹפְּטִי הַדַּקִּיק הֶמְיָה
נִשְׁמַעַת כְּמִבּוֹר שֵׁנָה: "אֲנִי אוֹהֶבֶת אוֹתְךָ"
מִלִּים וּמַלְאָכִים מִתּוֹךְ סִיבִים פּוֹרְחִים
קוֹרְנִים מֵאוֹת פְּרָחִים בִּמְהִירוּת כִּמְעַט הָאוֹר
וְזוֹ הִיא רַק שִׂיחָה שֶׁל אוֹר לֵייזֶר בְּבֶטֶן סִיב אוֹפְּטִי
מְהֵימָן וּמְעֻדָּן, דַּק וְחָלוּל כְּנִימָה
שָׁקוּף כִּזְכוּכִית וְאָטוּם כְּחִידָה.

1985

השירה

עַכְשָׁו כְּשֶׁהַפָּנִים שֶׁלָּהּ כְּבָר נְקִיִּים וּנְקוּבִים כִּכְבָרָה
בָּאַמְתּוֹת הֶכְרֵחִיּוֹת—הַשִּׁירָה יְכוֹלָה לָקוּם,
לְהִתְכּוֹפֵף רֶגַע עַל שֻׁלְחַן הָאִפּוּר שֶׁלָּהּ מוּל הַמַּרְאָה,
מַרְאָה מִזְדַּמֶּנֶת מֵאֵיזוֹ חֲנוּת, חֲנוּת בְּשׁוּק הַפִּשְׁפְּשִׁים אוֹ
שׁוּק הָעֲלִיָּה; וּלְזַנֵּק.
מְשַׁחֶקֶת לְתוֹכָהּ;
כְּדֵי לֹא לְהִכָּשֵׁל בַּמַּסֵּכוֹת שֶׁיִּצְטָרְכוּ לִמְחֹק
וּלְנַגֵּב אַחַר כָּךְ בְּמַיִם וְסַבּוֹן,
מִן הָרָאוּי שֶׁכָּל תְּנוּעָה כָּל קַו וְצֶבַע
בִּקְפִידָה יֵעָשׂוּ—
רַחֲבַת זִירָה הַמַּרְאָה כְּמוֹ פַּר דָּרוּךְ
תַּבִּיט בְּפָנֶיהָ שֶׁל גְּבֶרֶת הַשִּׁירָה הַנִּרְכָּנִים לְהִשְׁתַּקֵּף בָּהּ
תְּזוֹרֵר תַּרְכִּין קַרְנַיִם.
חַכּוּ נִרְאֶה לְאָן תַּגִּיעַ—
הַפַּר בַּמַּרְאָה וְהַשִּׁירָה לְעֻמָּתָהּ;

THE OPTICAL FIBER

Let there be let there be let there be
midway midway
to the star of the soul, riding
a transparent optical fiber,
I was a beam of light, a frequency—
a binary number; and inside me a word
and another word and another word
like beatings of light and darkness from an electric heart
sending quivering signals, waves, rows of waves as a story
from one end of the earth to another:
and there, at the end of the earth, the bewitched number will return
will be a regular number within a fraction of a second,
and from the thin optical fiber a cooing
is heard as if from a pit of sleep: "I love you"
words and angels out of blooming fibers
beaming hundreds of flowers in almost the speed of light
and all of this is only a laser light call inside the belly of an optical fiber
reliable and refined, thin and hollow as a string
transparent as glass and impenetrable as a riddle.

tr. Miri Kubovy

POETRY

Now that her skin is clean and pierced with essential truths like a sieve,
poetry can rise,
bend a moment over her make-up table and face the mirror—
any old mirror found in a store, a shop in some bazaar
or other—and leap.
Laughing to herself.
Each gesture, line and color
will be drawn with care
so as not to be misled by masks she'd have to erase
and wipe clean with water and soap—
the mirror a vast arena, a watchful bull
will look into the face of Mrs. Poetry leaning
into her own reflection,
will sneeze will dip horns.
Let's wait and see how far she'll go—
the bull in the mirror and poetry facing it;

הַפַּר יָכוֹל לָצֵאת מֵהַמַּרְאָה לִבְעֹל אוֹתָהּ בִּשְׁעַת רְכִינָתָהּ;
שִׁירָה בְּעוּלָה — זֶה מַה שֶּׁיִּהְיֶה לָנוּ,
אִם לֹא תִּצְלַח כָּאן הַשִּׁירָה הַמְאַלֶּפֶת
מוּל הַשּׁוֹר בַּמַּרְאָה;

1991

מצבי מלחמה

הַמִּבְנֶה הַנַּפְשִׁי,
הַגֵּאוֹלוֹגְיָה הַנַּפְשִׁית אֱנוֹשִׁית
כָּל הַזְּמָן כּוֹלֶלֶת לַבַּת אֵשׁ בְּתוֹכָהּ
כָּל הַזְּמָן שָׁם מְבַעְבַּעַת מִלְחָמָה
מִלְחָמָה כְּנָכְחוּת מַתְמֶדֶת
בְּהִתְפָּרְקוּת הַחֹמֶר;

מִתַּחַת לַסְּחַרְחֵרוֹת הַצִּבְעוֹנִיּוֹת, לְגַלְגַּלֵּי הַתַּעֲנוּגוֹת,
לְבָתֵּי הַקָּפֶה הַשְּׁקוּפִים אַפְלוּלִיִּים, הֵיכָן שֶׁיָּדַיִם מְנִיפוֹת
מַשֶּׁהוּ חָמוּד, טַעַם מְשַׁכֵּר וְזֶה יָכוֹל לִהְיוֹת תִּינוֹק גַּם;
מִתַּחַת לְבָמוֹת, לְאוּלַמּוֹת, לְכִסְאוֹת הַתַּלְמִידִים וְלוּחוֹת הַהוֹרָאָה,
מִתַּחַת לְכָרֵי הַשֵּׁנָה, לַשְּׁבִילִים הַבְּהִירִים לַשְּׁעוֹנִים,

מִתַּחַת לַחַיִּים
נִשְׁמַעַת כָּל הַזְּמָן הִתְפָּרְקוּת הַחֹמֶר הַלּוֹחֶמֶת אֶת נָכְחוּתָהּ
מִתַּחַת לְהָרֵי הַשִּׂכְחָה הַתּוֹקְפָנִית
לְהַר הָעִיר הַמְלֻבָּשׁ כְּתוּבוֹת
אֵיזוֹ חֲצָפָה וְרַהַב הָפְכוּ אוֹתָהּ וְנָתְנוּ לָהּ פֶּתַח מִלּוּט רָחָב
לָצֵאת לְהֵרָאוֹת וּלְהִשָּׁמַע, נִבְדֶּלֶת בְּכָל קַטְלָנוּתָהּ
בִּרְצוֹן אִישׁ־טִיל בְּמִין הַשְׁוָצָה בִּכְלֵי מַשְׁחִית —
יְצוּרִים חַד־מַשְׁמָעִיִּים, כֵּלִים מַסִּיגֵי גְּבוּל בְּהוֹנָאַת גְּבוּל
מַתְסִיסִים אוֹתָנוּ בִּתְחוּשׁוֹת אַנְשֵׁי הַבֶּטֶן
חַסְרֵי יִחוּד וְתֹאַר, אַנְשֵׁי הָעֹרֶף בְּמַדִּים מְחוּקִים
בְּנִסָּיוֹן לִבְרֹחַ שֶׁהוּא נִסָּיוֹן לִשְׁמֹר צוּרַת פָּנִים רִאשׁוֹנִים
נִדּוֹן לְכִשָּׁלוֹן.

הַמִּלְחָמָה מִשְׁתַּרְבֶּבֶת בְּכָל חוֹר
הַמִּלְחָמָה נִמְצֵאת בָּאֲוִיר
וְהַפֶּה שֶׁנִּפְצַע שָׁר אוֹתָהּ בְּכָל מְחִיר.

1993

the bull may leave the glass and ravage her as she bends over—
a ravaged poetry—that's what we'll have
if tamed poetry won't face up
to the bull in the glass

tr. Tsipi Keller

WAR SITUATIONS

The structure of the soul,
the human soul's geology
always includes burning lava
war always bubbling there
war as a constant presence
in the disintegration of matter;

under the colorful merry-go-rounds, the wheels of pleasure,
the dim gauzy coffeehouses, where hands toss
something sweet, an intoxicating flavor, and maybe an infant too;
under stages, concert halls, schoolroom chairs, and blackboards,
under pillows, well-lit trails, clocks,

under life
we always hear the disintegration of matter fighting to be
under mountains of aggressive forgetfulness
under the city mountain clothed in graffiti—
what nerve and pride turned it upside down and let it get away
to be seen and heard, distinguished in all its fatality
with the will of a rocket man showing off his weapon—
unequivocal creatures, tools for trespassing stealing over borders,
arousing gut feelings in gut people
nondescript and ordinary, home front people in erased uniforms
trying to escape trying to save the shape of a face that was,
and doomed to fail.

War twists itself into every hole
war is in the air
and the hurt mouth sings it at all costs.

tr. Lisa Katz

לאה איילון

מחשבות אפלות
ואני בכלל היפוך של מה שאתם חושבים

הַהוֹרָאוֹת הָיוּ לְהַטְמִין אֶת הַשּׁוֹשַׁנִּים הַצְּחֹרִים וְהַלַּבְקָנִיִּים הַלָּלוּ
בְּמֶרְחָק שֶׁל חֲמִשָּׁה־עָשָׂר עַל חֲמִשָּׁה־עָשָׂר ס״מ.
וּבְכֵן אֲנִי גְּחוּנָה עַל הָאֲדָמָה כְּמוֹ שְׁתֵּי רָשֻׁיּוֹת.
בְּפָנִים כָּל כָּךְ עֲדִינִים וּרְגִישִׁים וְיִחוּדִיִּים
וְכֹה רוֹמַנְטִיִּים בַּמַּבָּט הַמְחֻדָּד וְהַמִּסְתַּכֵּל בְּסַקְרָנוּת בְּכָל מַה שֶּׁקּוֹרֶה
לִפְנֵיהֶם
וְאִלּוּ הַגּוּף מִזְדַּקֵּר גָּחוּן וְהוֹפֵךְ לְמַיְחָם
מָשָׁל הוּא מִתְאַוֶּה שֶׁפִּקֵּק שֶׁעָם יִסְגֹּר אוֹתוֹ מֵאָחוֹר.
סֶרֶט הַמְּדִידָה הַגְּלִילִי נִמְתָּח וּמוֹדֵד בְּאֵיזֶה דִּיּוּק
חֲמִשָּׁה־עָשָׂר ס״מ
וְאָז מוּשָׂם בְּצֵל שׁוֹשָׁן צָחֹר מְפֹאָר בַּגֻּמָּה.
הַמַּחֲשָׁבוֹת וְהָרְצוֹנוֹת הֲכִי אֲפֵלִים יוֹצְאִים וּמִתְפַּתְּלִים מִמֹּחִי
מָשָׁל פְּקָעוֹת שֶׁל צִפְעוֹנִים עוֹלִים וּמִתְפַּתְּלִים
לְקוֹל חֲלִילוֹ שֶׁל פָּקִיר הֹדִּי שֶׁמְּנַגֵּן לִפְנֵיהֶם.
אֲנִי רוֹצָה לְהַפְשִׁיט וּלְהָסִיר אֶת הַבְּגָדִים מִכָּל הַנָּשִׁים הָאֵלֶּה
וּלְדַגְדֵּג לָהֶן בִּצְרוֹר שֶׁל עַנְפֵי הַשּׁוֹשָׁן הַצָּחֹר שֶׁלְּיָדִי
בֵּין הָרַגְלַיִם
אוֹ לִמְרֹחַ לָהֶן שָׁם מִשְׁחַת וָזֶלִין.
אַתְּ זוֹכֶרֶת רָצִינוּ כָּל כָּךְ לִשְׁתֹּל יָקִינְתוֹנִים וְסַלְסִלֵּי כֶּסֶף
בְּשׁוּם שֵׂכֶל בְּתוֹךְ הָעֲרָפֶל
וְלִהְיוֹת גַּנָּנוֹת וְלִהְיוֹת כֹּה מְתוּקוֹת
וְכֹה מַבִּיעוֹת אֵמוּן לָעוֹלָם.
בִּבְגָדִים נֶחְמָדִים שֶׁל צָהֹב וְכָחֹל
וּשְׁלַל וָזוֹת עֲמוּסוֹת וְרָדִים
עַל כַּנֵּי עֵץ מֻגְבָּהִים כּוֹנָנִיּוֹת וַאֲרוֹנוֹת.
וְעַתָּה הָעוֹלָם כָּל כָּךְ הֲפַכְפַּךְ
וַאֲנִי מְיַצֶּבֶת גִּבְעוֹל שׁוֹשָׁן צָחֹר בְּתוֹךְ גֻּמָּה
וַאֲנִי זֵידוֹנִית וּבוֹכָה.

1983

LEAH AYALON

DARK THOUGHTS
AND I AM EVEN THE OPPOSITE OF WHAT YOU THINK

The directions said to bury these pure and white lilies
at a distance of fifteen by fifteen centimeters.
And so I am bent over the ground like a two-headed authority.
With a face so delicate, sensitive and singular
and so romantic with the sharpened gaze that looks curiously at all that
occurs before it
while the bent body becomes erect and in heat
as though craving a cork that will close it from behind.
The rolled up tape measure is stretched and marks with great exactness
fifteen centimeters
and then the pure exquisite lily bulb is put in the hollow.
The darkest thoughts and desires turn and twist in my mind
like coils of poisonous snakes rising and twisting
to the sound of the Indian fakir's flute playing before them.
As a man I want to undress and remove the clothes from all those women
and tickle them with the bundles of white lily leaves beside me
between their legs
or spread vaseline there.
You remember we wanted so much to plant hyacinths
and silver ainsworthia
fragrance of wisdom in the fog
and be gardeners and be so sweet
and so believing in the world.
In lovely dresses of yellow and blue
and a myriad of vases filled with roses
on raised wooden bases, bookshelves and bureaus.
And now the world is so wayward
and I steady a lily stem in a hole
and I am wanton and crying.

tr. Rachel Tzvia Back

ילדה זהבה

אֲנִי לֹא אִמָּא יוֹתֵר
הִיא כָּל כָּךְ יָפָה
קְטַנְטֹנֶת זְהֵבָה
שׁוֹשָׁן בַּפֶּה
יָם בָּאֹזֶן
וְצִדְפָּה.
שֶׁאֲנִי לֹא יְכוֹלָה
לְהִתְיַחֵס אֵלֶיהָ כְּאִמָּא.
אֲנִי אוֹהֶבֶת אוֹתָהּ
כַּחַיִּים עַצְמָם.
אֲנִי אוֹהֶבֶת אוֹתָהּ כְּאִלּוּ אֲנִי לֹא אִמָּהּ.
רֵאשִׁית הִיא יוֹשֶׁבֶת
עַל סֶלַע אַרְנָבוֹת
כָּךְ שֶׁמֵּעוֹלָם לֹא הִצְלַחְתִּי
לְהַגִּיעַ אֵלֶיהָ.
וְיַלְדָּה קְטַנְטֹנֶת זְהֵבָה זוֹ
שׁוֹשָׁן בַּפֶּה
יָם בָּאֹזֶן
וְצִדְפָּה.
קָרְעָה אֶת לִבִּי.
רָצִיתִי לְהָמִיר אֶת עַצְמִי בָּהּ.
אַךְ כָּל מַה שֶּׁעָשׂוּי וּמְתֻקָּן
לִילָדִים,
אֵינוֹ עָשׂוּי וּמְתֻקָּן לִגְדוֹלִים.
אַךְ אֵינֶנִּי מַרְגִּישָׁה כָּךְ
אֵינֶנִּי מַרְגִּישָׁה.
עָלַי לְהִתְעַלֵּל בָּהּ
לְהוֹרִידָהּ מִמְּרוֹם שִׁבְתָּהּ
לִהְיוֹת שׁוּב אִמָּהּ
בְּזַעַף רַב לָתֵת לָהּ
חָלָב קַר.
הַתְּשׁוּבָה הִיא
מִלִּפְנֵי תְּרֵיסַר שָׁנָה.

1984

GOLDEN GIRL

I am not a mother anymore
she is so beautiful
golden little one
lily of lips
sea in ear
and an oyster
that I cannot
treat her like a mother.
I love her
as life itself.
I love her as though I weren't her mother.
From the first she sits
on a coney cliff
so I can never
reach her.
And this little golden girl
lily of lips
sea in ear
and an oyster.
She has ripped apart my heart.
I have wanted to become her.
But all that is made and mended
for children,
is not made and mended for adults.
But I don't feel this
I don't feel.
I must abuse her
bring her down from her heights
be again her mother
in great rage feed her
cold milk.
The answer
goes back a dozen years.

tr. Rachel Tzvia Back

אני אדבר אתך בספטמבר

כָּל מַה שֶׁתַּעֲשֶׂה יִגְרֹם לִי לֶאֱהֹב אוֹתְךָ
וַאֲנִי רוֹצָה לַעֲמֹד לְיָדְךָ כְּשֶׁתְּנַגֵּב אֶת הַזֵּעָה שֶׁלְּךָ בְּמַגֶּבֶת
וְלוֹמַר לְךָ כְּשֶׁאֲנִי אַבִּיט בְּכַדּוּרֵי הַשְּׁרִירִים שֶׁלְּךָ
שֶׁאֲנִי הוֹזָה בָּהֶם
שֶׁאִם תָּמוּת וְתַשְׁאִיר אוֹתִי בִּלְעָדֶיךָ
אֲנִי אַשְׁאִיר אוֹתְךָ מֵת אֶצְלִי בַּמִּטָּה
וְלֹא אֶתֵּן שֶׁיִּקְחוּ אוֹתְךָ מִמֶּנִּי.
אֲנִי אַשְׁאִיר אוֹתְךָ אֶצְלִי בַּבַּיִת
וְלֹא אֶפְתַּח אֲפִלּוּ לְגוֹבֶה הַמִּסִּים.
אֲנִי אֶגְרֹם לְךָ לְהִתְאַהֵב בִּי בַּמַּעֲשִׂים שֶׁלִּי
עַד שֶׁלֹּא תִּוָּתֵר יוֹתֵר אַהֲבָה.
אֲנִי אֶדְאַג לְהֵרָאוֹת
כְּשֶׁאַתָּה תִּסַּע עִם הַטֶּנְדֶּר שֶׁלְּךָ לְסַנְטָה מוֹנִיקָה
בָּז לְכָל הַנּוּבּוֹ רִישִׁים,
גַּם עֲדִינָה וְגַם מְלֵאַת חַיִּים וְסוֹעֶרֶת.
זֶה בֶּאֱמֶת לוֹחֵץ אוֹתִי
אֲבָל אֲנִי אֶת שֶׁלִּי חַיֶּבֶת לַעֲשׂוֹת.
אֲנִי חַיֶּבֶת לָתֵת לְךָ צְלִי בָּשָׂר עִם רֹטֶב תַּפּוּ"ע וּפִירֶה
כְּשֶׁתַּבִּיט בְּלִי הֶרֶף בַּשָּׁעוֹן שֶׁעַל הַקִּיר
בְּצִפִּיָּה לַמִּרְצָחִים.
וַאֲנִי חַיֶּבֶת לְהַבִּיט בַּתּוּגָה שֶׁל הָעוֹרְבִים.
פִּתְאֹם רָאִיתִי שֶׁמִּישֶׁהוּ הֶחְלִיט לָתֵת שִׁירוֹב שֶׁל חָלָב
לַמִּרְצָחִים,
וְשֶׁמִּישֶׁהוּ הֶחְלִיט שֶׁהַמָּן מֵהַמְּכוֹנָה יִהְיֶה רַק
לְאוֹהֲבוֹת מֵתִים,
וְשֶׁהַשּׁוֹשַׁנִּים יִהְיוּ מִזָּהָב.
אָז לָקַחְתִּי מָן וְהִסְתַּכַּלְתִּי עַל כַּדּוּרֵי הַשְּׁרִירִים שֶׁלְּךָ
שֶׁאֵדַע כַּמָּה לֹא אַסְכִּין לְמוֹתְךָ.

זֹאת הַכְרָזַת הָאַהֲבָה הֲכִי גְדוֹלָה חָשַׁבְתִּי
כְּשֶׁהִתְחַבַּקְנוּ לְיַד הַטֶּנְדֶּר הַיָּשָׁן
שֶׁנִּקְנָה כְּדֵי לְהַרְאוֹת כַּמָּה אֲנַחְנוּ עֲשִׁירִים
וְכַמָּה שֶׁלֹּא נַרְאֶה אֶת זֶה לַזּוּלַת.
וְאַחַר שׁוּב הִסְתַּכַּלְתִּי בְּךָ בִּמְעֻדָּן
וְרָאִיתִי שֶׁבְּחָכְמָתְךָ לֹא אֶשָּׁאֵר לְבַד.
שֶׁיִּהְיֶה פִּתְרוֹן.

1988

I'LL SPEAK WITH YOU IN SEPTEMBER

Everything you do will make me love you
and I want to stand next to you as you wipe off your sweat with a towel
and tell you—as I look at the bulges of your muscles
that I dream about—
that if you die and leave me without you
I'll keep your dead body by my side in bed
and won't let them take you from me.
I'll keep you with me at home
and won't even open the door for the tax man.
I'll make you fall in love with me
until there's no love left.
I'll make sure I'm seen
gentle yet full of life and storm
as you travel in your pickup truck to Santa Monica
scorning the *nouveau riches.*
It really puts pressure on me
but I have to do my thing.
I must give you roast beef with apple-sauce and mashed potatoes
as you stare non-stop at the clock on the wall
waiting for the killers.
And I must look at the sorrow of the crows.
Suddenly I noticed that someone decided to give the killers milk
    concentrate
and someone decided that manna from the machine would only be
for lovers of the dead,
and the roses would be made of gold.
Then I took the manna and looked at the bulges of your muscles
so I'd know to what extent I would not get accustomed to your death.

This is the greatest declaration of love I thought
as we embraced beside the old pickup
bought to show how rich we are
and how we won't show off to anyone.
And afterwards I looked at you again with tenderness
and saw that in your wisdom I would not remain alone,
that there would be a solution.

tr. Linda Zisquit

רבקה מרים

באותו לילה

א

בְּאוֹתוֹ לַיְלָה הֻבְרַר לוֹ שֶׁאִישׁ אֲנִי
אִישׁ כָּבֵד וּזְעוּם אֲרֶשֶׁת
שֶׁשִּׂיחָתוֹ מְהוּלָה בְּנִיבִים זָרִים
וְעַד כֹּה כְּשֶׁנָּגַע בִּי אַחֶרֶת
טָעָה.
אֲנִי אִישׁ.
כָּךְ רָאָה.
״אַתְּ אִישׁ״, כָּךְ אָמַר
שֶׁהֲרֵי מֻרְגָּל הָיָה לִקְרֹא לִי ״אַתְּ״
כָּל אוֹתָן הַשָּׁנִים.
לַחֲנוּת נִגַּשׁ יַחְדָּו
וְנִקְנֶה מִגְבָּעוֹת תּוֹאֲמוֹת
וּנְדַבֵּר אִישׁ אֶל רֵעֵהוּ
בְּקוֹלוֹת עָבִים.

ב

עַתָּה, מִשֶּׁהֻבְרַר שֶׁאִישׁ אֲנִי
נִמְצָא שֶׁאֲנִי אֲבִיהֶם שֶׁל יְלָדַי
וְגִדּוּלָם הָיָה בְּרֶחֶם שֶׁל אָב
שֶׁהוּא חַם וְשָׂעִיר. לְלֹא דֶּמַע.
יְלָדַי, קִרְאוּ לִי אִמָּא
וּבְדַבְּרִי אֲלֵיכֶם אָפִיק הַדַּק בְּקוֹלוֹתַי
וְכוֹבָעִים וְסִנָּרִים אוֹסִיף לְרַקֵּם
בְּאֶצְבְּעוֹתַי הַגְּדוֹלוֹת.
יְלָדַי, קִרְאוּ לִי אִמָּא
גַּם אִם הֶחָלָב קָפָא בִּקְצֵה פִּטְמוֹתַי.

ג

כָּל דְּבָרַי שֶׁכָּתַבְתִּי עַד כֹּה —
אִישׁ כְּתָבָם.
וַאֲנִי חָשַׁבְתִּי שֶׁהָיוּ כְּאִשָּׁה
תּוֹפְחִים וְצוֹמְקִים עִם הָעוֹנוֹת, כָּמוֹהָ.
וְלֹא הִיא.
יְשָׁרִים וּקְבוּעִים הֵמָּה, חַסְרֵי חַמּוּקִים.
נַעֲרָה כִּי תִּגַּשׁ אֲלֵיהֶם
בִּזְרוֹעַ בּוֹטַחַת אוֹתָהּ יַקִּיפוּ —
וְתִפָּעֵר.

1988

RIVKA MIRIAM

THAT VERY NIGHT

1

That very night it became clear to him that I'm a man
a heavy man with strict countenance
whose talk is mixed with strange dialects
and until now when he was touching me otherwise
he was wrong.
I'm a man.
So he saw.
"She's a man," he said,
for he was used to calling me "she"
all those years.
Together we'll go to the store
and buy matching hats
and speak to each other
in thick voices.

2

Now that it is clear that I'm a man
it turns out that I'm the father of my children
and their growth was in a father's womb
warm and hairy and tearless.
Children, call me mother
and when I speak to you I'll try
my thinnest voice
bonnets and aprons I'll continue to embroider
with my large fingers.
Children, call me mother
even if the milk froze at the tip of my nipples.

3

All the words I've written till now—
a man wrote.
Once I thought they were like a woman
swelling and shrinking with the seasons, like her.
It's not so.
They were straight and set, void of curves.
When a girl approaches them
with a confident arm, they'll embrace her
and she'll open up wide.

tr. Linda Zisquit

משירי אמות האבן

א

הֵם חָדְלוּ לִקְרֹא לִי.
גַּם בְּעָבְרִי בָּרְחוֹב אִי אַתָּה יָכוֹל לִרְאוֹת
אֶת קוֹלוֹתֵיהֶם מוּנָפִים לְעֶבְרִי.
הָפַכְתִּי לְאַחַת מֵאִמּוֹת הָאֶבֶן הַכְּבֵדוֹת
שֶׁגַּם בְּעֵת תְּנוּעָתָן הַתְּזוּזָה בָּהֶן נִבְלֶמֶת
וְאִי אַתָּה יָכוֹל לִרְאוֹת אוֹתִי נָעָה
אַף כְּשֶׁאֲנִי מְרַקֶּדֶת.

הֵם חָדְלוּ לִקְרֹא לִי.
גַּם כְּשֶׁנִּסָּה מִי מֵהֶם קוֹלוֹ אֵלַי לָשֵׂאת
נִתַּז קוֹלוֹ מִמֶּנִּי
שֶׁהֲרֵי אֲנִי מְרֻקֶּמֶת רַק לִשְׁמֹעַ
אֶת הָאֶבֶן הָרַבָּה.

ב

אֲנִי, מֵאִמּוֹת הָאֶבֶן הַכְּבֵדוֹת,
קוֹרֵאת לְאַבְרָהָם יִצְחָק וְיַעֲקֹב לֵישֵׁב בְּחֵיקִי
שֶׁמֵּרֹב אֶבֶן אֵינִי מִתְאֶמֶת לְתִינוֹקוֹת שֶׁל הַיּוֹם
וּנְחוּצִים לִי רַבָּנִים מִשֶּׁכְּבָר אוֹ רָאשֵׁי קָהָל
בַּעֲלֵי נוֹצוֹת אַמִּיצוֹת
שֶׁשְּׁתִיקָתָם הַמִּתְמַשֶּׁכֶת תָּבוֹא בְּדוּמִיַּת הָאֶבֶן.

1988

מירי בן-שמחון

נערה מן הרחם, לאן

נַעֲרָה מִן הָרֶחֶם
לְאָן הִיא הוֹלֶכֶת, אֵין רִשּׁוּם
שֶׁל צְעָדֶיהָ בָּאֲדָמָה אוֹתָהּ הִיא מְאַבֶּדֶת
הִיא מְבַקֶּשֶׁת לָתֵת הוֹ mal de tête
אֲבָל תֻּכִּים בֵּין שִׂפְתוֹתֶיהָ
הַצְּלִילִים שֶׁל שְׂפַת אִמָּהּ.
הַנְּסִבּוֹת הַטִּבְעִיּוֹת שֶׁלָּהּ
הֵן לֹא הַנְּסִבּוֹת הָאִידֵאָלִיּוֹת שֶׁלָּהּ
כֹּחַ מְשִׁיכָה מִשְׁתַּנֶּה וּמְבַכֵּר אֲרָעִיּוּת
מִתְחַוֵּר לָהּ.
מַה שֶּׁהִיא מַעֲבִירָה מִכְּלִי לִכְלִי אַחֵר
נִקְוָה לֹא לְשִׁמּוּשׁ מִחוּץ לַדְּפָנוֹת

POEMS OF STONE MOTHERS

1

They ceased calling me.
Even when I pass by, you cannot see
their voices waving in my direction.
I turned into one of the heavy stone mothers
whose motion is restrained even when they move
and you can't see me moving
even while I dance.

They ceased calling me
even when one of them tried to let his voice approach me
it splattered off
for I'm patterned to hear only
the abundant stone.

2

I, of the heavy stone mothers
call Abraham, Isaac, and Jacob to settle in my bosom.
Because of so much stone, I'm no longer suitable for today's babies
and I need rabbis of old or community heads
wearing brave feathers
whose continuous quiet will penetrate the silence of stone.

tr. Linda Zisquit

MIRI BEN-SIMHON

OUT OF THE WOMB, WHERETO

Girl out of the womb,
where is she going, no print
of her steps in the earth she's losing.
She wants to bestow, oh, a *mal de tête*
but there are parrots between her lips
the sounds of her mother tongue.
Her natural surroundings
aren't ideal,
gravity shifts, prefers the provisional,
it's clear to her.
She moves something from one bowl to another
saves what spills over the sides.

אֵין לָהּ קוֹאוֹרְדִּינַצְיָה בַּיָּדַיִם
וּבְכָל זֹאת שְׂפַת הַגּוּף שֶׁלָּהּ
הַלָּשׁוֹן שֶׁלָּהּ.
מוּל הַדַּף הָרֵיק הִיא מְכַסָּה אֶת מְבוּשֶׁיהָ
מַה שֶּׁמְּבַקֵּשׁ לְהִשְׁתַּלֵּחַ
מִתְבַּקֵּשׁ לְהִשָּׁאֵר
"הוֹ זֶה יָפֶה מְאֹד" אוֹמֶרֶת אִמָּהּ
רְכוּנָה לְהַקְשִׁיב
וְאֵינָהּ מְבִינָה דָּבָר
הִיא מְנַסָּה שׁוּב
הִיא בּוֹרֵאת בְּצַלְמָהּ אִמָּא אַחֶרֶת
לָמָּה הִיא צְרִיכָה לְאִמָּא עַכְשָׁו
נַעֲרָה מִן הָרֶחֶם
כְּשֶׁבִּפְנִים מַעֲרֶכֶת עִצְבִּית פָּרָה־סִמְפָּטִית
כְּרוּכָה הֲדוּקָה אֶל לֹבֶן חוּט שִׁדְרָתָהּ
מוֹלִיכָה חַשְׁמַל אֶל בִּטְנָהּ וּפְנִים יְרֵכֶיהָ
בִּזְרָמִים קוֹדְחִים.
לֹבֶן חוּט שִׁדְרָתָהּ אֵינוֹ עִנְיָן לִמְשׁוֹרְרִים
מַדְּעָנִים אוּלַי יְסַמְּנוּ אוֹתוֹ בְּאוֹתִיּוֹת יְעִילוֹת
chm אוֹ thm
זֶה קַל לְאֵין עֲרֹךְ עַכְשָׁו
כְּשֶׁהִיא מְנוּעָה מִמְּעֹרָבוּת נַפְשִׁית
כְּשֶׁהִיא פְּטוּרָה מִן הַוִּיזוּאָלִיּוּת שֶׁלָּהּ
כְּשֶׁהִיא נוֹשֵׂאת בָּאַחֲרָיוּת לְבַדָּהּ
שְׁוַת נֶפֶשׁ וּפַנְטַזְיוֹת
רוֹאָה גַּם כְּבִישִׁים וְקִירוֹת
מִתְבּוֹנֶנֶת בְּמַבָּע פָּסִיבִי נִימִי לֹא נִתְפָּס
בְּהִשְׁתָּרְגוּת שֶׁל חַיִּים אֲרוּגָה
מַאֲצִילָה מַצְלִילָה
מְשַׁנָּה זָוִיּוֹת
הֲרוּגָה מְפַנְטַזְיוֹת
נַעֲרָה בִּלְתִּי אֶפְשָׁרִית אֶפְשָׁרֻיּוֹתֶיהָ טְמוּנוֹת
אַהֲבוֹתֶיהָ עַכְשָׁו תְּמוּנוֹת.

1983

Her hands are clumsy
but despite this her body language
is her own tongue.
Facing the blank page she covers her parts
something that wants to thrust out
also demands to stay in.
"Oh, that's very nice," mother says
bent over listening
and not understanding at all
she tries again
she creates another mother in her own image
why does she need a mother now
girl out of the womb
while inside a para-empathetic nervous system
is wound tightly around her white spinal cord
conducting electricity to her stomach, face and thighs
in burning currents.
A white spinal cord isn't a subject for poets
perhaps scientists would mark it in bold letters
thm or *chm*
it's infinitely easy now
while she's kept from emotional involvement
while she's exempt from her visuality
while she alone takes indifferent responsibility
and sees fantasies
roads and walls too
staring with a reedy passive expression, unperceived
a life that intertwines
weaving, emanating, illuminating
changing angles
knocked out by fantasy
impossible girl whose possibilities are concealed
her loves are visuals now.

tr. Lisa Katz

שלי אלקיים

דיבור

״הַמַּחֲלָה שֶׁלָּךְ זֶה אַתְּ
עַכְשָׁו, לִמְדִי לֶאֱהֹב אוֹתָהּ.״
הָיְתָה אִמִּי אוֹמֶרֶת.

(מֵעֵבֶר לַשִּׂיחִים
עוֹבְרִים וְשָׁבִים שֶׁל שְׁעוֹת הָעֶרֶב
שָׂחִים הָיוּ בְּהִגָּיוֹן אַחֵר.)

וְאֵין נֶחָמָה בְּהֶגְיוֹנֶיהָ
אוֹ, לְהַבְדִּיל, רַחֲמִים.
אִמִּי
מְדַבֶּרֶת אֵלַי
כֹּחַ חַם
עוֹבֵר כַּפּוֹת יָדֶיהָ אֶל כְּתֵפַי.
לִפְעָמִים
נוֹגַעַת בְּמִצְחִי
לִמְדֹּד בְּרִיאוּת.

1983

חוה פנחס-כהן

הצבע בעיקר

כְּאִלּוּ הָיְתָה זוֹ בְּעָיָה שֶׁלִּי,
בְּדִידוּת. זֹאת לֹא שֶׁלִּי.
אֲנִי, לְבֵיתִי כְּבָר עָשִׂיתִי. וּבְכָל זֹאת
מִי יִתֵּן יָדַעְתִּי וְאָבוֹא עַד תְּכוּנָתוֹ
שֶׁל אוֹתוֹ חָלָל. נִסִּיתִי לָדַעַת בְּמִלִּים
וּדְבָרִים לְהָבִין; מַה יֹּאמַר לִי עַל עַצְמִי
עַל אוֹתוֹ חוֹר בְּתוֹכוֹ אֲנִי מֶרְכָּז בַּמַּעְגָּל
וּמִשְׁקֹלֶת הַמְטֻטֶּלֶת חוֹבֶקֶת צַוָּארִי.

הָרַדְיוֹ יָשִׁיר וְהַסֵּפֶר יֹאמַר;
יֵשׁ חַיִּים אֲחֵרִים.
כְּבִיסָה מְקֻפֶּלֶת. סְדִינִים מְצֻיָּרִים
גּוּפִיּוֹת יְלָדִים וּמַגֶּבֶת צִבְעוֹנִית
מִלִּים יְשָׁרוֹת בְּלִי צֵל וּבְלִי אוֹר.

SHELLEY ELKAYAM

TALK

"You are your illness
now, learn to love it,"
my mother used to say.

(Beyond the bushes
people strolling by at dusk
would talk with a different sense.)

And there's no consolation in her logic,
not to mention mercy.
My mother
speaks to me:
warm energy
through her palms to my shoulders.
Sometimes
she touches my forehead
to measure my health.

tr. Linda Zisquit

HAVA PINCHAS-COHEN

THE COLOR MOSTLY

As if it were my problem,
loneliness. It's not mine.
I've already taken care of myself. And still
I wish I knew and I'd get to the bottom
of that space. I tried to know in words
and to understand things; what it would tell me about myself
about that hole in which I am the center in the circle
and the pendulum weight clasps my neck.

The radio will sing and the book will say:
there is another life.
Folded laundry. Patterned sheets
babies' undershirts and a colored towel
straight words without shadow and without light.

אותו זְמַן, יֵשׁ דְּבָרִים שֶׁקּוֹרִים מֵעַצְמָם,
צְפוּיִים; כְּבָסִים רְטֻבִּים שֶׁהָרוּחַ מְיַבֵּשׁ.
שְׁתֵּי כּוֹסוֹת אֹרֶז יָבֵשׁ בְּמַיִם,
רֶבַע שָׁעָה עַל אֵשׁ נְמוּכָה.
גַּם יֶלֶד הֵכַנְתִּי שֶׁיְּמַלֵּא אוֹתִי,
לַמְרוֹת מַחְשְׁבוֹתַי. חַי.

וְזֶה נוֹתֵן שָׁהוּת לְהָבִין לְמָשָׁל,
פַּעֲמוֹנִים הַקְּשׁוּרִים בְּחוּטֵי תְּכֵלֶת
לְכַנְפוֹת הַכֹּהֲנִים. הַצֶּבַע בְּעִקָּר,
אַחַר־כָּךְ הַצְּלִיל.

1989

לאה איני

ניצול

אָבִי מִתְקַשֵּׁר לַמִּסְפָּר הַצָּלוּב לוֹ עַל זְרוֹעַ
וּמַקְשִׁיב־מַקְשִׁיב כְּדָרוּךְ
בָּאֹזֶן הַשְּׂמָאלִית אֵינוֹ מַקְשִׁיב
זֵכֶר לַסְּטִירָה מִכַּפּוֹ שֶׁל אֶס.אֶס.
בָּאֹזֶן הַזּוֹ הוּא שׁוֹמֵעַ
שׁוֹמֵעַ כְּמַחֲרִישׁ
אַךְ אֶת הָאֹזֶן הַבְּרִיאָה הוּא עוֹשֶׂה כַּאֲפַרְכֶּסֶת
לַסִּיּוּטִים שֶׁבָּאִים לוֹ
מְדוֹרָה, מְבוּנָה, מֵאַוּשְׁוִיץ
בִּקְרוֹנוֹת
אָבִי צוֹרֵחַ אַחַת לְשָׁבוּעַ כְּאוֹמֵר—
שְׁלוֹמִי טוֹב
וְאַחַר כָּךְ הוּא הוֹפֵךְ אֶת רֹאשׁוֹ עַל הַכַּר הָרָטֹב
וְנִרְדָּם עַל צִדּוֹ הַיְמָנִי
נוֹתֵן אֶת אָזְנוֹ הַמֵּתָה לְבִכְיִי
בִּכְיִי הַמְּהַלֵּךְ עַל בְּהוֹנוֹת.

1988

At the same time, there are things that happen by themselves,
expected; wet laundry that dries in the wind.
Two cups of dry rice in water,
a quarter of an hour on a low flame.
I also prepared a child to fill me,
despite my thoughts. Living.

And that gives time to understand for example,
bells tied with two blue threads
to the flaps of the Kohanim. The color mostly,
afterwards the sound.

tr. Linda Zisquit

LEAH AINI

SURVIVOR

My father dials the number crucified into his arm
and listens alert
he doesn't listen with his left ear
reminder of a slap from an S.S. hand
in this ear he hears
hears like a mute
uses the good ear as a receiver
for the nightmares
from Dora, Buna, Auschwitz
arriving on the trains
my father screams once a week as if to say
I feel fine
and afterwards he turns his head on the wet pillow
and falls asleep on his right side
turns his dead ear to my crying
crying that walks on tiptoes.

tr. Lisa Katz

קיר האימהות

שְׁנֵי
צִידָּיו
שֶׁל
קִיר
הַאִמָּהוֹת
שָׁוִים
כְּמוֹ
שְׁנֵי
צִידָּיו
שֶׁל
דַּף
נְיָר
מָתוּחַ

לֹא
בְּדִיוּק

כִּי
קִיר
הַאִמָּהוּ
ת כְּמוֹ
הַשִּׁיר הַזֶּה
הוּ
א גַּם
סִיבָּ
ה וְגַם
תוֹצָ
אָה שֶׁל
קִיר הַאִי
מָּהוּת

1994

EFRAT MISHORI

THE WALL OF MOTHERHOOD

The two
sides
of
the wall
of motherhood
are the same
as
the two
sides
of
a piece
of flat
paper

not
exactly

because
the wall
of motherhoo
d is like
this poem
it i
s
rea
son and also
res
ult
of
the wall of m
otherhood

tr. Rachel Tzvia Back

שרון אס

מתוך אם ההר נעלמה

69

נַעֲרָה־דָּג, יָפְיָהּ
נוֹתַר בְּאֶצְבְּעוֹתֶיהָ הָאֲרֻכּוֹת, הָאִטִּיּוֹת
כְּשׁוֹשַׁנּוֹת מַיִם בְּהִתְקָרְבִי. אֲנִי רוֹאָה אֶת שֶׁאָהֲבוּ
בָּהּ הַגְּבָרִים וּמְחַלֶּצֶת אוֹתָהּ מִקִּרְבָּהּ הָרֵיק
שֶׁל הָאֵם. בְּאֶצְבְּעוֹתֶיהָ עוֹבְרִים בַּחֲשַׁאי
מְחוֹזוֹת גְּשׁוּמִים כְּשֶׁהָאַהֲבָה
הוֹפֶכֶת אֵיבָרֶיהָ לְיָפִים וְנִפְרָדִים.
מִתְקָרֶבֶת אֲנִי הוֹזָה קַשְׂקַשֵּׂי כֶּסֶף שֶׁנּוֹצְצִים
בִּשְׂעָרָהּ וַאֲנִי הַגֶּבֶר מוּל נַעֲרָה־דָּג
רוֹאָה יָפְיָהּ שֶׁל אִמִּי שָׁבִיר כְּעוֹרֵק חַרְסִינָה כְּחַלְחַל.
הָרִים נִפְתָּחִים בְּגַבָּהּ
כְּשֶׁלּוֹחֶצֶת אוֹתִי אֵלֶיהָ כְּמוֹ חוֹסֶמֶת
בְּגוּפִי כָּבְדָּם שֶׁל שָׁמַיִם שְׁחוֹרִים
אוֹתָהּ נַעֲרָה־דָּג שֶׁלִּפְנֵי רֶגַע...
כָּעֵת צוֹעֶקֶת לְכָל אָרְכִּי, כִּלְעֵמֶק נִסְתָּר, וְקוֹלָהּ נִכְלָא בִּי, בִּי.
וְאַהֲבָתֵנוּ מְבֹעֶתֶת כִּי מֵעוֹלָם לֹא הָיְתָה אֵם
רַק נַעֲרָה חֲרֵדָה, מְמַלְמֶלֶת בְּשִׂמְלַת־דָּג
שֶׁלְּעִתִּים, אֲנִי, מְהַפְנֶטֶת מִתְּנוּעוֹתֶיהָ הָאַקְרָאִיּוֹת, הָעַצְמָאִיּוֹת, מִתְאַהֶבֶת—

וּנְסוֹגָה.

1997

SHARON HASS

from THE MOUNTAIN MOTHER IS GONE

69

Fish-girl, her beauty
remains in her long fingers, slow
as sea-anemones when I approach. I, a woman, see what
men have loved in her and save her from the empty center
of the mother. Between her fingers slip in secret
rainy districts when love
turns her limbs lovely and separate.
Nearing her I envision silver scales that sparkle
in her hair and I the man before a fish-girl
as a woman see my mother's beauty as fragile as a bluish porcelain vein.
Mountains open on her back
when she presses me to her as though blocking
with my body the weight of black skies
this same fish-girl who a moment before...
now screams the full length of me, as into a hidden valley, and her voice
is imprisoned in me, in me.
And our love is terrified for there never was a mother
only a frightened girl, murmuring in a fish-dress
that sometimes, hypnotized by her free and random movements, I fall in
love—

and retreat.

tr. Rachel Tzvia Back

BIOGRAPHICAL NOTES

Poets

These biographical notes begin with the nineteenth century. Women's voices in the Bible and rabbinic literature are discussed in the introduction, as are most of the known facts about the anonymous wife of Dunash ben Labrat, Merecina of Gerona, Asenath Barzani, Sarah Rebecca Rachel Leah Horowitz, and Freyha Bat Avraham Bar-Adiba.

Leah Aini (1962–) was born in the poorest section of Tel-Aviv, the third and youngest daughter of Holocaust survivors. The poem appearing here, "Survivor"—addressing the personal impact of her father's Holocaust experiences on her—is from her first collection, *Dyokan* (Portrait) (1988). Writing poetry and prose from the age of six, Aini has published two books of poems, two volumes of short stories, and a novel. She has been praised as one of the outstanding writers of fiction in Israel. In 1994 she won the Prime Minister's Award, a year-long fellowship enabling Israeli authors to devote themselves to their writing. Her latest book is *Hardufim (Sipurim Mura'lim al Ahava)* (Oleanders or poisoned love stories) (1997). She is married and has a daughter.

Devorah Amir (1948–) was born in Jerusalem during Israel's War of Independence. Her parents had emigrated from Poland to Israel, and were active in the left-wing Zionist workers' movement. Amir studied Jewish philosophy and kabbalah in Jerusalem, and English literature at the University of Illinois, before working at the Center for Educational Technology in Tel-Aviv, where she writes educational programs on language and literature. She began publishing poetry in several Hebrew literary journals before the appearance of her first and only book so far, *Be'era Itit* (Slow burning) (1994).

Ella Amitan (1900–1995), born in Dorpat, Estonia, replaced her family name Vilensky with her maternal grandfather's name. She published poems for children continuously from the mid-1930s, and many of these, set to music, are still sung today. She also worked as a translator, notably of children's classics, such as *Lassie.* During World War II, when she was in her forties, she was among the very few women in Mandatory Palestine who volunteered for the Women's Corps in the British Army, where she served for three years in Egypt and in Palestine. The poem about her army experience included here was first published in the socialist women's weekly *Dvar Ha-poelet* in 1945. In 1954 she won a prize in London for her play *Sabbath Eve.* Her adult poetry was collected in two volumes, *Lakh U-lekha* (For you and for you) (1948) and *Pirhei Neshiya* (Flowers of forgetfulness) (1963).

Leah Ayalon (c. 1951–) was born in Jerusalem where she attended Orthodox religious girls' schools, before studying at the Hebrew University of Jerusalem. Her first book, *Mi-tahat La-mayim* (Under water) appeared in 1983; the work's fantasy and eroticism caused something of a sensation since its themes seemed remote from Ayalon's religious upbringing. She has published six books of poetry, the most recent being *Kan Beitsim* (A nest of eggs) in 1998, and two collections of short stories (1992; 1996). Her poetry has been translated into several languages, and she has received a number of literary awards, including a 1990 Prime Minister's Award. She works at the Jewish National and University Library in Jerusalem.

Hamutal Bar-Yosef (1940–) was born in Mandatory Palestine on a kibbutz near the Sea of Galilee. During the War of Independence, she lost her only brother. By the age of eight she was writing poetry expressing the trauma of bereavement and the resilience of life. At twenty she married the playwright Yosef Bar-Yosef, with whom she had four children. Their youngest son committed suicide in 1985. Bar-Yosef has published six collections of poetry, most recently *Ha-lo* (The no / surely) (1998), as well as short stories, a book for children (1984), and a collection of her translations of the Russian poet Olga Sedakova (1998). She has also published five scholarly books; the latest is *Trends of Decadence in Modern Hebrew Literature* (Hebrew) (1997). Her literary research examines the relation of Russian culture to Hebrew literature. Bar-Yosef has won a number of poetry awards, and her work has been translated into several languages. She lives in Jerusalem and in Beersheva, where she has taught in the department of Hebrew Literature at Ben Gurion University since 1987.

Bat-Hamah (1898–1979) was born as Malka Schechtman in the village Lipniki in the province Volhynia, in northwest Ukraine. She was taught by her cousin, the author and critic Pesah Ginzburg, and was educated in Hebrew at home. She and her siblings spoke Hebrew with their father, a forester, who taught them the Bible, while they talked with their mother in Yiddish. Later Bat-Hamah studied directing at the Yiddish Theater Institute in Kiev and became assistant director and manager of the institute's theater, a position she held until it was closed down by Stalin in 1950. Her first poem was published in 1918, in the Hebrew journal *Ha-shiloah,* printed in Odessa. She was part of the "Hebrew Octoberists," who attempted to merge communist and Hebraic ideology. The group published an anthology, *Bereshit* (Genesis), which was printed in Austria, because no printing house in Russia would risk printing Hebrew poetry—even if it was communist—in 1926. In 1937, fearing for her safety, Bat-Hamah burned all her poems, and during the purges of the 1950s, she also destroyed parables and plays she had written in Yiddish. Although she wrote until the late 1970s, she never saw her work in print. Her work has survived in letters she sent to friends within and outside the Soviet Union. Some of her work was brought to Genazim, the Archive of the Association of Hebrew Writers, during the 1990s by emigrants from the former Soviet Union.

Yokheved Bat-Miriam (1901–1980) was born as Yokheved Zhelezniak in the small village of Kaplitch, Russia, where there were very few Jews. Her large family observed Hassidic traditions. She changed her name when she was seventeen. She studied pedagogy in Harkov, Moscow, and Odessa. Her first poems were published in 1922. Like Bat-Hamah, she was a member of the "Hebrew Octoberists." Unmarried, she had two children by two different men, and led a very unconventional life for her time. Her daughter, Mariasa, was born in 1925 in Moscow, and a year later Bat-Miriam went to Paris where her son, Nahum (Zuzik) Hazaz, was born in 1928. Soon after that she immigrated to Mandatory Palestine. Her early poems were collected in 1932 in *Me-rahok* (From afar) (reprint, 1985). She played an active role in the literary life of Mandatory Palestine during the 1930s and 1940s. Her writing reflects the symbolist direction of Hebrew poetry during this time. She published five collections of poems between 1937 and 1946, when *Shirim La-ghetto* (Poems for the ghetto) (1946) was published. When her son, Zuzik, died in Israel's 1948 War of Independence, she stopped writing and publishing poetry but continued to write daily letters to her daughter, who lived in the United States. She said she was no longer "Bat-Miriam" and was now only "Zuzik's mother." Her collected works (*Shirim*) were published in 1963 and were dedicated to the memory of her son. She received the Bialik Prize for literary achievement in 1968, and the Israel Prize in 1972, the highest honor awarded to Israelis who have made an outstanding contribution in their field.

Maya Bejerano (1949–) was born in kibbutz Eilon, near the northern border of Israel. She served in the army from 1967 to 1969, and completed a degree in library studies in 1977. During the 1970s she organized literary evenings with other poets, and her first book of poems, *Bat Ya'ana* (Ostrich), appeared in 1978. Since then she has produced eight volumes of poetry, as well as a collection of stories and a play, a storybook for children, and a long-playing record of her poems set to music (1989). From the outset she was highly praised by major critics for her daring and innovative language. She has won the Prime Minister's Award twice (1986, 1994) and the Israeli Literature Prize for Poetry for *Mizmorei Iyov* (The hymns of Job) (1993) and for her latest volume, *Anasse La-gaat Be-tabur Bitni* (Trying to touch my belly-button, 1997). A new project, *Optical Poem CD,* was completed in 1998 by the students of Camera Obscura Art School in Tel-Aviv. The CD includes thirteen poems by Bejerano and visual interactive works. She lives in Bat Yam, near Tel-Aviv, with her daughter, and works as a reference librarian at Beit Ariella, the Tel-Aviv municipal library.

Ruth Alpern Ben-David (1936–) was born in Tel-Aviv. When she was two years old she traveled with her parents on a family visit to Lithuania, and was trapped in the Kovno Ghetto when the Nazis invaded. She was orphaned in the Holocaust. After the war she returned to Israel, later served in the Israeli army, and taught art at the youth village in Nahalal until her retirement. Married, with two children and two grandchildren, she lives in Tivon in northern Israel. She has published two books, *Pahad Mavet* (Deadly fear) (1989) and *Heikhal Beniya Meuheret* (Temple of late building) (1994); both draw on her memories of the Holocaust and its aftermath.

Miri Ben-Simhon (1954–1996) was born in France and brought to Israel in the same year. She grew up in Jerusalem, studied Hebrew literature, and worked at an advertising agency and as an editor of the weekend newspaper *Yerushalaim,* later editing and translating for several institutions. She wrote three books of poems exploring her identity as a marginal woman, addressing, in particular, the discrimination that women from Arab countries suffer. She received a number of literary awards. She was run over by a car and killed in 1996. Her final book, *Eksistentsializm Hared* (Worried existentialism), was published posthumously in 1998.

Ruth Blumert (1943–) was born in Haifa. After studying microbiology and biochemistry at Bar-Ilan University, she turned to Hebrew literature and earned a master's degree from the Jewish Theological Seminary in 1976. She was director of the Israel Gur Theater Archive, and edited *Bama* (Stage), a drama quarterly. She has continued to edit and also to translate poetry into Hebrew. She has published a book of science fiction (1983), a collection of short stories (1987), two books for children, and two volumes of poetry—*Golim Al Kokhav Zar* (Exiles on a strange planet) (1991) and *Moda Mi-zman Aher* (Acquaintance from another age) (1996). Blumert has won several prizes, including a 1992 Prime Minister's Award.

Rahel Chalfi (c. 1945–) was born in Tel-Aviv, where she still lives with her husband and son. She attended high school in Mexico City, university in Jerusalem, and studied theater and film in the United States. She has worked for Israeli radio and television as a writer-director-producer. She has won several prizes for her poetry, plays, films, and work on the radio, both in Israel and in other countries, among them a 1989 Prime Minister's Award. Her first collection *Shirim Tat-Yamiyim Ve-aherim* (Underwater and other poems) appeared in 1975 (reprint, 1989). From the beginning Chalfi was clearly a feminist poet; in Israel, in 1975, however, no one viewed her as a feminist, even when Chalfi wrote about herself as a predatory barracuda or expressed tenderness for a woman's aging body. She has published six volumes of poetry since 1975; the latest are *Nosa'at Semuya* (Stowaway) (1999) and *Mikla'at Ha-shemesh* (Solar plexus: Collected poems) (1999).

Elisheva (Bihovski) (1888–1949) was born as Elisaveta Ivanovna Zirkowa in Riazan, Russia. Her father was a teacher. Her mother, who came from an English family that had settled in Russia during the Napoleonic wars, died when Elisheva was three years old. Elisheva was then brought up in her mother's sister's home in Moscow. She began to write poetry in Russian when she was nineteen. At that time she was strongly influenced by a close Jewish friend, and started to take an interest in Hebrew, Judaism, and Zionism, translating poetry from Yiddish and Hebrew into Russian. Her Russian poetry was printed in two books published in 1919, and a year later she began to write poetry in Hebrew. She married the Zionist activist Shimon Bihovski, and they had one daughter. In 1925 the Bihovskis emigrated to Mandatory Palestine, where Shimon helped Elisheva publish two books of poems in Hebrew, *Kos Ktana* (A small glass) (1926) and *Haruzim* (Rhymes) (1928). Elisheva became a colorful figure in literary bohemia in Tel-Aviv. She also wrote short stories (1928, reprinted 1976) and a novel, *Simtaot* (Side-Streets) (1929), about Russian and Jewish bohemia after the Russian revolution. In 1932, on a visit to Russia, Shimon Bihovsky died. Elisheva returned to Tel-Aviv, and lived there impoverished and alone. She died in 1949 in Tiberias, and because religious fundamentalists would not allow a non-Jew to be buried in the Jewish cemetery, she was buried in the nearby cemetery of kibbutz Kinneret, near the poet Rahel.

Shelley Elkayam (1955–) was born in Haifa, where her father's family had lived for six generations. Her mother's family came from Thessaloníki, Greece. She served in the Israeli army, and has worked as an organizational counselor and editor. Her first book of poetry *Tamtsit Atsmo* (The essence of one's self) appeared in 1981 to critical acclaim, commended, in particular, for its play with different levels of language, from the biblical to slang. Elkayam has since published three more books, and a selection of her poetry, *Simple Days,* was translated by Charles McGeehan into English (1984). A political and social activist, Elkayam was among the founders of the East for Peace movement, and in 1995 organized a women's poetry festival in Jerusalem. She lives in Jerusalem, is married to Surin Sandor, and has one son.

Esther Ettinger (1941–) was born in Jerusalem and grew up in Tel-Aviv. She has worked in the Ministry of Education and the Jewish National and University Library, and is now employed in the library of the law school of the Hebrew University of Jerusalem. Her first book, *Yarok Efshari* (Possible green), appeared in 1980. She has published four volumes of poetry, most recently *Hayai Burganiyim Le-hafli* (Poems) (1998). Her poetry, grounded in classical Hebrew literature and Jewish observance, often addresses the conflicts that arise between a woman's family obligations and writing. Ettinger has won several prizes, including a 1992 Prime Minister's Award. She is married and has four children.

Dahlia Falah (date of birth unknown) is a pen name, and the facts of her life are closely guarded by her publisher. Her first poems appeared in the late 1970s, and her only book so far, *Dodi Ha-shofet Ha-mehozi Dorban* (Poems) was published in 1997. Her poetry has been widely admired by critics who keep asking, Who is Dahlia Falah?

Haya Ginzburg (1900–1985), also known by her married name, Haya Friedman, was born in the village Lipniki in the province Volhynia, in northwest Ukraine. Her father was a teacher in a progressive Jewish primary school, and taught his daughter Hebrew. Ginzburg's family spoke Hebrew, as did the family of her cousin Bat-Hamah. Her elder brothers, the critics and authors Pesach and Simon Ginzburg, left Russia before World War I. Between 1918 and 1919, Haya emigrated from Russia to the United States, where she married and settled in Miami. Only a few of her poems have survived; after her immigration to the United States she stopped writing poetry.

Lea Goldberg (1911–1970), one of the most significant Israeli poets of the early twentieth century, was the first woman to be admitted into the canon of modern Hebrew poetry. She is still among the most widely read and admired Israeli poets. Goldberg was born in Königsberg and grew up in Kovno, Lithuania. She won a scholarship for study in Germany in 1930, and completed her doctoral dissertation on the Samaritan translation of their Bible at the University of Bonn. In 1935, when the British were preventing Jewish immigration to Palestine, she received, with the help of the poet Avraham Shlonsky, a certificate allowing her to enter Mandatory Palestine. Her first book of poems, *Tabaot Ashan* (Smoke rings), was published the same year. Her mother soon managed to join her, and they lived together until Goldberg's death. In Tel-Aviv Goldberg was one of two women (Bat-Miriam was the other), who, along with Alterman and others, formed a modernist poets' group around Shlonsky. Goldberg worked for socialist daily newspapers as a drama and literature critic. In 1952 she was invited to teach in the department of comparative literature at the Hebrew University of Jerusalem, which she later chaired. Considered an outstanding teacher and critic, she directed a poetry workshop for several of her gifted students, and had a significant influence on the early careers of poets such as Ravikovitch, Harechavi, and Chalfi. Her first poem was published in 1928, and she published continuously until her death, nine volumes of poetry in all. She has been translated into many languages, and was herself a prolific translator. Among her classic translations into Hebrew are Tolstoy's *War and Peace,* Petrarch's sonnets, Ibsen's *Peer Gynt,* and Shakespeare's *As You Like It.* She is also among the most popular writers for children in Israel, and was children's literature editor of Sifriat Poalim Publishing House. She published three works of prose, among them an autobiographical novel (1946); three plays, one of which, *Ba'alat Ha-armon* (The lady of the palace) (1955), was performed successfully on Broadway, in London, and in Japan as well as in Israel; and numerous essays. Her critical writing covered poetry, short stories, drama, fine arts, and notably, Russian literature, including Dostoevsky, Tolstoy, and Pushkin. Goldberg was also a recognized painter, and her drawings often illustrated her books. She received the Israel Prize posthumously.

Hedva Harechavi (1941–) was born in kibbutz Degania Bet, and has lived in Jerusalem from a young age. A painter, she graduated from Bezalel Art Academy, and her works have been exhibited in Israel and abroad. She has published four volumes of poetry, the most recent *Ha-aher* (The other) (1993). Her early work was colorful and surrealistic, and somewhat idiosyncratic. Using repetition, anaphora, and rhyme, Harechavi is known for her rhythmic litanies of self-analysis and reflection. Her poems have been translated into several languages and anthologized. She has won the Prime Minister's Award twice, in 1981 and 1993.

Shulamith Hareven (1932–) was born in Warsaw and brought to Mandatory Palestine when she was nine years old. She volunteered for the Haganah prestate military organization in Jerusalem and served during the siege of 1947–

48. Later, as an officer, she participated in founding the Israel Defense Force's broadcasting service, and was in charge of transit camps for immigrants to Israel. She was the first woman elected to the Academy of Hebrew Language in 1979. As a political activist, she has served as a spokesperson for Peace Now, and expressed her views in a regular newspaper column. She has been a writer in residence at several universities in Israel and abroad, and in 1995 was selected by the Parisian *L'Express* as one of "one hundred women who make the world move." She is the author of sixteen books and her work has been translated into seventeen languages. She has published three books of poetry, three collections of short stories, a novel (*A City of Many Days*, 1979), novellas, and suspense stories. Her most recent publications in English are *The Vocabulary of Peace* (essays, 1995) and *Thirst—The Desert Trilogy* (prose fiction, 1996). She lives in Jerusalem with her husband Alouph Hareven, and has a son and a daughter.

Galit Hasan-Rokem (1945–), *see* Editors.

Sharon Hass (1966–), born in Ramat Gan, has taught literature and philosophy at the University of Tel-Aviv, and at Camera Obscura Art School. She runs writing workshops in poetry and prose for children and adults. One of the founders of a writing program for gifted adolescents, she is in charge of its poetry workshops. Her first volume of poetry, *Em Ha-har Ne'elma* (The mountain mother is gone) (1997), is a long poem that creates a mythology of mother-daughter relations. The book won a Hezy Leskli scholarship and a debut prize from the Israeli Council for Culture and Art. She was invited to represent Israel at the International Poetry Festival in Rotterdam in 1996, and has read at other festivals and poetry events in Israel. She lives in Tel-Aviv.

Amira Hess (1943–) was born in Baghdad, Iraq, and immigrated to Israel when she was nine years old. She is descended from a family of poets and mystics, among them the poet Asenath Barzani. Overcoming feelings of rejection in a society that marginalized Jews of Eastern origin, she enrolled in a poetry workshop and began publishing when she was thirty-nine years old. Her poetry was praised from the start for its deconstructive play, its fantastic dreamlike quality, and its social and ethnic commitment. She has published four books: *Ve-yareah Notef Shiga'on* (And a moon dripping madness) (1984), *Shney Susim Al Kav Ha-or* (Two horses on the light line) (1987), *Bole'a Ha-informatsia* (The information eater) (1993) and *Yovel* (Yovel, poems) (1998). In 1991 she won the Prime Minister's Award. During the Intifada she taught literature at a Palestinian girls' school in east Jerusalem. She has two daughters.

Judith Kafri (1935–) was born and raised in kibbutz Ein Ha-Horesh, where her parents were among the founders. She has worked as a translator and editor of books related to education and psychology. In recent years she has concentrated on writing poetry and biographies. She has published eight volumes of poetry, beginning with *Ha-zman Yerahem* (Time will pity) (1962), as well as a memoir about her childhood, *Kol Ha-kayits Halakhnu Yehefim* (We were barefoot all summer) (1996). She has won several awards, among them a

1986 Prime Minister's Award and the 1993 Rahel Prize. Married, a mother of three, and a grandmother of four, she is a member of the peace movements Peace Now and Four Matriarchs. She lives in Mazkeret Batya in central Israel.

Shulamit Kalugai (1891–1972) was born in Poltava, Ukraine. Having studied at the Sorbonne in Paris, and in Pittsburgh, Pennsylvania, she joined her brothers—Yitzhak Ben-Zvi, Israel's second president, and Aharon Reuveni, a prominent Hebrew novelist—in Ottoman Palestine in 1910. She was among the founding teachers of the Hebrew Gymnazia (high school) of Jerusalem. After marriage to Yitzhak Kalugai, she moved to Haifa, where she taught French in a high school. She was a close friend of Rahel, who was also from Poltava. Her early writing was in prose; her short stories were collected in *Gimnazistit* (A schoolgirl) (1938). She also wrote children's literature and was a translator. "Jezebel," the poem appearing here, is from *Nashim* (Women) (1941), a cycle of portrait poems dedicated to female characters in the Bible and Jewish midrashic folktales.

Sabina Messeg (1942–) was born in Sofia, Bulgaria, and immigrated to Israel as a child. She grew up in Jaffa. Messeg divides her time between the agricultural settlement Hemed and Galilee, together with her husband, the painter Aharon Messeg. Her first book of poetry, *Kolot Mashak* (Flutter sounds), appeared in 1984 and won the Newman Debut Prize. She has since published four more volumes of poetry. During the Gulf War she spent time at a monastery in Ein Kerem, a period of seclusion which produced her book of poems *Yemey Minzar* (Monastery days) (1997). She also writes for children and is a translator. She has translated Ted Hughes into Hebrew (1996).

Miri (Halperin, later Dor) (1911–1945) was born in Warsaw and immigrated with her parents to Mandatory Palestine when she was nine years old. Her Russian Jewish parents, Yehiel and Penina Halperin, pioneered Hebrew preschool education. Her older brother, Uriel, was the renowned Hebrew poet Yonatan Ratosh (see biographical note for Shin Shifra). Her first poems, including the poem printed here, were written in 1926, at the age of sixteen. The few poems that followed were mostly long and influenced by expressionism, unlike the style of most women's Hebrew poetry at the time. Her poetic career was short lived. In 1936 she went to Paris to study zoology and linguistics. On her return to Mandatory Palestine, in 1938, she wrote children's stories about animals. Her marriage to Menahem Dor, who identified with the political left, caused a rift in her extreme right-wing family. She died during pregnancy, for lack of medical attention. Her poems were collected in a posthumous volume, *Sholal* (Plunder) (1949).

Rivka Miriam (1952–) was born in Jerusalem, where she still lives. She is the daughter of the Yiddish author Leib Rochman, and the mother of three children. Miriam is one of the early poets to combine religious conviction, mysticism, and Jewish erudition with a feminist consciousness—a mix that has become prominent in contemporary women's Hebrew poetry. She was fourteen when her first book, *Kutanti Ha-tsehuba* (My yellow coat) (1966), appeared and has since published eight more volumes of poetry; the most recent is *Mi-karov Haya Ha-mizrah* (Nearby was the East) (1996). Miriam has also published two collections of short stories and two books for children. She paints and has displayed her paintings in several art exhibits, conducts study groups, and teaches creative writing. She has won several literary awards, including a Prime Minister's Award.

Agi Mishol (1947–) was born in Hungary and was brought to Israel in 1950. She is the only daughter of Holocaust survivors. Her first book, *Nani Ve-shneinu* (Nani and the two of us) appeared in 1971 and established her as a unique poetic voice. One of the prominent poets publishing in Israel today, two of her recent books—*Yonat Faksimilia* (Fax pigeon) (1991, reprint 1995) and *Ha-shfela Ha-pnimit* (The interior plain) (1995, reprint 1997)—have gone into second printings. Her sixth and latest book is *Re'e Sham* (titled *Look There* in English) (1999). Her poetry has been translated and anthologized. In November 1998 a bilingual Hebrew-English edition of her poetry appeared, produced by Poetry Ireland Review, the work of ten Irish poet-translators. She has won several literary awards, including a 1995 Prime Minister's Award. She teaches literature at high schools and at university level, conducts poetry workshops, is a literary critic for the radio, a translator, and a farmer.

Efrat Mishori (1964–) was born in Tiberias, and now lives in Tel-Aviv. She has made a name for herself as a performance poet. She writes essays and criticism on poetry and art. She has published two collections of her poetry—*Efrat Mishori: Shirim 1990–1994* (Poems: 1990–1994), which won the Ron Adler Prize for a debut book, and *Mi-merhakei Efrat* (As far as Efrat (1996)—and a book for children, *Sefer Ha-halomot* (The book of dreams) (1988). She has presented her poetry in a performance called *Ani Ha'dugmanit Shel Ha-shira* (I am the poetry model), a title which distinguishes the body language of a poet from the exploited body of a fashion model. She is married to a visual artist and has one son.

Rachel (Luzzatto) Morpurgo (1790–1871) was born in Trieste. She was descended from a line of great Italian poets and scholars; the most widely acclaimed is the poet and messianic mystic RaMHaL, Rabbi Moses Haim Luzzatto (1707–1747). Her early education was in Hebrew, at home, under the instruction of her brother's tutors. She evidently studied very little outside the Jewish tradition. Until she was twelve, she studied the Bible and biblical exegeses with her uncles. When she was fourteen, she began to study the Talmud with a rabbi, and mathematics with her uncle. Later she read kabbalah on her own, and spent many hours of study with her cousin Shmuel David Luzzatto (ShaDaL), who became a Hebrew poet and renowned scholar. Her parents opposed her match with Yaakov Morpurgo, and she refused to marry anyone else until they finally assented, when she was twenty-nine years old. She wrote two poems about this, one of them addressed to ShaDaL, who sent the poem to the Vienna-based Haskalah periodical *Kokhavey Yizhak* (Isaac's stars). The poem was received with enthusiasm by both the editor and the periodical's readers. Morpurgo's poems are few, and were written far apart. In a note to one poem she apologizes for neglecting to perfect the meter, because "the children are young" (a daughter and three sons); and in a letter to Mendel Stern, the editor of *Kokhavey Yizhak,* she apologizes for not sending him more poems because it is three hours past midnight and she is tired. Biographical accounts stress her devotion to good housekeeping and her skill as a seamstress, as if to forgive Morpurgo for her studies and her poetry, which women did not engage in. Her poetry was first collected in a posthumous book in 1890, to mark her centenary. The book was reissued in Israel in 1953. In recent years, the development of feminist criticism of Hebrew literature has encouraged new scholarly interest in Morpurgo.

Judith Mossel-Eliezerov (1944–) was born in Jerusalem to a family that had lived in Palestine for ten generations. She is the daughter of a rabbi, and the mother of three. She teaches literature at teachers' colleges. She has published three books: *Kefafot, Mishkafaim U-mitria* (Gloves, glasses, and an umbrella) (1980), *Toladot* (Chronicles) (1988), and *Akeret Ha-bait* (Housewife) (1997). She has won several prizes, among them a 1990 Prime Minister's Award. Her poetry reveals her religious faith and sometimes her struggle with it, as well as her mystical experience.

Hava Pinchas-Cohen (1955–) was born in Jaffa. Her first book of poetry, *Ha-tseva Be-ikar* (Mainly the color) (1990), won the Luria Prize. She has since published another two books of poetry—*Massa Ayala* (The passage of the doe) (1995) and *Nahar Ve-shikheha* (A river and forgetfulness) (1998)—and has become a prominent figure in a group of mostly religious poets. Her poems have been described by critics as "personal Midrashim," which use the discourse of traditional belief without compromising a contemporary woman's empowerment. She is recipient of a 1995 Prime Minister's Award, edits the cultural journal *Dimui* (Image), and publishes children's literature and literary reviews. A mother of four, she lives in Rehovot.

Anda Pinkerfeld-Amir (1902–1981) was born in Rzesza in western Galicia, Austria-Hungary, to an assimilated Jewish family. She studied natural sciences and microbiology in Poland before settling in Mandatory Palestine in 1924. After World War II she was sent by the Jewish Agency to work in Displaced Persons' camps in Europe. Later she worked in the Ministry of Defense's archives, documenting the lives of people who died in the Israeli War of Independence. Her first book of poetry—*Pie'sni Zycia* (Song of life) (1921)—was written in Polish. In Mandatory Palestine she began to write in Hebrew. Her early poems were published at the end of the 1920s, and were well received by poet-critics such as Elisheva and Rahel who praised the poetry's free meter and absence of rhyme, which differentiated Pinkerfeld-Amir from the major trend of Hebrew modernism of the time. Rahel also admired the space Pinkerfeld-Amir's poems provided for a woman's emotional experience. Other critics rejected her for the same reasons. Recently, critical interest in Pinkerfeld-Amir is growing as feminists relate to her wide range of personae, from biblical characters to Japanese geishas, and to her sensitive perception of women's lives. *Yamim Dovevim* (Whispering days) appeared in 1929, and although she published continuously until the 1980 publication of *U-v-khol Zot* (And yet), she is recognized primarily as a beloved and prolific writer of children's books, for which she has received the Bialik Award for children's literature in 1936 and the Israel Prize in 1978.

Esther Raab (1894–1981) was born in Petah Tikva, a town that began as a small agricultural settlement. Her parents were among its founders. In her teens Raab joined the pioneering labor collective Degania, and later taught in the agricultural school at Ben Shemen. In 1921 she moved to Cairo, where she married her cousin Isaac Green. Her first poems were published the following year in a leading literary journal in Tel-Aviv and established her as a "native" poet, remarkably at home in Hebrew and in the Palestinian landscape. She returned to Tel-Aviv in 1925, and her home became a center of cultural life in the city. Green stayed in Cairo, managing his family's business, and died in 1930, the same year in which Raab's first book, *Kimshonim* (Thistles), appeared. Raab gradually retired from her active social and cultural life and stopped writing for eleven years. In 1963 *Kimshonim* was reprinted, with new poems. Raab won enthusiastic critical reception. Two more books were printed during her lifetime: *Tefila Aharona* (Last prayer) (1972) and *Hemyat Shorashim* (The murmur of roots) (1976). Her prose and memoirs were published posthumously by her nephew, the author Ehud Ben-Ezer, who has also written her biography. Raab was considered a marginal poet by her contemporaries, unlike Bat-Miriam and Rahel. But current scholarship, especially among feminists, has established her as one of the leading voices in Hebrew modernism. Secure in her empowered sexuality when she began writing early in Mandatory Palestine, she is also recognized as a virtuoso of rhythm and sound.

Rahel (Bluwstein) (1890–1931), an Israeli cult figure and romantic icon, was born in Saratov, and grew up in Poltava, Ukraine. Her father served in the czar's army for twenty-five years and later became a prosperous businessman. Her mother was well-educated, corresponded with Tolstoy, and devoted herself to the education of her children. Rahel studied in Russian at a Jewish school, and had private tutoring at home in basic Hebrew. As a child she wrote poetry in Russian. After her mother died and her father remarried for the third time, Rahel grew estranged from her home and moved to Kiev with her sisters to study painting. In 1909 she traveled to Ottoman Palestine. She worked in agriculture on the Carmel, and later in the women's farming school on the Sea of Galilee, and perfected her knowledge of Hebrew. In 1913 she went to France to study agriculture. World War I prevented her return to Palestine and cut her off from her father's financial support. Rahel graduated with honors and returned to Russia, where the lung disease that had plagued her from childhood worsened. She returned to Mandatory Palestine on the first available boat after the war, in 1919. She joined the Degania collective close to the Sea of Galilee, but, when she was diagnosed with tuberculosis, was forced to leave. Eventually she settled in Tel-Aviv. Most of her poems were written there during the last six years of her life, many of them published in the labor movement's daily newspaper, *Davar*. Two books were published during her life: *Safiah* (After-growth) (1927) and *Mi-neged* (At a distance) (1930). *Nevo* (Nebo) (1932) was published posthumously, and her collected poetry, first printed in 1935, has since appeared in numerous editions. Her critical writing was charged with modernist values—what she called "simplicity." Outstanding in their prosody, many of her poems were set to music and are still among the most popular Israeli songs. A selection of her poems, *Flowers of Perhaps*, translated into English by Robert Friend, was published in London by Menard Press in 1995.

Dahlia Ravikovitch (1936–), the most acclaimed woman poet writing in Israel today, was born in a suburb of Tel-Aviv. Her father was a Russian Jewish engineer, who emigrated from China to Mandatory Palestine in the early 1930s. He taught Ravikovitch to read and write when she was four years old. In 1942 he was run over and killed by a drunk driver. The loss has permeated Ravikovitch's writing. She moved with her mother to kibbutz Geva, but at thirteen Ravikovitch chose to leave the kibbutz, and lived with a series of foster families in Haifa. She began publishing poetry when she was eighteen, and her first book, *Ahavat Tapuah Ha-zahav* (Love of the golden apple), was published in 1959, winning immediate admiration. Critics praised her command of traditional Hebrew sources and poetic forms, and later her conversational diction. Her active political protest against the Israeli occupation of Palestinian lands and of Lebanon has produced some of the finest political poetry written in Israel in the last decades. A journalist and a high school teacher, she has translated Yeats, T. S. Eliot, and children's classics into Hebrew. She has published eight volumes of poetry, including three selected, and most recently *Hatsi Sha'a Lifnei Ha-monsun* (Half an hour before the monsoon) (1998). A collection of short stories appeared in 1976 and was lately reissued, with new stories, as *Kvutsat Ha-kaduregel Shel Winnie Mandela* (Winnie Mandela's football team) (1997). Ravikovitch has also written two poetry books for children. She has won several awards, among them the prestigious Israel Prize in 1998. She has a son and lives in Tel-Aviv. The American poet and translator, Chana Bloch, with Ariel Bloch, has edited and translated into English three volumes of her selected poems, the most recent *The Window* (1989).

Bracha Serri (c. 1942–) was born in San'a, Yemen, and brought to Israel in the mass exodus of Jews from Yemen soon after the state was established. She studied linguistics and Hebrew literature at the Hebrew University of Jerusalem, and has a master's degree in linguistics and education. Often adopting, as in the poem included here, the "naive" first-person voice of a Yemenite woman crushed between an oppressive patriarchal background and the discriminatory nature of her everyday life, Serri has produced an effective literature of protest and has exposed many injustices, especially against women, in Israeli society. She lived in Berkeley for seven years and now has returned to her home in

Jerusalem. Her books include *Seventy Wandering Poems* (a bilingual edition in Hebrew and English, 1983) and *Para Aduma* (Red heifer) (1990). She has also written short stories and a play.

MALKA SHAKED (1933–) was born in Czechoslovakia and immigrated to Mandatory Palestine with her parents when she was one year old. She was brought up in a traditional religious home. She first published poetry during the Gulf War, in 1991. Her first volume of poetry, *Tmunot Matsav* (States of mind) (1996) won the WIZO award for creative women. Shaked taught literature at high schools and colleges and now teaches in the teacher training program in the School of Education of the Hebrew University in Jerusalem. She has published literary criticism on S. Y. Agnon, Anton Chekhov, and contemporary writers, and a book about family saga novels, *Huliyot Ve-shalshelet* (Links and a chain) (1990). She is married to Gershon Shaked, a professor of Hebrew Literature; they have two daughters and five grandchildren, and live in Jerusalem.

SARAH SHAPIRA (c. 1870–c. 1930) was born in Dünaburg, near Vitebsk, currently Latvian Daugavpils, and often referred to by Jews by its Russian name, Dvinsk. It is known that Shapira was living in Moscow in 1927. Her grandfather was a rabbi, and her father was a strong advocate of learning Hebrew. Shapira signed the poem printed here, "Sarah, daughter of Dr. Shapira of Dnaburg." Dnaburg had two private Jewish girls' schools, which Shapira may have attended, and an active Zionist group, which may have influenced her. She corresponded with the major Hebrew poet of the time, Yehuda Leib Gordon, who encouraged her.

SHIN SHIFRA (1931–) was born and grew up in Bnei-Brak, an Orthodox town on the outskirts of Tel-Aviv. Her first poems were published when she was twenty-one. Shifra was affiliated with a group named the "Canaanites," led by the poet Yonatan Ratosh. The "Canaanites" adopted an ancient "Hebrew" ideology, rejecting the Jewish diaspora, and favoring political and cultural identification with ethnic groups who inhabited the Middle East prior to the appearance of Judaism (and, consequently, Christianity and Islam as well). Ratosh's influence on Shifra is clear in her early choice of miniature chantlike forms, mythological themes, and archaic words. Her steadfast feminist conviction and her study of Hebrew literature and Jewish philosophy with Gershom Scholem were at odds with the "Canaanite" movement. Her books include *Shir Isha* (Woman's poem) (1962), *Shirei Midbar* (Poems of the desert) (1972), *Hatsavim Nerot Neshama* (Poems) (1987), and a collection of short stories, *Rehov Ha-hol* (The sand street) (1994). Shifra has also translated from the original Accadian and Sumerian, and has edited, together with Ya'akov Klein, an anthology of Mesopotamian literature, *Ba-yamim Ha-rehokim Ha-hem* (In those distant days) (1997). She has won several literary prizes, among them a 1989 Prime Minister's Award.

AYIN TUR-MALKA (Aliza Greenberg) (1926–) was born in Jerusalem. She took the name Tur-Malka when she married the famous, politically active poet Uri Zvi Greenberg, who had adopted the Hebrew name of Tur-Malka. They had five children. Since her husband's death in 1981, she has been intensely engaged in the publication of his complete works and has also published essays about his poetry. Her first poems were published when she was sixteen. She has since published three books: *Ken Shel Zeradim* (A nest of twigs) (1963), *Shirat Ha-Be'erot* (The wells' song) (1972), and *Ashmora Ha'Shlishit* (The morning watch) (1989).

Haya Vered (1922–1998) was born in Chelmno, Poland, and was brought to Mandatory Palestine when she was three years old. She joined a communist youth movement and later kibbutz Gevar Am (1944–57). After having been an active editor of and contributor to literary publications of the kibbutz movement, she left the kibbutz and taught literature in high school. Vered's rhetorical and often admonishing poetry was harshly reviewed and rejected. She did not publish after the late 1950s and would have been completely forgotten had not Hannan Hever's critical work restored her to readers' attention. In an interview in the early 1960s, she revealed that she had written over two hundred poems that she would not publish. Her only book, *Shirim Al Herev U-meitar* (Poems about a sword and a cord), appeared in 1956.

Yona Wallach (1944–1985), almost fifteen years after her death, is still a living presence. The impact of her fantastic imagery and liberating sexuality on Hebrew poetry still resonates today. She was born in Kfar Ono, a suburb of Tel-Aviv. Her parents had emigrated from Bessarabia to Mandatory Palestine in 1932. Her father was killed in Israel's War of Independence in 1948. Wallach grew up on a street named after her father. Wallach did not finish high school but studied art in Tel-Aviv at the Avni Institute of Art. Her mother was a part-owner of a movie theater where Wallach spent many hours. Wallach started writing as a young girl, and her first poems were published when she was twenty. In 1965 she committed herself to a psychiatric hospital and experimented there with LSD. Her first book, *Devarim* (Poems), appeared one year later. She was hospitalized again in 1972 following a suicide attempt. She published four more volumes of poetry before her death, and also wrote plays, as well as personal columns for a number of magazines. She lived with her mother, Esther. They died in the same year—the mother of Parkinson's disease, the daughter of breast cancer. Wallach won several awards, among them a 1978 Prime Minister's Award. Wallach, along with Meir Wieseltier and Ya'ir Hurvitz, was a major force in the Israeli avant-garde of the 1960s and 1970s, and her popularity continues to grow. Two books have been published posthumously: *Mofa* (Appearance) (1985) and her selected poems in 1992. An English translation by Linda Zisquit of her selected poems, *Wild Light,* was published in 1997.

Nurit Zarchi (1941–) was born in Jerusalem and grew up in kibbutz Geva, where the family moved after the death of her father, author Israel Zarchi, when she was six years old. Her mother taught at the kibbutz school. Her first book, *Yarok Yarok* (Green green), appeared in 1966, and she has since published six more books; the most recent is *Melon Hipnodrom* (Hypnodrom hotel) (1998). A pronounced feminist, Zarchi has devoted essays and fiction to questions of gender and creativity. She is considered a leading voice in contemporary postmodern Israeli fiction and children's literature as well, and has published two collections of short stories and an autobiography. She was twice the recipient of the Prime Minister's Award (1980, 1991), and has won the International Andersen Medal for Children's Literature three times. A mother of two daughters, she is an instructor in workshops of prose and poetry.

Simcha Zarmati-Atzta (1927–1992) was born in the Yemenite neighborhood of Tel-Aviv. Her parents had emigrated from Yemen to Ottoman Palestine. She was active in the prestate anti-British right-wing underground military organizations ETZEL (Irgun Tzevai Leumi) and LEHI (the Stern Gang or Lohamei Herut Yisrael), and was arrested by the British. She was a teacher and volunteer and lectured about women in the Bible. She wrote both poetry and prose, exploring social, class, and ethnic conflicts in Israel, and the generation gap between parents who had emigrated from Yemen and children who had grown up in Israel, like herself. She also wrote political poetry identified with the Israeli Right and opposed the trading of occupied lands for peace. Her poetry books include *Mi-tock He-anan She-ba-har* (From the cloud at the mountain: Poems) (1986) and *Arav Ve-ma'arav* (Arabia and West) (1992).

Zelda (Schneersohn Mishkovsky) (1914–1984) was descended from prominent rabbinic Hassidic scholars. She was born in Yekaterinoslav and brought up in her grandfather's home in Cheringov. The Russian revolution left her parents impoverished because the rabbinic family was perceived as an enemy of the new regime. In 1925 the family immigrated to Mandatory Palestine and settled in Jerusalem, where Zelda completed her studies. She worked as a teacher and painted. During the 1940s, she began to write and publish poetry. In 1950 she married Haim Mishkovsky, quit teaching and, encouraged by her husband, dedicated herself to poetry. Her first book, *Pnai* (Leisure), did not appear until 1967. It won immediate and wide critical acclaim. Most striking perhaps were the enthusiastic reviews written by poets who represented the poetic avant-garde—Yona Wallach, Meir Wieseltier, Mordechai Geldman, and others. She was adored by religious, nationalistic, messianic, and secular audiences alike. Zelda published six books and a collection of selected poems (1979), and received the Brenner Prize in 1971, the Bialik Prize in 1977, and the Wertheim Prize in 1982.

Translators

Rachel Tzvia Back was born in 1960 in Buffalo, New York, and has lived in Israel since 1981. Her poetry has appeared in numerous journals including *The American Poetry Review, Sulfur, Tikkun, Modern Poetry in Translation,* and *Ariel.* Her chapbook, *Litany,* was published in 1995, and she was a 1996 recipient of the Israeli Absorption Minister's Award for Immigrant Writers. She currently teaches American literature at the Hebrew University in Jerusalem.

Chana Bloch has published three books of poems—*The Secrets of the Tribe, The Past Keeps Changing,* and *Mrs. Dumpty* (winner of the 1998 Felix Pollak Prize in Poetry at the University of Wisconsin)—as well as translations of the biblical Song of Songs and of the Israeli poets Dahlia Ravikovitch and Yehuda Amichai. She lives in Berkeley and teaches at Mills College, where she is professor of English and director of the creative writing program.

Peter Cole was born in 1957 in Paterson, New Jersey, and first came to Jerusalem in 1981. He has published two books of poems—*Rift* (1989) and *Hymns and Qualms* (1998)—and four volumes of translations, including *Selected Poems of Shmuel Hanagid* (1996), *Love and Selected Poems of Aharon Shabtai* (1997), and *From Island to Island: Poems by Harold Schimmel* (1998). Among his many awards are fellowships from the National Endowment for the Arts and the National Endowment for Humanities, and the 1998 Modern Language Association Scaglione Prize for Translation. His translation of selected poems of the Hebrew-Andalusian poet Solomon ibn-Gabirol is forthcoming.

Marcia Falk, poet, translator, and Judaic scholar, is the author of *The Book of Blessings: New Jewish Prayers for Daily Life, the Sabbath, and the New Moon Festival* (1996), and the translator of *Song of Songs: A New Translation and Interpretation* (1990) and *With Teeth in the Earth: Selected Poems of Malka Heifetz Tussman* (translated from Yiddish) (1992).

Bernhard Frank teaches comparative literature and creative writing at Buffalo State College. He edited and translated *Modern Hebrew Poetry* in the Iowa Translation Series in 1980, a comprehensive anthology of the translated works of forty-nine Hebrew poets. He was editor-translator of the Israel issue of the *International Poetry Review* (spring 1996). His poetry and articles have recently appeared in *Judaism, Response,* and *Explicator,* among other journals.

Robert Friend, poet and translator, born in Brooklyn, New York, lived in Jerusalem from 1950 until his death in 1998. He lectured in American and English literature at the Hebrew University. He published four volumes of translations of Hebrew poetry by Nathan Alterman, Lea Goldberg, Gabriel Preil, and Rahel, as well as translations from Yiddish and other languages. His most recent volume of translations is *The Book of the Alphabet,* children's verse by S. Y. Agnon (1998), and the last collection of his own poems is *The Next Room* (1995). The editors are especially grateful to Robert Friend, who completed, during his final illness, three new translations of rhymed poems for this volume.

Kinereth Gensler grew up in Chicago and Jerusalem, where she spends her summers. She lives in Cambridge, Massachusetts, and has taught in the Radcliffe Seminars for more than twenty years. In addition to her books of poetry—*Threesome Poems* (1976), *Without Roof* (1981), and *Journey Fruit* (1997)—she is co-author, with Nina Nyhart, of *The Poetry Connection,* a text for teaching poetry writing to children.

Miriyam Glazer (also known as Myra) is chair of the literature department and director of the Dortort Writers Institute at the University of Judaism in Los Angeles. Her *Burning Air and a Clear Mind* (1981) was among the earliest collected volumes of contemporary Israeli women's poetry translated into English. She has edited an anthology of poetry and fiction *Dreaming the Actual: Israeli Women Writers at the Turn of the Twenty-first Century,* which will appear in 2000, with many of her own translations.

Barbara Goldberg has published five books of poetry, including *Cautionary Tales* (1990), and has won numerous awards for her poetry and fiction. Two of her books have appeared in Hebrew translation, and she has co-edited, with Moshe Dor, two anthologies of contemporary Israeli poetry. She lives in Chevy Chase, Maryland.

Kathryn Hellerstein teaches Yiddish language and literature at the University of Pennsylvania. Her books of translations from Yiddish include Moyshe-Leyb Halpern's poems, *In New York: A Selection* (1982) and *Paper Bridges: Selected Poems of Kadya Molodowsky* (forthcoming). She is co-editor of the forthcoming *Jewish American Literature: A Norton Anthology.*

Zvi Jagendorf was born in Vienna, grew up in England, and has lived and worked in Israel since 1958. He is professor of English and theater at the Hebrew University. His essays and stories have appeared in journals and anthologies in many countries. His translations of Hebrew poetry have been published in collections in England and the United States.

Lisa Katz, born in 1949 in New York, has lived in Jerusalem since 1983. The winner of a New York State Creative Artists Public Service grant, her poems and stories have been published in *Fiction* and *Shenandoah* magazines, and her translations from the Hebrew have appeared in *Modern Hebrew Literature, Ariel,* and *Modern Poetry in Translation* (London). She is completing a doctorate on Sylvia Plath at the Hebrew University, where she teaches in the English department.

Shirley Kaufman, *see* Editors.

Tsipi Keller is a writer and translator. She is a recipient of a National Endowment for the Arts translation fellowship, an Armand G. Erpf translation award from the Translation Center at Columbia University, and a Creative Artists Public Service grant and a New York Fiction Award. Her translation of Dan Pagis's posthumous collection, *Last Poems,* was published by *The Quarterly Review of Literature* (1993), and her novels, *The Prophet of Tenth Street* (1995) and *Leverage* (1997) were published in Hebrew by Sifriat Poalim, Israel. She lives in New York City.

Miri Kubovy is professor of Near Eastern languages and civilizations, and director of modern Hebrew studies at Harvard University, and also teaches at the Free University of Berlin. She has translated three books and published numerous articles on modern Hebrew literature, especially on the narrative of S. Y. Agnon, on the young writers of the 1990s, and on Israeli women's poetry.

Gabriel Levin was born in France, grew up in the United States and Israel, and has lived in Jerusalem since 1972. He is the author of two collections of poems: *Sleepers of Beulah* (1992) and *Ostraca* (1999). He has written a book-length essay on Jerusalem *Hezekiah's Tunnel* (1997) and has published two volumes of translations: *The Little Bookseller Oustaz Ali* (from the French), a collection of the early-twentieth-century Egyptian poet and prose writer Ahmed Rassim; and *On The Sea* (from the Hebrew), a collection of the acclaimed Hebrew poet of twelfth-century Andalusia, Yehuda Halevi.

Elaine Magarrell works as a poet in the Washington, D.C., public schools. The author of two volumes of poetry, most recently *Blameless Lives* (1991) and winner of the Word Works Poetry Prize (1992), she is also the recipient of grants from the Washington, D.C., Commission of Arts.

Yaffah Berkovits Murciano studied French, Spanish, and Arabic at the Polytechnic of Central London, and social administration at the London School of Economics and Political Science. She emigrated to Israel in 1980, where she works as a translator. She has translated several works on Jewish history and philosophy, as well as the Arabic section of *Voices Within the Ark,* an international anthology of modern Jewish poetry, edited by Howard Schwartz and Anthony Rudolf (1980). She is currently translating a book on Jewish women in the sixteenth-century Levant.

Ilana Pardes, completed her doctorate at the University of California, Berkeley, and teaches at the Hebrew University in the department of comparative literature. She is the author of *Countertraditions in the Bible: A Feminist Approach* (1992) and *The Biography of Ancient Israel* (forthcoming).

Catherine Harnett Shaw lives in Washington, D.C., and works with the federal criminal justice system. She is the author of one volume of poetry, *Still Life* (1983).

Chava Weissler holds the Philip and Muriel Berman Chair of Jewish Civilization at Lehigh University in Pennsylvania. She is the author of *Voices of the Matriarchs* (1998), a study of the religious lives of central and eastern European Jewish women in the seventeenth and eighteenth centuries.

Linda Stern Zisquit, born in Buffalo, New York, has lived in Israel since 1978. She has published several volumes of translations from the Hebrew, including *Open-Eyed Land: Desert Poems* by Yehuda Amichai (1992), and *The Book of Ruth,* with woodcuts by Maty Grunberg (1996). She received a National Endowment for the Arts Translation Grant and a PEN Translation Award nomination for *Wild Light: Selected Poems of Yona Wallach* (1997). Her own collections of poetry are *Ritual Bath* (1993) and *Unopened Letters* (1996). She teaches at the Hebrew University and for the Wesleyan-Brown Overseas Program, and runs an art gallery in Jerusalem.

Editors

Shirley Kaufman was born in Seattle, lived for many years in San Francisco, and moved to Jerusalem in 1973, when she married H. M. Daleski, a professor of English at the Hebrew University. She has published seven volumes of her own poetry in the United States, the most recent being *Roots in the Air: New and Selected Poems* (1996); and books of translations from the Hebrew of the poetry of Amir Gilboa and Abba Kovner, and from the Dutch of Judith Herzberg. The Herzberg collection won a Columbia University translation prize. Among her awards are a National Endowment for the Arts fellowship, and the 1991 Shelley Memorial Award of the Poetry Society of America. Her own work has been translated into Hebrew by Aharon Shabtai, with Dan Pagis and Dan Miron (*Me-hayim Le-hayim Aherim,* 1995), and into many other languages. She has taught at the Hebrew University and as poet-in-residence and visiting professor at several American universities.

Galit Hasan-Rokem was born in 1945 in Helsinki, Finland, and immigrated with her family to Israel in 1957. She is Max and Margarethe Grunwald Professor of Folklore at the Hebrew University of Jerusalem, where she lectures in the departments of Hebrew literature and Jewish and comparative folklore. She has lectured and published extensively in Europe and the United States. She translates poetry from Swedish, Finnish, and English into Hebrew, and translations of her own poetry have been published in English, Swedish, and Spanish. She has written and edited several scholarly books, most recently *Untying the Knot: On Riddles and Other Enigmatic Modes,* edited with David Shulman (1996), and *Riqmat Hayim* (The web of life: folklore in rabbinic literature) (1996; forthcoming in English). She has published two volumes of her poetry, *Eshet Lot* (Lot's wife) (1989), which won the Tel-Aviv Foundation Award, and *Shiur Be-fituah Kol* (Voice training) (1998). She is the literary editor of the *Palestine-Israel Journal,* a founding member of Women's Peace Net in Israel and of Bat-Shalom. She serves as the president of the International Society for Folk Narrative Research. She is married to the theater scholar Freddie Rokem and the mother of three.

Tamar S. Hess was born in Rehovot, Israel, in 1966 and grew up in Jerusalem. She teaches in the department of Hebrew literature of the Hebrew University of Jerusalem, and is completing her Ph.D. dissertation on autobiographical writings by women of the early-twentieth-century immigration to Ottoman Palestine. In 1996 she received the Feinsod-Sukenik Prize of the Lafer Center for Gender Studies at the Hebrew University, where she has also taught introductory courses in feminist theory. She was awarded the prestigious national Nathan Rotenstreich Scholarship for doctoral students in 1997.

Author of the Foreword

Alicia Suskin Ostriker is a distinguished Jewish American poet-critic. The author of nine volumes of poetry, she has twice been a National Book Award finalist. Her writing on women poets includes *Writing Like a Woman* (1983) and the controversial *Stealing the Language: The Emergence of Women's Poetry in America* (1986). She is also the author of *The Nakedness of the Fathers: Biblical Visions and Revisions* (1994).

BIBLIOGRAPHY OF ISRAELI WOMEN'S HEBREW POETRY IN ENGLISH TRANSLATION

Books by Individual Poets

Elkayam, Shelley. *Simple Days*. Translated by Charles McGeehan. Amsterdam: Boaz Press, 1984.

Goldberg, Lea. *Selected Poems*. Translated by Robert Friend. London: Menard Press, 1976.

Mishol, Agi. *The Swimmers*. Translated by seven poets at the Tyrone Guthrie Center, Annaghmakerrig. Dublin: Poetry Ireland, 1998.

Rahel. *Flowers of Perhaps: Selected Poems of Ra'hel*. Translated by Robert Friend with Shimon Sandbank. London: Menard Press, 1995.

Ravikovitch, Dahlia. *A Dress of Fire*. Translated by Chana Bloch. London: Menard Press, 1976.

———. *The Window: New and Selected Poems*. Translated and edited by Chana Bloch and Ariel Bloch, with a foreword by Robert Alter. Riverdale-on-Hudson, N.Y.: Sheep Meadow Press, 1989.

Serri, Bracha. *Wandering Poems*. Bilingual selections, translated by Yaffah Berkovits. Jerusalem: Bracha Serri, P. O. Box 7882, Jerusalem 91077, Israel, 1983.

Wallach, Yona. *Wild Light*. Translated by Linda Zisquit, with an introduction by Aharon Shabtai. Riverdale-on-Hudson, N.Y.: Sheep Meadow Press, 1997.

Anthologies

Alcalay, Ammiel, ed. and trans. *Keys to the Garden: New Israeli Writing*. Includes poems by Shelley Elkayam, Amira Hess, and Bracha Serri, and a short story by Simcha Zarmati-Atzta. San Francisco: City Lights Books, 1996.

Glazer, Myra [Miriyam], ed. *Burning Air and a Clear Mind: Contemporary Israeli Woman Poets*. With an Introduction by Myra Glazer, and with drawings by Shirley Faktor. Athens, Ohio: Ohio University Press, 1981.

Glazer, Miriyam, ed. and trans. *Dreaming the Actual: Contemporary Fiction and Poetry by Israeli Writers at the Turn of the Twenty-first Century*. New York, N.Y.: SUNY Press, forthcoming spring 2000.

Moshe Dor, Goldberg, Barbara, eds. *After the First Rain: Israeli Poems on War and Peace*. Syracuse, N.Y.: Syracuse University Press in association with Dryad Press, 1998.

Seneca Review, ed. Eighteen poems by Israeli women, translated by Tsipi Keller. *Seneca Review* (spring 1997).

PUBLICATION CREDITS

For permission to reprint and translate the Hebrew poems in this anthology, we gratefully acknowledge the Association of Composers, Authors, and Publishers of Music in Israel (ACUM). The rights for the Hebrew poems not in the public domain, unless otherwise indicated, reside with ACUM. We thank ACUM, the poets, and publishers for sharing their work. For the English-language translations, most of which were commissioned for this edition, we are grateful for the financial assistance provided by the Institute for the Translation of Hebrew Literature, as well as the generosity of the publishers, poets, and translators. Unless otherwise stated, the English-language translation copyright for all poems included in this anthology resides with the translator.

Leah Aini, "Survivor," from *Dyokan* (Portrait) (Tel-Aviv: Hakibbutz Hameuchad Publishing House Ltd., 1988). Translation by Lisa Katz.

Devorah Amir, "What Sinks In," from *Be'era Itit* (Slow burning) (Tel-Aviv: Hakibbutz Hameuchad Publishing House Ltd., 1994). Translation by Shirley Kaufman.

Ella Amitan, "In the Army," first published as "Bashana Ha-shlishit" (On the third year), *Dvar Ha-poelet* 11 (5), nos. 1–2 (February 1945). Here taken from *Lakh U-lekha* (For you and for you) (Tel-Aviv: Masada, 1948). Translation by Rachel Tzvia Back.

Leah Ayalon, "Dark Thoughts and I'm Even the Opposite of What You Think," from *Mi-tahat La-mayim* (Under water) (Tel-Aviv: Hakibbutz Hameuchad Publishing House Ltd., 1983); "Golden Girl," from *Zehu Gan Ha-eden* (This is a paradise) (Tel-Aviv: Sifriat Poalim Publishing House Ltd., 1984); "I'll Speak with You in September," from *Dani'el Dani'el* (Daniel Daniel) (Jerusalem: Keter Publishing House, 1988). "Dark Thoughts . . ." and "Golden Girl," translations by Rachel Tzvia Back; "I'll Speak with You in September," translation by Linda Zisquit.

Babylonian Talmud, excerpts titled "'Lore for Healing'" and "'The First Night'" translations by Shirley Kaufman with Galit Hasan-Rokem; "'Songs for the Dead,'" translation by Peter Cole.

Freyha Bat Avraham Bar-Adiba, "[Lift up my steps]," first published in *AlYahudi,* 26 November 1936, p. 1; here taken from *Pe'amim* 55 (1993); "Hear My Voice in the Morning," from *Pe'amim* 4 (1980) (original from the Simhon Halwah manuscript, private collection). Translations by Peter Cole.

Hamutal Bar-Yosef, "Jaffa, July 1948," from *Rak Ha-yarok* (Poems) (Tel-Aviv: Hakibbutz Hameuchad Publishing House Ltd., 1981); "Vise," from *U-va-tsfifut* (In the crush) (Tel-Aviv: Hakibbutz Hameuchad Publishing House Ltd., 1990). Translations by Shirley Kaufman.

Asenath Barzani, "Asenath's Petition," first published (in Hebrew) by Jacob Mann, ed., in *Texts and Studies in Jewish History and Literature,* vol. 1 (Cincinnati: Hebrew Union College Press, 1931). Translation by Peter Cole.

Bat-Hamah, "The Vigil," from *Gehalim Lohashot* (Anthology of Hebrew and Yiddish literature from the Soviet Union), ed. Yehoshua Gilboa (Tel-Aviv: M. Newman Publishers Ltd., 1954). Translation by Peter Cole.

Yokheved Bat-Miriam, "[Just as you see me, that's how I am]," from *Me-rahok* (From afar) (Tel-Aviv: Hakibbutz Hameuchad Publishing House Ltd., 1985); "Miriam" and "Hagar," from *Shirim* (Poems) (Tel-Aviv: Sifriat Poalim Publishing House Ltd., 1963). "[Just as you see me, that's how I am]," translation by Bernhard Frank, reprinted by permission of the publisher and translator, from *Modern Hebrew Poetry,* edited by Bernhard Frank (Iowa City: University of Iowa Press, 1980); "Miriam," translation by Ilana Pardes, reprinted, in revised form, by permission of the translator, from "Yocheved Bat-Miriam: The Poetic Strength of a Matronym" in *Gender and Text in Modern Hebrew and Yiddish Literature,* edited by Naomi B. Sokoloff, Anne Lapidus Lerner, and Anita Norich (New York and Jerusalem: The Jewish Theological Seminary of America, 1992); "Hagar," translation by Zvi Jagendorf.

Maya Bejerano, "Data Processing 60" and "The Optical Fiber," from *Retsef Ha-shirim 1986–1972* (Selected poems) (Tel-Aviv: Am Oved Publishing Ltd., 1987); "Poetry," from *International Poets Festival Anthology,* edited by Eyal Megged and Vivian Eden (Jerusalem: Mishkenot Sha'ananim, 1993); "War Situations," from *Mizmorei Iyov* (The hymns of Job) (Tel-Aviv: Hakibbutz Hameuchad Publishing Ltd., 1993). "Data Processing 60" and "The Optical Fiber," translations by Miri Kubovy, reprinted, in revised form, by permission of the translator, from *Women of the Word: Jewish Women and Jewish Writing,* edited by Judith R. Baskin (Detroit: Wayne State University Press, 1994); "Poetry," translation by Tsipi Keller; "War Situations," translation by Lisa Katz.

Ruth Alpern Ben-David, "Setting Out for Convalescence," from *Iton 77* 209 (July 1997). Translation by Lisa Katz.

ben Labrat, the wife of Dunash, "[Will her love remember]," first published by Ezra Fleischer, "Dunash Ben Labrat, Wife and Son," (in Hebrew) *Jerusalem Studies in Hebrew Literature* (1985). The original manuscript is held in the Taylor-Schechter collection, Cambridge University (accession no. 143.46); a copy of the manuscript is also held by the Institute of Copies of Hebrew Manuscripts at the Jewish National and University Library, Jerusalem. Translation by Peter Cole.

Miri Ben-Simhon, "Out of the Womb, Whereto," from *Me'unyenet Lo Me'unyenet* (Poems) (Tel-Aviv: Hakibbutz Hameuchad Publishing House Ltd., 1983). Translation by Lisa Katz.

Ruth Blumert, "Collisions," from *Helicon Poetry Quarterly* 22 (1997). Translation by Tsipi Keller.

Rahel Chalfi, "Such Tenderness," from *Homer* (Matter: Poems) (Tel-Aviv: Hakibbutz Hameuchad Publishing House Ltd., 1990); "'I Went to Work as an Ostrich' Blues," from *Zikit O Ikron I-havada'ut* (Poems: 1970–1981) (Tel-Aviv: Hakibbutz Hameuchad Publishing House Ltd., 1986); "Tel-Aviv Beach, Winter '74," from *Shirim Tat-Yamiyim Ve-aherim* (Underwater poems and others) (Tel-Aviv: Hakibbutz Hameuchad Publishing House Ltd., 1989); "The Water Queen of Jerusalem," from *Nefila Hofshit* (Free fall) (Israel: Marcus Publishers with Ah'Shav, 1979). "Such Tenderness" and "The Water Queen of Jerusalem," translations by Tsipi Keller; "'I Went to Work as an Ostrich' Blues," translation by Shirley Kaufman; "Tel-Aviv Beach, Winter '74," translation by Elaine Magarell, reprinted by permission of the publisher and translator, from *After the First Rain: Israeli Poems on War and Peace,* edited by Moshe Dor and Barbara Goldberg (Syracuse, N.Y.: Syracuse University Press in association with Dryad Press, 1998), copyright 1997 Dryad Press.

Deborah, Song of Deborah, Judges 5.1–31, translation (with adaptations) from *Tanakh: The Holy Scriptures, According to the Traditional Hebrew Text* (Philadelphia: The Jewish Publication Society of America, 1985).

Elisheva, "What's Left," from *Haruzim: Shirim* (Rhymes: Poems) (Tel-Aviv: n. p., 1928). Translation by Robert Friend.

Shelley Elkayam, "Talk," from *Nitsat Ha-limon* (Poems) (Jerusalem: Quality Edition and Adam Books, 1983). Translation by Linda Zisquit.

Esther Ettinger, "The Sadness Cage," from *Hashalat Ha-aman* (Lent by the artist) (Jerusalem: Maxwell-Macmillan-Keter Publishing House Ltd., 1991). Translation by Lisa Katz.

Dahlia Falah, "Adult-Wisdom," from *Dodi Ha-shofet Ha-mehozi Dorban* (Poems) (Tel-Aviv: Am Oved Publishing Ltd., 1997). Translation by Rachel Tzvia Back.

Haya Ginzburg, "[Why, my Lord]," from *Ha'Toren* 5 (April 1918). Translation by Peter Cole.

Lea Goldberg, all poems from *Ktavim* (Collected works) (Tel-Aviv: Sifriat Poalim Publishing House Ltd., 1973, 1986), copyright by Sifriat Poalim Publishing House Ltd. "To Mother's Picture," translation by Zvi Jagendorf; "The Flowering," verse 2, translation by Shirley Kaufman; "The Love of Teresa De Meun," verse 2, "A Look at a Bee" and "Toward Myself," translations by Robert Friend, reprinted by permission of the publisher and Jean Shapiro Cantu (for the estate of Robert Friend), from *Leah Goldberg: Selected Poems* (London: Menard Press, 1976), translation copyright 1976 by Robert Friend; "The Love of Teresa De Meun," verse 9, translation by Robert Friend.

Hedva Harechavi, "When She Goes Out Alone," from *Adi* (Poems) (Tel-Aviv: Sifriat Poalim Publishing House Ltd., 1981); "A Very Cheerful Girl," from

Ani Rak Rotsa Le'hagid Lakh (I just want to tell you) (Tel-Aviv: Sifriat Poalim Publishing House Ltd., 1985). Translations by Tsipi Keller.

Shulamith Hareven, "New Life," from *Yerushalaim Dorsanit* (Poems) (Jerusalem: Sifriat Poalim Publishing House Ltd., 1962). Translation by Shirley Kaufman.

Galit Hasan-Rokem, "[This child inside me]," from *Eshet Lot* (Lot's wife) (Tel-Aviv: Hakibbutz Hameuchad Publishing House Ltd., 1989); "Black Pearls," from *Shiur Be-fituach Kol* (Voice training) (Tel-Aviv: Hakibbutz Hameuchad Publishing House Ltd., 1998). "[This child inside me]," translation by Kathryn Hellerstein; "Black Pearls," translation by Shirley Kaufman.

Sharon Hass, "The Mountain Mother Is Gone," verse 69, from *Em Ha-har Ne'elma* (The mountain mother is gone) (Tel-Aviv: Sharon Hass and Tag Publishers Ltd., 1997). Translation by Rachel Tzvia Back.

Amira Hess, "[Menopause toward daylight], "from *Ve-yare'ah Notef Shiga'on* (And a moon dripping madness) (Tel-Aviv: Am Oved Publishing Ltd., 1984); "When Nightingales Will Pass the Depths of Despair," verses 6–10, from *Bole'a Ha-informatsia* (The information eater) (Tel-Aviv: BITAN Publishers Ltd., 1993). Translations by Lisa Katz.

Sarah Rebecca Rachel Leah Horowitz, "The *Tkhine* of the Matriarchs," first published in Aramaic in a *bichlech* (booklet). Translation by Chava Weissler, reprinted by permission of the publisher and translator, from *Voices of the Matriarchs* (Boston: Beacon Press, 1998).

Judith Kafri, "The Woman," from *Malan Shel Kayits* (Awn of summer) (Tel-Aviv: Sifriat Poalim Publishing House Ltd., 1988). Translation by Tsipi Keller.

Shulamit Kalugai, "Jezebel," from *Nashim* (Women) (Tel-Aviv: Yavne Publishing House, 1941). Translation by Robert Friend.

Lamentations 1.12–16, 19–22, translation from *The Holy Scriptures, According to the Masoretic Text* (Philadelphia: The Jewish Publication Society of America, 1916), copyright 1917, 1945, 1955.

Merecina of Gerona, "[Blessed, majestic and terrible]," from Avraham M. Haberman, *Studies in Sacred and Secular Poetry of the Middle Ages* (in Hebrew) (Jerusalem: Ruben Moss 1972). Translation by Peter Cole.

Sabina Messeg, "If It's True That Lakes Get Old," from *Ha-Ba'it Be'Migdal* (The house in Migdal) (Tel-Aviv: Hakibbutz Hameuchad Publishing House Ltd., 1987). Translation by Shirley Kaufman.

Midrash Lamentations Rabbah, Proem 24, Rome ms., Casanata no. J. I. 4, compared with British Museum no. 27089, printed in the edition of Solomon Buber (Vilnius: Widow and Brothers Romm, 1899), 28. "Rachel Stands Before the Holy One," translation by Shirley Kaufman with Galit Hasan-Rokem.

Midrash Leviticus Rabbah, 14.8, London ms., British Museum no. 34, printed in the edition of Mordechai Margulies: *Midrash Wayyikra Rabba—A Critical Edition* (Jerusalem: Wahrmann Books, 1972) 312–14. "Unborn," translation by Shirley Kaufman with Galit Hasan-Rokem.

Miri, "Gallop," from *Sholal: Tsror Shirim* (Astray: Poems) (Tel-Aviv: Mahbarot Le'Sifrut Publishing Ltd., 1949). Translation by Gabriel Levin.

Miriam, Song of Miriam, Exodus 15.20–21, translation from *The Holy Bible, King James Version* (1611; reprint, New York: Oxford University Press, 1967).

Rivka Miriam, "That Very Night" and "Poems of Stone Mothers," from *Mi-shirei Imot Ha-even* (Poems of stone mothers) (Tel-Aviv: Sifriat Poalim Publishing House Ltd., 1987). Translations by Linda Zisquit.

Agi Mishol, "[The transistor muezzin]," from *Yoman Mata* (Plantation notes) (Jerusalem: Keter Publishing Ltd., 1986); "Estate," "In the Supermarket," and "Turning to Rest in Sappho's Poems," from *Ha-shfela Ha-pnimit* (The interior plain: Poems) (Tel-Aviv: Hakibbutz Hameuchad Publishing House Ltd., 1995). "[The transistor muezzin]," translation by Linda Zisquit, reprinted by permission of the translator, from *Delos* 2, no. 1 (spring 1989) [first published with the title "Over the Fire"], copyright 1989 by Center for World Literature; "Estate" and "Turning to Rest in Sappho's Poems," translations by Tsipi Keller, reprinted by permission of the translator, from *The Seneca Review* 17, no. 1 (1997), copyright 1997 by Hobart and William Smith Colleges; "In the Supermarket," translation by Tsipi Keller.

Efrat Mishori, "The Wall of Motherhood," from *Efrat Mishori: Shirim 1990–1994* (Efrat Mishori: Poems) (Tel-Aviv: Efrat Mishori and Artifact Gallery, 1994). Translation by Rachel Tzvia Back.

Rachel Morpurgo, all poems from *Ugav Rahel* (Poems and letters) (Tel-Aviv: Mahbarot Le-sifrut (1890), reprint 1953). Translations by Peter Cole.

Judith Mossel-Eliezerov, "The Dress," from *Toladot: Shirim* (Chronicles) (Tel-Aviv: Sifriat Poalim Publishing House Ltd., 1988). Translation by Gabriel Levin.

Hava Pinchas-Cohen, "The Color Mostly," from *Ha-tseva Be-ikar* (Poems) (Tel-Aviv: Am Oved Publishing Ltd., 1990). Translation by Linda Zisquit.

Anda Pinkerfeld-Amir, "[Like every woman]," from *Yuval: Shirim* (Brook) (Tel-Aviv: Davar Publishers Ltd., 1932). Copyright © 1932 by Dvir Publishers. Translation by Shirley Kaufman.

Esther Raab, all poems from *Kol Ha-shirim* (Collected poems) (Tel-Aviv: Zmora-Bitan Publishers, 1994). "[I'm under the bramble]," "She-Fox," and "Last Prayer," translations by Kinereth Gensler; "[Holy grandmothers in Jerusalem]," translation by Shirley Kaufman; "Night," translation by Shirley Kaufman, reprinted by permission of the publisher and translator, from *New Writing in Israel,* edited by

Ezra Spicehandler (New York: Schocken Books, 1976), copyright 1976 by American-Israel Publishing Co. Ltd. and The Institute for the Translation of Hebrew Literature, Ltd.; "Requests," translation by Catherine Harnett Shaw, reprinted by permission of the publisher and translator, from *After the First Rain: Israeli Poems on War and Peace*, edited by Moshe Dor and Barbara Goldberg (Syracuse, N.Y.: Syracuse University Press in association with Dryad Press, 1998), copyright 1997 by Dryad Press.

Rahel, all poems from *Rahel,* edited by Uri Milstein (Tel-Aviv: Zmora-Bitan Publishers, 1985). "To My Country," "Rachel," "Our Garden," "[I have only known]," and "Tenderness," translations by Robert Friend, reprinted by permission of the publisher and Jean Shapiro Cantu (for the estate of Robert Friend), from *Flowers of Perhaps: Selected Poems of Ra'hel* (London: Menard Press, 1995), translation and copyright 1994 by Robert Friend and Shimon Sandbank; "A Way of Speaking," translation by Shirley Kaufman.

Dahlia Ravikovitch, all poems from *Kol Ha-shirim Ad Ko* (The complete poems so far) (Tel-Aviv: Hakibbutz Hameuchad Publishing House Ltd., 1995). "Clockwork Doll," "A Dress of Fire," "Little Child's Head on the Pillow," and "Hovering at a Low Altitude," translations by Chana Bloch and Ariel Bloch, reprinted by permission of the publisher and Chana Bloch, from *The Window* (Riverdale-on-Hudson, N.Y.: The Sheep Meadow Press, 1986), copyright 1989 by Chana Bloch and Ariel Bloch; "We Had an Understanding," translation by Rachel Tzvia Back; "Lying upon the Water," translation by Tsipi Keller; "A Mother Walks Around," translation by Chana Bloch and Ariel Bloch.

Ruth 1.16–17, 19–21, translation from *The Holy Bible, King James Version* (1611; reprint, New York: Oxford University Press, 1967).

Bracha Serri, "Illiterate," from *Shiv'im Shirei Shotetut* (Wandering poems) (Jerusalem: Bracha Serri, 1983); "Aliza Says," from *Para Aduma* (Red heifer) (Tel-Aviv: Breirot Publishers, 1990). "Illiterate," translation by Yaffah Berkovits, reprinted, by permission of Yaffah Berkovits Murciano, from *Wandering Poems,* copyright 1983 by Bracha Serri. "Aliza Says," translation by Rachel Tzvia Back.

Malka Shaked, "Shame," from *Tmunot Matsav* (States of mind) (Tel-Aviv: Hakibbutz Hameuchad Publishing House Ltd., 1996). Translation by Shirley Kaufman.

Sarah Shapira, "Remember the Horn," from *Ha-boker Or* 7 (January 1886). Translation by Shirley Kaufman.

Shin Shifra, "Goat" and "Moonstruck," from *Hatsavim Nerot Neshama: Shirim* (Poems, 1973–1985) (Tel-Aviv: Am Oved Publishing Ltd., 1987); "A Woman Who Practices How to Live," verse 2, 3, 5, from *Iton 77* 21 (April 1997). Translations by Tsipi Keller.

Song of Songs is reprinted, with warmest gratitude, by permission of the translator Chana Bloch, from *The Song of Songs,* translated by Ariel Bloch and

Chana Bloch (New York: Random House, 1995; reprint, Berkeley and Los Angeles: University of California Press, 1998).

Ayin Tur-Malka, "Memorial Service," from *Shirat Ha-be'erot* (Poems) (Tel-Aviv: Ya'ir Publishers Ltd., 1972, reprint 1989). Translation by Shirley Kaufman.

Haya Vered, "The Zero Hour," from *Shirim Al Herev U-meitar* (Poems about a sword and a cord) (Tel-Aviv: Hakibbutz Hameuchad Publishing House Ltd., 1956). Translation by Lisa Katz.

Yona Wallach, all poems from *Tat Hakara Niftahat Kmo Menifa* (Selected Poems, 1963–1985) (Israel: Hakibbutz Hameuchad Publishing House Ltd., 1992). "Absalom," "[A grizzly she-bear reared me]," "Tefillin," and "I No Longer Really Love Being Afraid," translations by Linda Zisquit, reprinted by permission of the publisher and translator, from *Wild Light* (Riverdale-on-Hudson, N.Y.: Sheep Meadow Press, 1997), copyright 1997 by Linda Zisquit; "Hebrew," translation by Lisa Katz.

Nurit Zarchi, "She Is Joseph," from *Isha Yalda Isha* (A woman brought woman: Poems) (Tel-Aviv: Sifriat Poalim Publishing House Ltd., 1983); "Lightly," from *Kefar Ha-ruhot* (Village of the spirits) (Tel-Aviv: Nurit Zarchi and BITAN Publishers Ltd., 1994); "Night Is a Powerful Day," verse 1, and "Baby Blues," from *Melon Hipnodrom* (Hypnodrom hotel) (Tel-Aviv: Nurit Zarchi and Tag Publishers Ltd., 1998). "She Is Joseph," translation by Shirley Kaufman; "Lightly" and "Baby Blues," translations by Tsipi Keller; "Night Is a Powerful Day," verse 1, translation by Lisa Katz.

Simcha Zarmati-Atzta, "To Your Image," from *Mitokh He-anan She-ba-har* (From the cloud at the mountain: Poems) (Tel-Aviv: Sifriat Afikim, Forum for Spiritual and Social Awakening, 1986). Translation by Gabriel Levin.

Zelda, all poems from *Shirei Zelda* (Zelda's poems) (Tel-Aviv: Hakibbutz Hameuchad Publishing House Ltd., 1985). "Each Rose," translation by Barbara Goldberg, reprinted by permission of the publisher and translator, from *After the First Rain: Israeli Poems on War and Peace*, edited by Moshe Dor and Barbara Goldberg (Syracuse, N.Y.: Syracuse University Press in association with Dryad Press, 1998), copyright 1997 by Dryad Press; "Leisure," translation by Shirley Kaufman; "A Woman Who's Arrived at a Ripe Old Age," translation by Myra [Miriyam] Glazer, reprinted by permission of the publisher and the translator, from *Burning Air and a Clear Mind* (Athens, Ohio: Ohio University Press, 1981), copyright 1981 by Ohio University Press; "Place of Fire," translation by Marcia Falk, reprinted by permission of the publisher and translator, from *The Stones Remember,* edited by Moshe Dor, Barbara Goldberg, Giora Leshem (Washington, D. C.: The Word Works, 1991), copyright 1991 by The Word Works.

THE DEFIANT MUSE SERIES

The Defiant Muse: Dutch and Flemish Feminist Poems from the Middle Ages to the Present
Edited and with an introduction by Maaike Meijer; co-editors: Erica Eijsker, Ankie Peypers, and Yopie Prins

The Defiant Muse: French Feminist Poems from the Middle Ages to the Present
Edited and with an introduction by Domna C. Stanton

The Defiant Muse: German Feminist Poems from the Middle Ages to the Present
Edited and with an introduction by Susan L. Cocalis

The Defiant Muse: Hebrew Feminist Poems from Antiquity to the Present
Edited and with an introduction by Shirley Kaufman, Galit Hasan-Rokem, and Tamar S. Hess, with a foreword by Alicia Suskin Ostriker

The Defiant Muse: Hispanic Feminist Poems from the Middle Ages to the Present
Edited and with an introduction by Ángel Flores and Kate Flores

The Defiant Muse: Italian Feminist Poems from the Middle Ages to the Present
Edited by Beverly Allen, Muriel Kittel, and Keala Jan Jewell, with an introduction by Beverly Allen